D1461870

Microsoft® ADO.NET 4
Step by Step

Tim Patrick

Microsoft Press titles may be purchased for educational, business or sales promotional use. Online editions are also available for most titles (*http://my.safaribooksonline.com*). For more information, contact our corporate/institutional sales department: (800) 998-9938 or *corporate@oreilly.com*. Visit our website at *microsoftpress.oreilly.com*. Send comments to *mspinput@microsoft.com*.

Acquisitions and Development Editor: Russell Jones
Production Editor: Kristen Borg
Production Services: Octal Publishing, Inc.
Technical Reviewer: Sahil Malik
Indexing: Potomac Indexing, LLC
Cover: Karen Montgomery
Compositor: Susan Brown
Illustrator: Robert Romano

978-0-735-63888-4

To Abel Chan, a good friend and a good programmer.

Contents at a Glance

Table of Contents

What do you think of this book? We want to hear from you!

Microsoft is interested in hearing your feedback so we can continually improve our books and learning resources for you. To participate in a brief online survey, please visit:

www.microsoft.com/learning/booksurvey/

Part V **Presenting Data to the World**

Acknowledgments

An open-ended thank you goes to Microsoft, not only for developing some of the products that have kept me gainfully employed for nearly three decades, but for welcoming me into their book-writing fold. It was also a pleasure to work again with the team at O'Reilly Media, Microsoft's publishing partner. Editors Russell Jones and Kristen Borg kept all the trains running on time, which wasn't easy given the busy technical and publishing traffic. Rounding out the group were Meghan Blanchette, Sumita Mukherji, and Adam Witwer. Thank you all.

Sahil Malik, ADO.NET expert and fellow author, has the distinction of having read through every single word of this book looking for technical concerns. Nancy Sixsmith did the same for the mechanics of language, grammar, and consistency. The book is richer for their involvement.

Claudette Moore once again worked her agenting magic, somehow always managing to make everyone on both sides of a contract happy. This book would be nothing more than a series of discarded emails were it not for her hard work and dedication. Thank you, Claudette, for yet another adventure.

Thanks to all my friends at Harvest, especially fellow food and movie lovers Alice, Brenda, Andy, Suzy, Matt, Tiffany, Jeff, and Monica. Love and appreciation in heaps to my wife Maki and my son Spencer, both of whom exude patience and care. And thanks once again to God for making all these other acknowledgments possible in the first place.

Tim Patrick
October 2010

Introduction

ADO.NET is Microsoft's core data access library for .NET developers, and is the heart of many data-centric technologies on the Windows development platform. It works with C#, Visual Basic, and other .NET-enabled languages. If you are a .NET developer looking to interact with database content or other external data sources, then ADO.NET is the right tool for you.

Microsoft ADO.NET 4 Step by Step provides an organized walkthrough of the ADO.NET library and its associated technologies. The text is decidedly introductory; it discusses the basics of each covered system, with examples that provide a great head start on adding data features to your applications. While the book does not provide exhaustive coverage of every ADO.NET feature, it does offer essential guidance in using the key ADO.NET components.

In addition to its coverage of core ADO.NET library features, the book discusses the Entity Framework, the LINQ query system, and WCF Data Services. Beyond the explanatory content, each chapter includes step by step examples and downloadable sample projects that you can explore for yourself.

Who Is This Book For?

As part of Microsoft Press's "Developer Step By Step" series of training resources, *Microsoft ADO.NET 4 Step by Step* makes it easy to learn about ADO.NET and the advanced data tools used with it.

This book exists to help existing Visual Basic and C# developers understand the core concepts of ADO.NET and related technologies. It is especially useful for programmers looking to manage database-hosted information in their new or existing .NET applications. Although most readers will have no prior experience with ADO.NET, the book is also useful for those familiar with earlier versions of either ADO or ADO.NET, and who are interested in getting filled in on the newest features.

Assumptions

As a reader, the book expects that you have at least a minimal understanding of .NET development and object-oriented programming concepts. Although ADO.NET is available to most, if not all, .NET language platforms, this book includes examples in C# and Visual Basic only. If you have not yet picked up one of those languages, you might consider reading John Sharp's *Microsoft Visual C# 2010 Step by Step* (Microsoft Press 2010) or Michael Halvorson's *Microsoft Visual Basic 2010 Step by Step* (Microsoft Press 2010).

With a heavy focus on database concepts, this book assumes that you have a basic understanding of relational database systems such as Microsoft SQL Server, and have had brief exposure to one of the many flavors of the query tool known as SQL. To go beyond this book and expand your knowledge of SQL and Microsoft's SQL Server database platform, other Microsoft Press books such as Mike Hotek's *Microsoft® SQL Server® 2008 Step by Step* (Microsoft Press, 2008) or Itzik Ben-gan's *Microsoft® SQL Server® 2008 T-SQL Fundamentals* (Microsoft Press, 2008) offer both complete introductions and comprehensive information on T-SQL and SQL Server.

Organization of This Book

This book is divided into five sections, each of which focuses on a different aspect or technology within the ADO.NET family. Part I, "Getting to Know ADO.NET," provides a quick overview of ADO.NET and its fundamental role in .NET applications, then delves into the details of the main ADO.NET library, focusing on using the technology without yet being concerned with external database connections. Part II, "Connecting to External Data Sources," continues that core library focus, adding in the connectivity features. Part III, "Entity Framework," introduces the Entity Framework, Microsoft's model-based data service. Another service layer, LINQ, takes center stage in Part IV, "LINQ." Finally, Part V, "Presenting Data to the World," covers some miscellaneous topics that round out the full discussion of ADO.NET.

Finding Your Best Starting Point in This Book

The different sections of *Microsoft ADO.NET 4 Step by Step* cover a wide range of technologies associated with the data library. Depending on your needs and your existing understanding of Microsoft data tools, you may wish to focus on specific areas of the book. Use the following table to determine how best to proceed through the book.

If you are	Follow these steps
New to ADO.NET development, or an existing ADO developer	Focus on Parts I and II and on Chapter 21 in Part V, or read through the entire book in order.
Familiar with earlier releases of ADO.NET	Briefly skim Parts I and II if you need a refresher on the core concepts. Read up on the new technologies in Parts III and IV and be sure to read Chapter 22 in Part V.
Interested in the Entity Framework	Read Part III. Chapter 22 in Part V discusses data services built on top of Entity Framework models.
Interested in LINQ data providers	Read through the chapters in Part IV.

Most of the book's chapters include hands-on samples that let you try out the concepts just learned. No matter which sections you choose to focus on, be sure to download and install the sample applications on your system.

Conventions and Features in This Book

This book presents information using conventions designed to make the information readable and easy to follow.

- In most cases, the book includes separate exercises for Visual Basic programmers and Visual C# programmers. You can skip the exercises that do not apply to your selected language.

- Each exercise consists of a series of tasks, presented as numbered steps (1, 2, and so on) listing each action you must take to complete the exercise.

- Boxed elements with labels such as "**Note**" provide additional information or alternative methods for completing a step successfully.

- Text that you type (apart from code blocks) appears in bold.

- A plus sign (+) between two key names means that you must press those keys at the same time. For example, "Press Alt+Tab" means that you hold down the Alt key while you press the Tab key.

- A vertical bar between two or more menu items (e.g. File | Close), means that you should select the first menu or menu item, then the next, and so on.

System Requirements

You will need the following hardware and software to complete the practice exercises in this book:

- One of Windows XP with Service Pack 3 (except Starter Edition), Windows Vista with Service Pack 2 (except Starter Edition), Windows 7, Windows Server 2003 with Service Pack 2, Windows Server 2003 R2, Windows Server 2008 with Service Pack 2, or Windows Server 2008 R2

- Visual Studio 2010, any edition (multiple downloads may be required if using Express Edition products)

- SQL Server 2008 Express Edition or higher (2008 or R2 release), with SQL Server Management Studio 2008 Express or higher (included with Visual Studio, Express Editions require separate download)

- Computer that has a 1.6GHz or faster processor (2GHz recommended)

- 1 GB (32 Bit) or 2 GB (64 Bit) RAM (add 512 MB if running in a virtual machine or SQL Server Express Editions; more for advanced SQL Server editions)

- 3.5GB of available hard disk space

- 5400 RPM hard disk drive

- DirectX 9 capable video card running at 1024 x 768 or higher-resolution display

- DVD-ROM drive (if installing Visual Studio from DVD)

- Internet connection to download software or chapter examples

Depending on your Windows configuration, you might need Local Administrator rights to install or configure Visual Studio 2010 and SQL Server 2008 products.

Code Samples

Most of the chapters in this book include exercises that let you interactively try out new material learned in the main text. All sample projects, in both their pre-exercise and post-exercise formats, are available for download from the book's catalog page on the web site for Microsoft's publishing partner, O'Reilly Media:

http://oreilly.com/catalog/0790145300034/

Click the Examples link on that page. When a list of files appears, locate and download the *ADO.NET 4 SBS Examples.zip* file.

> **Note** In addition to the code samples, your system should have Visual Studio 2010 and SQL Server 2008 installed. The instructions below use SQL Server Management Studio 2008 to set up the sample database used with the practice examples. If available, install the latest service packs for each product.

Installing the Code Samples

Follow these steps to install the code samples on your computer so that you can use them with the exercises in this book.

1. Open the *ADO.NET 4 SBS Examples.zip* file that you downloaded from the book's web site.

2. Copy the entire contents of the opened .zip file to a convenient location on your hard disk.

Installing the Sample Database

Follow these steps to install the sample database used by many of the book's practice examples.

> **Note** You must first download and install the Code Samples using the instructions listed above. Also, you must have both SQL Server 2008 and SQL Server Management Studio 2008 installed, any edition.

1. Start SQL Server Management Studio 2008 and open a new Object Explorer connection to the target database instance using the File | Connect Object Explorer menu command.

2. In the Object Explorer panel, right-click on the Databases branch of the connection tree, and select New Database from the shortcut menu.

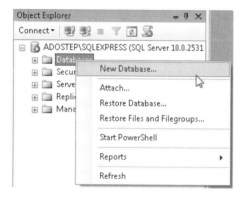

3. When the New Database dialog box appears, enter **StepSample** in the Database Name field. Click OK to create the database.

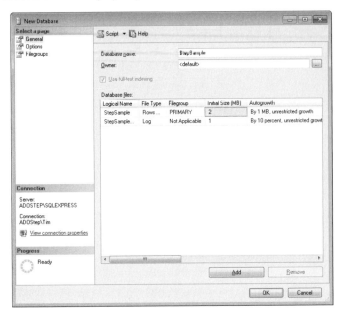

4. Select File | Open | File from the main SQL Server Management Studio menu, and locate the *DB Script.sql* file installed with the book's sample projects. This file appears in the *Sample Database* folder within the main installation folder.

5. Click the Execute button on the SQL Editor toolbar to run the script. This will create the necessary tables and objects needed by the practice examples.

6. Close SQL Server Management Studio 2008.

Using the Code Samples

The main installation folder extracted from the *ADO.NET 4 SBS Examples.zip* file contains three subfolders.

- *Sample Database*   This folder contains the SQL script used to build the sample database. The instructions for creating this database appear earlier in this Introduction.

- *Exercises*   The main example projects referenced in each chapter appear in this folder. Many of these projects are incomplete, and will not run without following the steps indicated in the associated chapter. Separate folders indicate each chapter's sample code, and there are distinct folders for the C# and Visual Basic versions of each example.

- *Completed Exercises*   This folder contains all content from the Exercises folder, but with chapter-specific instructions applied.

To complete an exercise, access the appropriate chapter-and-language folder in the *Exercises* folder, and open the project file. If your system is configured to display file extensions, Visual Basic project files use a .vbproj extension, while C# project files use .csproj as the file extension.

Uninstalling the Code Samples

To remove the code samples from your system, simply delete the installation folder that you extracted from the .zip file.

Software Release

This book was written for use with Visual Studio 2010, including the Express Editions products. Much of the content will apply to other versions of Visual Studio, but the code samples may be not be fully compatible with earlier or later versions of Visual Studio.

The practice examples in the book use SQL Server 2008, including the Express Edition products. Many of the examples may work with SQL Server 2005 or earlier versions, but neither the installation script nor the sample projects have been tested with those earlier releases.

Errata and Book Support

We've made every effort to ensure the accuracy of this book and its companion content. If you do find an error, please report it on our Microsoft Press site at *oreilly.com*:

1. Go to *http://microsoftpress.oreilly.com*.
2. In the Search box, enter the book's ISBN or title.
3. Select your book from the search results.
4. On your book's catalog page, under the cover image, you'll see a list of links.
5. Click View/Submit Errata.

You'll find additional information and services for your book on its catalog page. If you need additional support, please e-mail Microsoft Press Book Support at *mspinput@microsoft.com*.

Please note that product support for Microsoft software is not offered through the addresses above.

We Want to Hear from You

At Microsoft Press, your satisfaction is our top priority, and your feedback our most valuable asset. Please tell us what you think of this book at:

http://www.microsoft.com/learning/booksurvey

The survey is short, and we read every one of your comments and ideas. Thanks in advance for your input!

Stay in Touch

Let's keep the conversation going! We're on Twitter: *http://twitter.com/MicrosoftPress*.

Part I

Getting to Know ADO.NET

Chapter 1: Introducing ADO.NET 4

Chapter 2: Building Tables of Data

Chapter 3: Storing Data in Memory

Chapter 4: Accessing the Right Data Values

Chapter 5: Bringing Related Data Together

Chapter 6: Turning Data into Information

Chapter 7: Saving and Restoring Data

Chapter 1
Introducing ADO.NET 4

After completing this chapter, you will be able to:

- Identify what ADO.NET is

- Explain ADO.NET's role in an application

- Identify the major components that make up ADO.NET

- Create an ADO.NET link between a database and a .NET application

This chapter introduces you to ADO.NET and its purpose in the world of Microsoft .NET application development. ADO.NET has been included with the .NET Framework since its initial release in 2002, playing a central role in the development of both desktop and Internet-targeted applications for programmers using C#, Visual Basic, and other Framework languages.

What Is ADO.NET?

ADO.NET is a family of technologies that allows .NET developers to interact with data in standard, structured, and primarily disconnected ways. If that sounds confusing, don't worry. This book exists to remove the confusion and anxiety that many developers experience when they first learn of ADO.NET's multiple object layers, its dozens of general and platform-specific classes, and its myriad options for interacting with actual data.

Applications written using the .NET Framework depend on *.NET class libraries*, which exist in special DLL files that encapsulate common programming functionality in an easy-to-access format. Most of the libraries supplied with the .NET Framework appear within the *System* namespace. *System.IO*, for instance, includes classes that let you interact with standard disk files and related data streams. The *System.Security* library provides access to, among other things, data encryption features. ADO.NET, expressed through the *System.Data* namespace, implements a small set of libraries that makes consuming and manipulating large amounts of data simple and straightforward.

ADO.NET manages both internal data—data created in memory and used solely within an application—and external data—data housed in a storage area apart from the application, such as in a relational database or text file. Regardless of the source, ADO.NET generalizes the relevant data and presents it to your code in spreadsheet–style rows and columns.

> **Note** Although ADO.NET manipulates data in tabular form, you can also use ADO.NET to access nontabular data. For instance, an ADO.NET provider (discussed later in the chapter, on page 7) could supply access to hierarchical data such as that found in the Windows Registry, as long as that provider expressed the data in a tabular structure for ADO.NET's use. Accessing such non-tabular data is beyond the scope of this book.

If you are already familiar with relational databases such as Microsoft SQL Server, you will encounter many familiar terms in ADO.NET. Tables, rows, columns, relations, views; these ADO.NET concepts are based loosely on their relational database counterparts. Despite these similarities, ADO.NET is not a relational database because it doesn't include key "relational algebra" features typically found in robust database systems. It also lacks many of the common support features of such databases, including indexes, stored procedures, and triggers. Still, if you limit yourself to basic create, read, update, and delete (CRUD) operations, ADO.NET can act like a miniature yet powerful in-memory database.

As an acronym, "ADO.NET" stands for—nothing. Just like the words "scuba," "laser," and "NT" in Windows NT, the capital letters in ADO.NET used to mean something, but now it is just a standalone term. Before Microsoft released the .NET Framework, one of the primary data access tools Windows developers used in their programs was known as *ADO*, which did stand for something: ActiveX Data Objects. After .NET arrived on the scene, ADO.NET became the natural successor to ADO. Although conceptual parallels exist between ADO.NET and ADO, the technologies are distinct and incompatible.

> **Note** ADO is based on Microsoft's older COM technology. The .NET Framework provides support for COM components, and therefore enables .NET programs to use ADO. This is especially useful for development teams transitioning legacy applications to .NET. Although ADO and ADO.NET components can appear in the same application, they can interact only indirectly because their object libraries are unrelated.

When communicating with external data stores, ADO.NET presents a disconnected data experience. In earlier data platforms, including ADO, software developers would typically establish a persistent connection with a database and use various forms of record locking to manage safe and accurate data updates. But then along came the Internet and its browser-centric view of information. Maintaining a long-standing data connection through bursts of HTTP text content was no longer a realistic expectation. ADO.NET's preference toward on-again, off-again database connections reflects this reality. Although this paradigm change brought with it difficulties for traditional client-server application developers, it also helped usher in the era of massive scalability and n-tier development that is now common to both desktop and Web-based systems.

Why ADO.NET?

In the early days of computer programming, the need for a data library like ADO.NET didn't exist. Programmers had only a single method of accessing data: direct interaction with the values in memory. Permanently stored data existed on tape reels in fire-resistant, climate-controlled, raised-floor rooms. Data queries could take hours, especially if someone with more clout had a higher-priority processing need.

Over time, computers increased in complexity, and (as if to fill some eternal maxim) data processing needs also expanded to consume all available computing resources. Businesses sought easier ways to manage entire records of numeric, text, and date-time values on their mainframe systems. Flat-file and relational database systems sprang up to establish proprietary management of millions of data values. As personal computers arrived and matured, developers soon had several database systems at their disposal.

This was great news for data consumers. Businesses and individuals now had powerful tools to transform data bits into usable information, to endow seemingly unrelated values with meaning and purpose. But it was bad news for developers As technology marched on, companies purchased one proprietary system after another. Programming against such systems meant a reinvention of the proverbial wheel each time a middle manager asked for yet another one-time report. Even the standard SQL language brought little relief because each database vendor provided its own spin on the meaning of "standard."

What programmers needed was a way to generalize different data systems in a standard, consistent, and powerful way. In the world of .NET application development, Microsoft ADO.NET meets that need. Instead of worrying about the minutiae associated with the different database systems, programmers using ADO.NET focus on the data content itself.

Major Components of ADO.NET

The *System.Data* namespace includes many distinct ADO.NET classes that work together to provide access to tabular data. The library includes two major groups of classes: those that manage the actual data within the software and those that communicate with external data systems. Figure 1-1 shows the major parts that make up an ADO.NET instance.

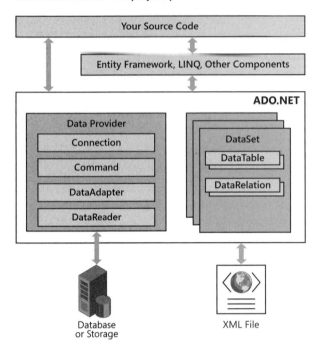

FIGURE 1-1 Key ADO.NET elements.

At the data-shaped heart of the library is the *DataTable*. Similar in purpose to tables in a database, the *DataTable* manages all the actual data values that you and your source code ultimately care about. Each *DataTable* contains zero or more rows of data, with the individual data values of each row identified by the table's column definitions.

- Each table defines *DataColumn* items, each representing the individual data values that appear in the table's records. *DataColumn* definitions include a data type declaration based on the kind of data destined for each column. For instance, a *CustomerLastName* column might be defined to use data of type *System.String*, whereas an *OrderSalesTax* column could be crafted for use with *System.Decimal* content.

- One *DataRow* entry exists for each record of data stored within a table, providing access to the distinct columnar data values. ADO.NET includes methods that let you add to, delete from, modify, and query each *DataTable* object's rows. For tables connected to an external data storage area, any changes made can be propagated back to the source.

- You can optionally establish links between the tables of data using *DataRelation* entries.

- Programmatic limitations can be placed on tables and their data values using *Constraint* instances.

- *DataView* instances provide a limited or modified view of the rows in a *DataTable*.

- Tables can be grouped together into a *DataSet*. Some tools that interact with ADO.NET data require that any tables be bound within a *DataSet*, but if you plan to do some limited work with only a single table, it's fine to work with just the *DataTable* instance.

DataTable instances and their associated objects are sufficient for working with internal data. To connect with external data from a database, ADO.NET features multiple *data providers*, including a custom provider for Microsoft SQL Server. Database platforms without a specific provider use the more generic ODBC and OLE DB providers, both included with ADO.NET. Several third-party providers can be purchased or obtained free of charge, which target specific platforms, including Oracle.

- All communication with the external data source occurs through a *Connection* object. ADO.NET supports connection pooling for increased efficiency between queries.

- SQL queries and data management statements get wrapped in a *Command* object before being sent to the data source. Commands can include optional *Parameter* instances that let you call stored procedures or create fill-in-the-blank queries.

- The *DataAdapter* object stores standard query definitions for interacting with a database, removing the tedium of constantly needing to build SQL statements for each record you want to read or write, and helping to automate some ADO.NET-related tasks.

- The *DataReader* object provides fast, read-only access to the results of a query for those times when you just need to get your data quickly.

ADO.NET also includes features that let you save an entire *DataSet* as an XML file and load it back in later. And that's just the start. You'll learn how to use all these elements—and more—throughout the upcoming chapters.

Extensions to ADO.NET

Generalizing access to data is a key benefit of using ADO.NET. But an even greater advantage for .NET developers is that all values managed through ADO.NET appear as objects, first-class members of the .NET data world. Each data field in a table is a strongly typed data member, fully compliant with .NET's Common Type System. Individual fields can be used just like any other local variable. Data rows and other sets of objects are standard .NET collections and can be processed using standard iteration methods.

Because ADO.NET values exist as true .NET objects and collections, Microsoft has enhanced the core ADO.NET feature set with new tools. Two of these technologies, the Entity Framework and LINQ, are not formally part of ADO.NET. But their capability to interact with and enhance the ADO.NET experience makes them essential topics for study.

The *Entity Framework*, the focus of Part III of this book, emphasizes the conceptual view of your data. Although the data classes in ADO.NET are programmer-friendly, you still need to keep track of primary keys and relationships between tables and fields. The Entity Framework attempts to hide that messiness, and restores the promise of what object-oriented programming was supposed to be all about. In the Entity Framework, a customer object includes its orders; each order includes line item details. Instead of working with the raw table data, you interact with logically designed entities that mimic their real-world counterparts, and let the Framework worry about translating it all into SQL statements.

LINQ, introduced in Part IV, brings the joy of English-like queries to your favorite programming language. Microsoft enhanced both Visual Basic and C# with new LINQ-specific language features. Now, instead of building string-based SQL statements to query data, the syntax of each programming language becomes the query language. LINQ is a generic data tool, enabling you to easily mix ADO.NET data and other content sources together into a single set of results.

Connecting to External Data

Chapter 8, "Establishing External Connections," introduces the code elements that support communications between ADO.NET and external sources of data. Although using only code to establish these connections is quite common, Visual Studio also includes the *Data Source Connection Wizard*, a mouse-friendly tool that guides you through the creation of a ready-to-use *DataSet*. Here's an example of using the Connection Wizard.

Creating a Data Source Using the Connection Wizard

1. Start Visual Studio 2010. Select File | New | Project from the main menu.

   ADO.NET is supported in most common project types. To keep things simple for now, create a Windows Forms application using either C# or Visual Basic as the language. The following figures show the process using a Visual Basic Windows Forms application, although the steps are identical in C#.

2. In the New Project dialog box, provide a name for the project.

3. Click OK.

   Visual Studio will create a project.

4. Select Data | Add New Data Source from the menu.

   Visual Studio displays the Data Source Configuration Wizard.

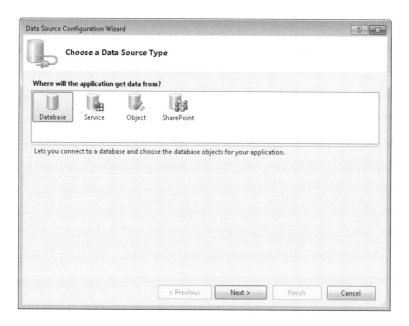

The Database choice should already be selected in the Choose A Data Source Type panel.

5. Click Next.

6. In the Choose a Database Model panel, choose Dataset.

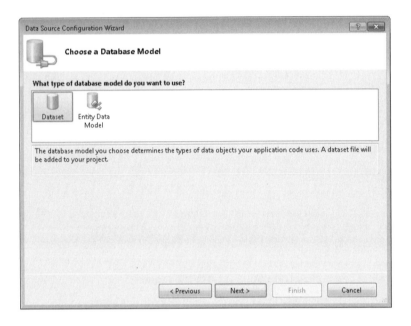

7. Click Next.

The Wizard displays the Choose Your Data Connection panel. If you previously configured data sources, they will appear in the Which Data Connection Should Your Application Use To Connect To The Database? list.

8. Because you are setting up a connection to the test database for the first time, click the New Connection button.

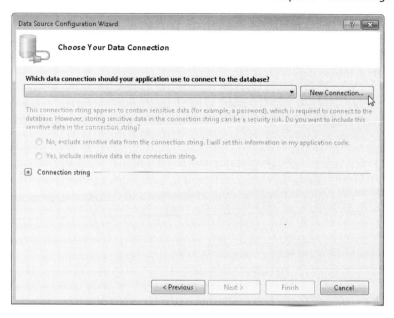

9. When the Choose Data Source dialog box appears, select Microsoft SQL Server from the Data Source list.

The Data Provider field will automatically choose the SQL Server data provider. For maximum flexibility, clear the Always Use This Selection field.

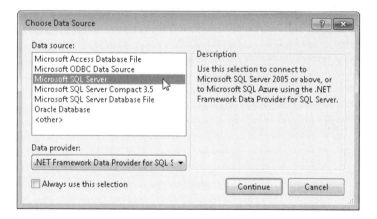

Note Choosing Microsoft SQL Server will access a database that has previously been attached to a SQL Server database instance. To create a data source that directly references a database file not necessarily attached to the engine instance, select Microsoft SQL Server Database File from the Data Source list instead. The wizard will then prompt you for the disk location of the file.

10. Click Continue to accept the data source.

11. In the Add Connection dialog box, select the server from the Server Name field.

For SQL Server 2008 Express Edition instances, this is typically the name of the local computer with **\SQLEXPRESS** appended to the name. If you are using the full SQL Server product, leave off the **\SQLEXPRESS** suffix. For SQL Server instances hosted on the same system as your Visual Studio installation, you can use **(local)** as the server name.

For SQL Server instances configured with database-managed authentication, select Use SQL Server Authentication and supply the appropriate user name and password. For databases managed with Windows authentication (the likely choice for the test database), select Use Windows Authentication instead.

The Select Or Enter a Database Name field should now include the available databases within the test database file. (If not, confirm that you have supplied the right server name and authentication values and that SQL Server is running on your system.)

12. Select StepSample (or the name of your primary test database) from the list. Then click OK to complete the connection configuration.

Control returns to the wizard with the new data connection selected in the list on the Choose Your Data Connection panel.

Note ADO.NET uses *connection strings*, short, semicolon-delimited definition strings, to iden-tify the data source. As you develop new applications, you will probably forgo the Data Source Configuration Wizard as a means of building connection strings. If you are curious about what appears in a connection string, expand the Connection String field in the Choose Your Data Connection panel.

13. Click the Next button to continue.

The next wizard panel asks if the connection string should be stored in the application's configuration file. The field should already be selected, which is good, although you might want to give it a more programmer-friendly name.

Note .NET applications use two types of configuration files (although it varies by project type): *application configuration files* and *user configuration files*. Although your application has access to the settings in both files, if you plan to include a feature in your program that modifies these saved settings, make sure that you place such settings in the user configuration file. Application configuration files can't be modified from within the associated application.

14. Click the Next button once more to continue.

SQL Server will perform a quick analysis of your database, compiling a list of all avail-able data-exposing items, including tables, views, stored procedures, and functions. The Choose Your Database Objects panel displays all items found during this discovery process.

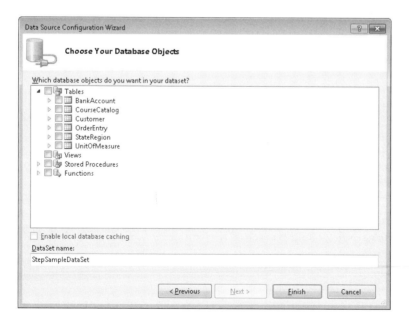

15. For this test, include the Customer table in the DataSet by expanding the Tables section and marking the Customer table with a check mark.

You can optionally modify the DataSet Name field to something that will be easier to repeatedly type in your source code. Click Finish to exit the wizard and create the data source. The data source is now available for use in your application.

16. Select Data | Show Data Sources from the Visual Studio menu to see the data source.

The wizard also added a new .xsd file to your project; it appears in the Solution Explorer with your other project files. This XML file contains the actual definition of the data source. Removing this file from the project removes the Wizard-created data source.

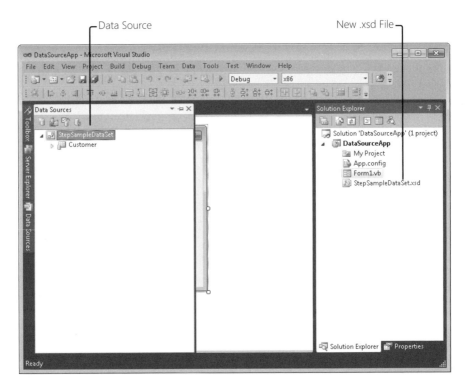

Visual Studio also lets you preview the data records within the data source.

17. Select Data | Preview Data from the Visual Studio menu to open the Preview Data dialog box.

The menu choice might be hidden depending on what is currently active in the Visual Studio IDE. If that menu choice does not appear, click the form in the design window and then try to select the menu item again.

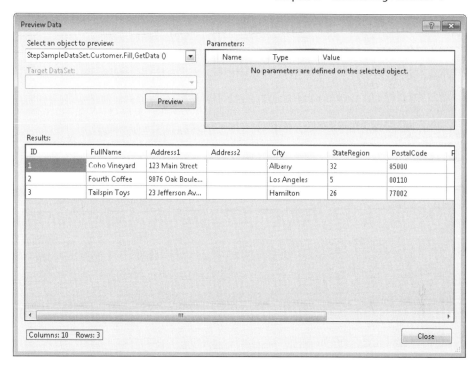

Summary

This chapter provided an overview of Microsoft's ADO.NET technology and its major data management components. At its heart, computer programming is all about data manipulation, whether the data values represent customer records, characters and objects in a 3D interactive video game, or the bits in a compressed audio file. With this inherent focus on data, it makes sense that Microsoft would provide a great tool for interacting with tabular data, one of the most useful ways of organizing data, especially in a business setting.

As you will see in upcoming chapters, the concepts included in this opening chapter have direct ties to specific ADO.NET classes and class members. As a .NET developer, you already have a core understanding of how ADO.NET can be used in an application because everything in the library is expressed as standard .NET objects. The only things you still need to learn are some of the details that are specific to ADO.NET—the very subjects covered in the rest of this book.

Chapter 1 Quick Reference

To	Do This
Create a new data source	Create or open a project in Visual Studio.
	Select Data | Add New Data Source.
	Follow the steps in the Connection Wizard.
Preview data in an existing data source	Select Data | Preview Data.
	Select the target data source from the Select An Object To Preview list.
	Click the Preview button.
Remove a data source from a project	Select the .xsd file in the Solution Explorer.
	Press the Delete key or right-click on the file and select Delete from the shortcut menu.

Chapter 2
Building Tables of Data

After completing this chapter, you will be able to:

- Understand the ADO.NET classes used to create tables

- Create strongly typed columns within a table

- Indicate the primary key for a table

- Design a table graphically or in code

The focus of all data in ADO.NET is the table—or more correctly, the *DataTable*. This class, located at *System.Data.DataTable*, defines a single table in which strongly typed column definitions and runtime data rows appear. By itself, a *DataTable* isn't very interesting; it's just a memory-based repository for data. It becomes useful only when you start employing ADO.NET and standard .NET Framework methods and tools to process the data stored in each table and data row.

 Note Some of the exercises in this chapter use the same sample project, a tool that exposes the structure of a *DataTable*. Although you can run the application after each exercise, the expected results for the full application might not appear until you complete all related exercises in the chapter.

Implementing Tables

As with everything else in .NET, tables in ADO.NET exist as instantiated objects. Whether hand-written by you, produced by dragging and dropping items in the development environment, or generated by one of the Visual Studio tools, the ADO.NET code you include in your application exists to create and manage *DataTable* objects and other related objects.

Logical and Physical Table Implementations

ADO.NET's *DataTable* object represents a *logical implementation* of a table of data. When you visualize the data values within the table, you have an image of a spreadsheet-like table, with distinct cells for each text, numeric, date/time, or other type of value.

The *physical implementation* of a *DataTable* object is somewhat different. Instead of one large grid layout, ADO.NET maintains tabular data as a collection of collections. Each *DataTable* object contains a collection of ordered rows, each existing as an instance of a *DataRow* object. Each row contains its own collection of items that holds the row's (and ultimately the table's) actual data values. A set of column definitions exists separately from the actual column values, although the definitions influence the values. Figure 2-1 shows the difference between the logical and physical structures of a data table.

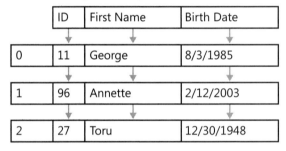

Logical Implementation

Row	ID	First Name	Birth Date
0	11	George	8/3/1985
1	96	Annette	2/12/2003
2	27	Toru	12/30/1948

Physical Implementation

	ID	First Name	Birth Date
0	11	George	8/3/1985
1	96	Annette	2/12/2003
2	27	Toru	12/30/1948

FIGURE 2-1 Logical and physical table layouts.

The *DataTable* Class

The three main classes that make up a data table are *DataTable*, *DataColumn*, and *DataRow*. As expected, these classes define a table, its columns, and its data rows, respectively. The main discussion for the *DataRow* class appears in Chapter 3, "Storing Data in Memory."

To define a table, create a new *DataTable* object, optionally supplying a table name.

```
C#
System.Data.DataTable unnamedTable = new System.Data.DataTable();
System.Data.DataTable namedTable = new System.Data.DataTable("Customer");
```

```
Visual Basic
Dim unnamedTable As New System.Data.DataTable()
Dim namedTable As New System.Data.DataTable("Customer")
```

After you create a *DataTable*, you can modify its *TableName* property and other relevant properties as needed.

> **Note** Both Visual Basic and C# include features that let you use namespace elements as if they were globally named elements. Visual Basic accomplishes this on a file-by-file basis with the *Imports* keyword; C# includes the *Using* keyword for the same purpose. Visual Basic also includes a project-specific setting that automatically applies an *Imports*-like rule to each indicated namespace. (To use this feature, modify the items in the Imported Namespaces list on the References panel of Project Properties.) From this point forward, all code will assume that the *System.Data* and *System.Data.SqlClient* namespaces have been globalized in this way.

The *DataTable* class implements several useful events that it fires whenever data is added to, removed from, or modified in the table. Table 2-1 shows the data-related events you can plug into your code.

TABLE 2-1 Data-Related Events in the DataTable Class

Event Name	Triggering Action
ColumnChanging, ColumnChanged	During and after a single data value change within a row's collection of data.
RowChanging, RowChanged	During and after any data change within a row of data.
RowDeleting, RowDeleted	During and after a row is being deleted from a table.
TableClearing, TableCleared	During and after all rows are being deleted from a table at once.
TableNewRow	When a new row is inserted into a table's collection of rows. This event is not raised when calling the table's *NewRow* method, but instead when that new row is added to the table.

Creating a *DataTable*: C#

1. Open the "Chapter 2 CSharp" project from the installed samples folder. The project includes two *Windows.Forms* classes: *Switchboard* and *TableDetails*.

2. Open the source code view for the *Switchboard* form. Locate the *GetNoColumnTable* function. Add the following statement to that function to create a new *DataTable*:

    ```
    return new DataTable("BoringTable");
    ```

3. Open the source code view for the *TableDetails* form. Locate the *TableDetails_Load* routine. Just below the comment, "Show the table name," add the following statement to access the *TableName* property of the *DataTable*:

    ```
    this.TableName.Text = ActiveTable.TableName;
    ```

4. Run the application. When the switchboard appears, click the Show Table with No Columns button. The *TableDetails* form opens with a structural view of the columnless table.

Creating a *DataTable*: Visual Basic

1. Open the "Chapter 2 VB" project from the installed samples folder. The project includes two *Windows.Forms* classes: *Switchboard* and *TableDetails*.

2. Open the source code view for the *Switchboard* form. Locate the *GetNoColumnTable* function. Add the following statement to that function to create a new *DataTable*:

```
Return New DataTable("BoringTable")
```

3. Open the source code view for the *TableDetails* form. Locate the *TableDetails_Load* routine. Just below the comment, "Show the table name," add the following statement to access the *TableName* property of the *DataTable*:

```
Me.TableName.Text = ActiveTable.TableName
```

4. Run the application. When the switchboard appears, click the Show Table with No Columns button. The *TableDetails* form opens with a structural view of the columnless table.

Adding Data Columns

Creating a *DataTable* instance is an essential first step in using ADO.NET, but a table that contains no columns is rarely useful. The next task in table building is in populating the *DataTable* object's *Columns* collection with one or more *DataColumn* instances that represent the table's columnar values.

Database Normalization

Before rushing into the task of adding columns, it is important to think about the nature of the columns being added. If you are creating a standalone table that won't interact with other *DataTable* objects or some of the more abstract data tools that work with ADO.NET, it is fine to throw any columns you need into the table. However, if you are trying to replicate the types of table interactions frequently found in traditional relational databases, you should ensure that your tables are optimized to take advantage of key ADO.NET features.

Normalization is the process of crafting tables that ensure data integrity and take advantage of the processing power of relational database systems. E.F. Codd, inventor of the relational database model, proposed normalization as a method of eliminating data anomalies that infect data during certain types of insert, update, and delete operations. A discussion of normalization is beyond the scope of this book. If you're not familiar with the normalization process or the various "normal forms," a few moments spent reading about this essential craft will help support your data management needs.

The *DataColumn* class, found in the same *System.Data* namespace as the *DataTable* class, defines a single column in your table's schema. *DataColumn* objects can be created as independent instances for inclusion in a *DataTable* object's *Columns* collection, one for each column in the table. At a useful minimum, you must provide at least the name and data type of each column. The following code block creates a table with a single long-integer field:

C#

```csharp
DataTable customer = new DataTable("Customer");
DataColumn keyField = new DataColumn("ID", typeof(long));
customer.Columns.Add(keyField);
```

Visual Basic

```vb
Dim customer As New DataTable("Customer")
Dim keyField As New DataColumn("ID", GetType(Long))
customer.Columns.Add(keyField)
```

The following *System* types are officially supported by *DataColumn* instances:

- *Boolean*
- *Byte*
- *Char*
- *DateTime*
- *Decimal*
- *Double*
- *Int16*
- *Int32*
- *Int64*
- *SByte*
- *Single*
- *String*
- *TimeSpan*
- *UInt16*
- *UInt32*
- *UInt64*
- Arrays of *Byte* (although there are some limitations)

You can also use the equivalent Visual Basic and C# data types.

Note You can use any other data types as the column type, but ADO.NET will place limita-tions—sometimes significant limitations—on a column if you don't use one of the supported types. Also, nonsupported types are likely to be incompatible with the available data types found in any connected database. See the Visual Studio 2010 online documentation entry for "DataColumn.DataType Property" for full details on these and other limitations.

The *DataTable* object's *Columns* collection includes an *Add* overload that simplifies the cre-ation of columns. In this syntax, you pass the standard *DataColumn* arguments directly to the *Add* method.

C#

```csharp
DataTable customer = new DataTable("Customer");
customer.Columns.Add("ID", typeof(long));
customer.Columns.Add("FullName", typeof(string));
customer.Columns.Add("LastOrderDate", typeof(DateTime));
```

Visual Basic

```vb
Dim customer As New DataTable("Customer")
customer.Columns.Add("ID", GetType(Long))
customer.Columns.Add("FullName", GetType(String))
customer.Columns.Add("LastOrderDate", GetType(Date))
```

The *DataColumn* class includes several useful properties that let you customize each column to suit your processing needs. Many of these properties enable features that parallel those common in relational database tables. Table 2-2 documents these helpful properties.

TABLE 2-2 Useful Properties in the DataColumn Class

Property	Description
AllowDBNull	A Boolean value that indicates whether database-style NULL values are permitted in this column in the actual data rows.
	A database-style NULL value is not the same as the Visual Basic *Nothing* value, nor is it equal to the *null* value in C#. Instead, they are more akin to the nullable data types available in both languages—but still not exactly the same.
	The .NET Framework includes a *System.DBNull* class that you can use to test for NULL values in ADO.NET fields. Use this object's *Value.Equals* method to test a value for equivalence to *DBNull*.
	C#
	`if (DBNull.Value.Equals(fieldValue))...`
	Visual Basic
	`If (DBNull.Value.Equals(fieldValue)) Then...`
	Visual Basic also includes an intrinsic function, *IsDBNull*, that provides similar functionality.
	Visual Basic
	`If (IsDBNull(fieldValue)) Then...`
	By default, all ADO.NET fields allow NULL values.
AutoIncrement, AutoIncrementSeed, AutoIncrementStep	These three properties control the auto-increment functionality of a column. When enabled, new rows added to a *DataTable* automatically generate new values for auto-increment columns, with these new values based on the rules established by the *AutoIncrementSeed* and *AutoIncrementStep* properties. By default, the *AutoIncrement* property is set to *False*, which disables the functionality.

Property	Description
Caption	Provides a place to store a user-friendly title or description for the column. If unassigned, this property returns the value of the *ColumnName* property. Not all database platforms support the idea of a column caption. When connecting an ADO.NET *DataTable* instance to a database, this property might or might not be supported.
ColumnName	This is the name of the column, which is typically assigned through the *DataColumn* class's constructor.
DataType	This property identifies the data type of the column, which is also normally assigned through the *DataColumn* class's constructor. After data has been added to a *DataTable*, the data type for each column is set and can't be modified.
DateTimeMode	For columns that track date and time information, this property defines the rules for storing the time and its related time-zone information.
DefaultValue	Any column in a *DataTable* can include a default value. This value is assigned to the relevant column any time a new row is created. You can replace the default value in a specific data row as needed.
MaxLength	For columns that store text data, this property indicates the maximum length of the text. By default, the maximum length is set to -1, which indicates no maximum length.
ReadOnly	Read-only columns cannot be modified in any data row that has already been added to a table. By default, columns can be updated as needed.
Unique	This Boolean property, when set to *True*, establishes a "unique value" constraint on the field. No two rows within the table will be allowed to have the same value. Also, NULL values aren't allowed in columns marked as unique.

In addition to these column-level properties, the containing *DataTable* class includes a *PrimaryKey* property that lets you indicate the column (or multiple columns) that make up the table's primary key. This property hosts an array of *DataColumn* objects taken directly from the *Columns* collection of the same *DataTable*.

```csharp
C#
DataTable customer = new DataTable("Customer");
customer.Columns.Add("ID", typeof(long));
customer.Columns.Add("FullName", typeof(string));
// ----- Use ID for the primary key.
customer.PrimaryKey = new DataColumn[] {customer.Columns["ID"]};
```

Visual Basic

```vb
Dim customer As New DataTable("Customer")
customer.Columns.Add("ID", GetType(Long))
customer.Columns.Add("FullName", GetType(String)
' ----- Use ID for the primary key.
customer.PrimaryKey = {customer.Columns("ID")}
```

Note The table-level *PrimaryKey* setting, the column-specific *Unique* property, and other similar limitations on the table's data are known as *constraints*. ADO.NET includes a *Constraint* class that works in tandem with these property settings. Constraints are discussed in Chapter 5, "Bringing Related Data Together."

Although each *DataColumn* added to the *Columns* collection of a *DataTable* defines the columns that appear in a table, they don't hold any actual row data. The individual column-specific data values for each row are added through the *DataTable* object's *Rows* collection. Chapter 3 contains details on adding data to a table.

Adding Columns to a *DataTable*: C#

Note This exercise uses the "Chapter 2 CSharp" sample project and continues the previous exercise in this chapter.

1. Open the source code view for the *Switchboard* form. Locate the *GetColumnTable* function. This routine already contains a single statement.

   ```csharp
   return null;
   ```

2. Replace that line with the following statements to create a new *DataTable* with columns and a primary key:

   ```csharp
   // ----- Return a table that has columns.
   DataTable theTable = new DataTable("Customer");

   // ----- Add some basic columns.
   theTable.Columns.Add("ID", typeof(long));
   theTable.Columns.Add("FullName", typeof(string));
   theTable.Columns.Add("LastOrderDate", typeof(DateTime));

   // ----- Create a primary key for the table.
   theTable.PrimaryKey = new DataColumn[] {theTable.Columns["ID"]};

   // ----- Finished.
   return theTable;
   ```

3. Open the source code view for the *TableDetails* form. Locate the *TableDetails_Load* routine. Just below the comment, "Add the columns to the display list," add the following statements to access individual columns of the *DataTable*:

```
foreach (DataColumn oneColumn in ActiveTable.Columns)
    this.AllColumns.Items.Add(oneColumn);
if (this.AllColumns.Items.Count == 0)
    this.AllColumns.Items.Add("No columns available");
```

4. Locate the *AllColumns_DrawItem* event handler. Just below the comment, "Extract the column details," add the following statements to access members of the *DataColumn*:

```
columnName = itemDetail.ColumnName;
dataTypeName = itemDetail.DataType.ToString();
isPrimaryKey = ((ActiveTable.PrimaryKey != null) &&
    (ActiveTable.PrimaryKey.Contains(itemDetail) == true));
```

5. Run the application. When the switchboard appears, click the Show Table with Columns button. The *TableDetails* form opens with a structural view of the table and its column details.

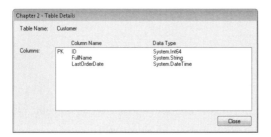

Adding Columns to a *DataTable*: Visual Basic

> **Note** This exercise uses the "Chapter 2 VB" sample project and continues the previous exercise in this chapter.

1. Open the source code view for the *Switchboard* form. Locate the *GetColumnTable* function. This routine already contains a single statement.

```
Return Nothing
```

2. Replace that line with the following statements to create a new *DataTable* with columns and a primary key:

```
' ----- Return a table that has columns.
Dim theTable As New DataTable("Customer")
```

```
' ----- Add some basic columns.
theTable.Columns.Add("ID", GetType(Long))
theTable.Columns.Add("FullName", GetType(String))
theTable.Columns.Add("LastOrderDate", GetType(Date))

' ----- Create a primary key for the table.
theTable.PrimaryKey = {theTable.Columns("ID")}

' ----- Finished.
Return theTable
```

3. Open the source code view for the *TableDetails* form. Locate the *TableDetails_Load* routine. Just below the comment that says "Add the columns to the display list," add the following statements to access individual columns of the *DataTable*:

```
For Each oneColumn In ActiveTable.Columns
    AllColumns.Items.Add(oneColumn)
Next oneColumn
If (AllColumns.Items.Count = 0) Then _
    AllColumns.Items.Add("No columns available")
```

4. Locate the *AllColumns_DrawItem* event handler. Just below the comment that says "Extract the column details," add the following statements to access members of the *DataColumn*:

```
columnName = itemDetail.ColumnName
dataTypeName = itemDetail.DataType.ToString()
isPrimaryKey = ((ActiveTable.PrimaryKey IsNot Nothing) AndAlso
    (ActiveTable.PrimaryKey.Contains(itemDetail) = True))
```

5. Run the application. When the switchboard appears, click the Show Table with Columns button. The *TableDetails* form opens with a structural view of the table and its column details.

Dataset Designer

Visual Studio includes the *Dataset Designer*, a drag-and-drop tool through which you can design your own ADO.NET data sets, including multiple data tables within the set. As with the data sets created using the Data Source Connection Wizard (refer to the "Connecting to External Data" section, on page 8 in Chapter 1), the Dataset Designer creates ADO.NET objects that reside within your Visual Basic or C# project.

You can use *DataTable* objects created with the Dataset Designer in your code just like the *DataTable* objects you built using code earlier in this chapter. However, rather than being built with C# or Visual Basic source code, you create the tables with your mouse. These tables are stored as XML, in a file with an .xsd extension. (Visual Studio will also add a few other files that it requires to support the Dataset Designer environment. Visual Studio generates these files automatically, and you shouldn't change them manually.)

Using the Dataset Designer is straightforward. You add a *DataSet* item to your project, which induces Visual Studio to display the designer. Using designer-specific toolbox items, you create your data tables and the relationships between them. You can also drag existing database tables from the Solution Explorer onto the design surface and customize them to meet your application's needs. The following two examples take you through the process of building a *DataTable* using the Dataset Designer.

Creating a Custom Table in the Dataset Designer

1. Start a new Visual Basic or C# project. A Windows Forms application might be the most convenient for this demonstration, but most other project types will work as well. (The images shown in this example use a C# project, but the process is identical for Visual Basic.)

2. Add a new *DataSet* item to your project. Select Project | Add New Item from the Visual Studio menu. When the Add New Item dialog box appears, select the Data item from the Installed Templates panel and then select DataSet from the main list of items. Provide a file name with an .xsd extension in the Name field and then click the Add button. Visual Studio creates the necessary files and opens the designer.

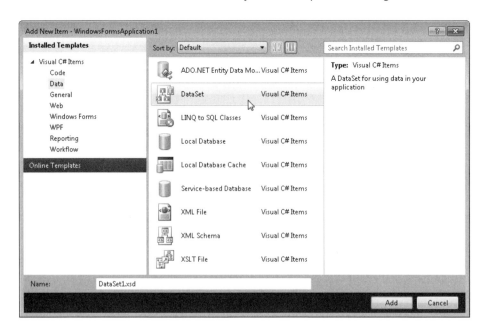

3. The designer displays a blank surface on which you will craft your table.

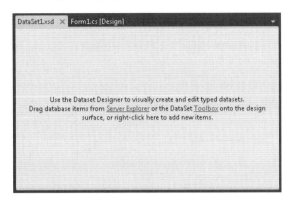

The Toolbox (accessible through the View | Toolbox menu or possibly already visible within the development environment), which is commonly used in Windows Forms projects and other projects with a visual focus, now displays items specific to the designer: *DataTable*, *Query*, *Relation*, and *TableAdapter*.

For this example, you will focus on the *DataTable* element. Add a *DataTable* to the designer by double-clicking the *DataTable* tool or by dragging the *DataTable* tool to the designer surface. A new table named *DataTable1* appears on the surface.

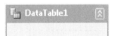

4. Modify the name of the table either by clicking the name in the table's image or through the *Name* entry in the Properties panel. Changes to the table name are reflected in the *TableName* property of the resulting *DataTable* object. Rename the sample table to **Customer**.

5. Add columns to the table (and in turn, to the underlying *DataTable* object's *Columns* collection) by right-clicking the title bar of the table image and selecting Add | Column from the shortcut menu that appears. When the table is selected, you can also use the keyboard shortcut Ctrl+L to add new columns.

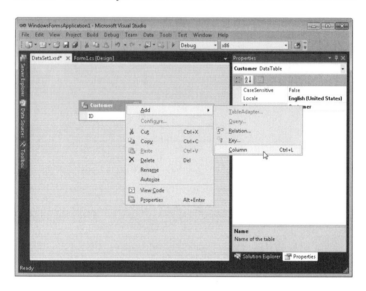

Add three columns to the Customer table. Name them **ID**, **FullName**, and **LastOrderDate**.

6. Adding a primary key is just as easy. The same Add menu used to create a new column includes a Key menu command. After you have added one or more columns to the table's definition, selecting the Add | Key shortcut menu displays the Unique Constraint dialog box. This dialog box serves two purposes: to indicate which columns should have their *Unique* properties enabled and to establish the primary key for the table.

Bring up the Unique Constraint dialog box for the Customer table. To create a primary key using the ID column, select the ID check box in the Columns list and then select the Primary Key check box underneath the Columns list. Click OK to add the key constraint to the table.

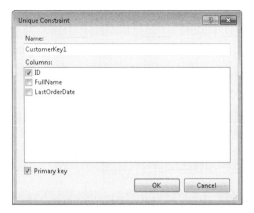

7. To set the properties of each column, select the column name in the designer's view of the table and then use the development environment's Properties panel to modify the relevant settings. If you click the ID column in the Customer table, you will see that the designer already set this column's *AllowDBNull* property to *False* and its *Unique* property to *True*, two requirements for any primary key column.

   Select the ID column from the table's image and change its *DataType* property to **System.Int64**. Alter the *LastOrderDate* column in the same way, so that its *DataType* property is set to **System.DateTime**.

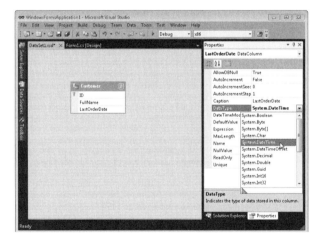

8. The designer includes features for establishing relationships between tables and for building custom data queries. These ADO.NET features will be discussed in later chapters. For now, save the changes you made in the designer by choosing File | Save in the Visual Studio menu.

Adding an existing database table to the designer surface is as simple as creating a new table. The main difference is that instead of obtaining new designer items from the Toolbox, you get them from the Server Explorer, another toolbox-like panel in Visual Studio.

Adding a Database Table to the Dataset Designer

1. In a C# or Visual Basic project, open the Dataset Designer by adding a *DataSet* item to the project, as detailed in the previous exercise.

Note If the Server Explorer is not already visible in the development environment, access it by choosing View | Server Explorer. If you completed the exercise in Chapter 1 that added a connection to the StepSample example database, that connection will appear in the Server Explorer. (If not, you can add a connection to the database by right-clicking Data Connections in the Server Explorer and following the prompts, as discussed in the Chapter 1 example.)

Some editions of Visual Studio include a Database Explorer instead of a Server Explorer. Although this example uses the Server Explorer, completing the steps using the Database Explorer is a nearly identical process. Access the Database Explorer by choosing View | Database Explorer.

2. Expand the Data Connections item in the Server Explorer. Then expand the StepSample database entry and the Tables item within it.

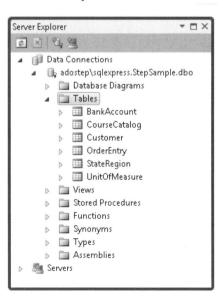

3. To add one of the tables to the designer, drag it from the Server Explorer to the design surface. For example, dragging the Customer table places a representation of that table's structure on the design surface. The designer also sets all the correct properties for the table and its columns in the Properties panel.

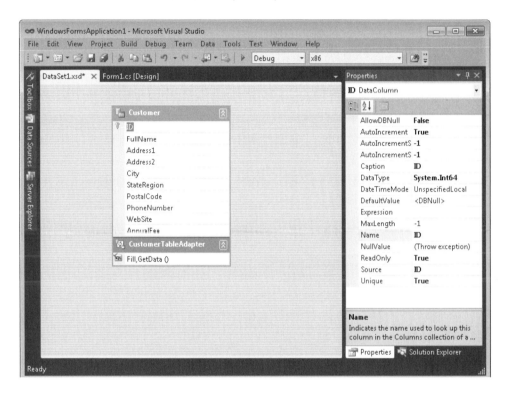

After you have added a complete .xsd file to a project through the Dataset Designer, its member tables are immediately available to the project's source code. In this exercise, you will complete the sample project started earlier in this chapter.

Using Dataset Designer Tables in Code

> **Note** If you have not yet done so, follow the coding steps for the "Chapter 2 VB" or "Chapter 2 CSharp" project documented previously.

1. Using the steps in the prior example, add the Customer table to a new Dataset Designer file named ExternalTable.xsd.

2. Open the source code for the Switchboard form. Locate the *GetDesignerTable* function. The code currently includes a single source code line that returns *null* (in C#) or *Nothing* (in Visual Basic). Replace this line with the following source code:

C#
```
return new ExternalTable.CustomerDataTable();
```

Visual Basic
```
Return New ExternalTable.CustomerDataTable
```

3. Run the application. When the switchboard appears, click the Show Designer Table button. The *TableDetails* form opens with a structural view of the Customer table from the StepSample database.

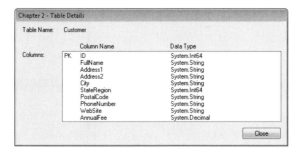

Summary

This chapter introduced the *DataTable* class, the focus of data activity in ADO.NET. To be useful, the *DataTable* class requires support from additional objects, especially the *DataColumn* class that defines the columns for a table. There are many ways to create data tables in .NET applications. Direct coding of the relevant table objects in Visual Basic or C# source code is quite common, but you can also build new tables visually by using the Visual Studio Dataset Designer. Adding existing table designs from external databases is also an option.

After the table structures exist in code, they can be processed and analyzed just like any other set of objects. In the example in the preceding section, you added *DataColumn* objects from a data table as items in a *ListBox* control, and the control displayed various properties from each column in its list of items.

Chapter 2 Quick Reference

To	Do This
Design a *DataTable* in code	Create a *System.Data.DataTable* object.
	Create one or more objects and add them to the table's *Columns* collection.
Add a primary key in code	Assign to the *DataTable* object's *PrimaryKey* property an array of items from the table's *Columns* collection.
Build a new table visually	Create or open a project.
	Select Project | Add New Item.
	Add a *DataSet* item to your project.
	Drag *DataTable* items from the Toolbox to the Dataset Designer design surface.
	Use Ctrl+L to add new columns quickly.
Add an external database table visually	Create or open a project.
	Select Project | Add New Item.
	Add a *DataSet* item to your project.
	Drag the table from the Server Explorer (or Database Explorer) to the Dataset Designer design surface.

Chapter 3
Storing Data in Memory

After completing this chapter, you will be able to:

- Explain how a *DataTable* stores data

- Add new data rows to a table

- Examine, update, and remove existing values in a table row

- Explain how ADO.NET differentiates between pending and final data values

- Integrate data verification code into your *DataTable* object

Adding columns to a *DataTable* is an essential step in managing data in ADO.NET, but the columns themselves contain no data. To store actual data values in an ADO.NET table, you must use the *DataRow* class. After you place one or more data rows in a table, the real work of managing application-specific information begins. This chapter introduces the *DataRow* class and its role in data storage within each data table.

> **Note** The exercises in this chapter all use the same sample project, a simple editor of *DataRow* records within a single *DataTable*. Although you will be able to run the application after each exercise, the expected results for the full application might not appear until you complete all exercises in the chapter.

Adding Data

Adding new data rows to a table is a three-step process:

1. Create a new row object.

2. Store the actual data values in the row object.

3. Add the row object to the table.

Creating New Rows

The *DataColumn* objects you add to a *DataTable* let you define an unlimited number of column combinations. One table might manage information on individuals, with textual name fields and dates for birthdays and driver-license expirations. Another table might exist to track the score in a baseball game, and contain no names or dates at all. The type of information you store in a table depends on the columns included in that table, along with the name, data type, and field constraints for each column.

The *DataRow* class lets you store a single row of data in a table. However, a row of data that tracks customers or medical patients is not the same as a row that tracks baseball scores. The columns differ in number, data types, and even their names and positions. Therefore, each ADO.NET *DataRow* must be configured to work with a specific *DataTable* and its collection of *DataColumn* instances.

The *DataTable* class includes the *NewRow* method to generate table-specific data rows. Whenever you want to add a new row of data to a table, the first step always involves generating a new *DataRow* with the *NewRow* method.

C#

```csharp
DataRow oneRow = someTable.NewRow();
```

Visual Basic

```vb
Dim oneRow As DataRow = someTable.NewRow()
```

The generated row includes information about each data column defined for the table. Typically, the data associated with each column in the new row is initially NULL, the database state for an unassigned field. However, if a *DataColumn* definition includes a *DefaultValue* setting, that initial value will appear immediately in the generated row for the named column. Also, any column that has its *AutoIncrement* and related fields set (typically a primary key field) will include generated sequential values for that column.

Defining Row Values

The *DataRow* class includes an *Item* property that provides access to each defined column, by name, zero-based index number, or reference to the physical *DataColumn* instance. When writing code with a specific table format in mind, programmers generally use the column-name method because it makes clear which field is being referenced in a code statement.

C#

```csharp
oneRow.Item["ID"] = 123;              // by column name
oneRow.Item[0] = 123;                 // by column position
DataColumn whichColumn = someTable.Columns[0];
oneRow.Item[whichColumn] = 123;  // by column instance
```

Visual Basic

```vb
oneRow.Item("ID") = 123          ' by column name
oneRow.Item(0) = 123             ' by column position
Dim whichColumn As DataColumn = someTable.Columns(0)
oneRow.Item(whichColumn) = 123   ' by column instance
```

Because *Item* is the default member for the *DataRow* class, you can omit the name when referencing row values, as shown here:

C#
```
oneRow["ID"] = 123;
```

Visual Basic
```
oneRow("ID") = 123
```

Visual Basic includes a special "exclamation point" syntax that condenses the statement even more, but you can use it only with column names, not with column indexes.

Visual Basic
```
oneRow!ID = 123
```

 Note Members of the *Item* class are defined as the generic *Object* type; they are not strongly typed to the data type defined for the columns. This means that you can store data of an incorrect type in any field during this assignment phase. Errors will not be reported until you attempt to add the *DataRow* object to the table's *Rows* collection, as described in the "Storing Rows in a Table" section of this chapter on page 40.

As you assign values to a row, they become available immediately for use in other expressions.

C#
```
orderData["Subtotal"] = orderRecord.PreTaxTotal;
orderData["SalesTax"] = orderRecord.PreTaxTotal * orderRecord.TaxRate;
orderData["Total"] = orderData["Subtotal"] + orderData["SalesTax"];
```

Visual Basic
```
orderData!Subtotal = orderRecord.PreTaxTotal
orderData!SalesTax = orderRecord.PreTaxTotal * orderRecord.TaxRate
orderData!Total = orderData!Subtotal + orderData!SalesTax
```

Fields with no default or auto-increment value are automatically set to NULL. If for any reason you need to set a field to NULL from a non-NULL state, assign it with the value of .NET's *DBNull* class.

```
C#
oneRow["Comments"] = System.DBNull.Value;
```

```
Visual Basic
oneRow!Comments = System.DBNull.Value
```

As mentioned in Chapter 2, "Building Tables of Data," you can test field values in C# using the *DBNull.Value.Equals* method or in Visual Basic with the *IsDBNull* function. The *DataRow* class includes its own *IsNull* method; it is functionally equivalent to the methods from Chapter 2. Instead of passing the *IsNull* method a field value to test, you pass it the column's name, the column's position, or an instance of the column.

```
C#
if (oneRow.IsNull("Comments"))...
```

```
Visual Basic
If (oneRow.IsNull("Comments") = True)...
```

 Note *System.DBNull* is not the same as *null* in C#, or *Nothing* in Visual Basic. Those keywords indicate the absence of an object's value. *System.DBNull.Value* is an object that presents a value.

Storing Rows in a Table

After you have assigned all required data values to the columns in a new row, add that row to the *DataTable* using the table's *Rows.Add* method.

```
C#
someTable.Rows.Add(oneRow);
```

```
Visual Basic
someTable.Rows.Add(oneRow)
```

An overload of the *Add* method lets you skip the formal row-object creation process; instead, you supply the final field values directly as arguments. All provided values must appear in the same order and position as the table's *DataColumn* instances.

C#

```
// ----- Assumes column 0 is numeric, 1 is string.
someTable.Rows.Add(new Object[] {123, "Fred"});
```

Visual Basic

```
' ----- Assumes column 0 is numeric, 1 is string.
someTable.Rows.Add(123, "Fred");
```

Whichever method you employ, the *Add* process tests all data values to be added to the table for data type compliance before adding the row. If the new row contains any values that can't be stored in the target column-specific data type, the *Add* method throws an exception.

Adding Rows to a *DataTable*: C#

1. Open the "Chapter 3 CSharp" project from the installed samples folder. The project includes two *Windows.Forms* classes: *AccountManager* and *AccountDetail*.

2. Open the source code view for the *AccountManager* form. Locate the *AccountManager_Load* event handler. This routine creates a custom *DataTable* instance with five columns: *ID* (a read-only, auto-generated long integer), *FullName* (a required 30-character unique string), *Active* (a Boolean), *AnnualFee* (an optional decimal), and *StartDate* (an optional date).

3. Add the following statements just after the "Build some sample data rows" comment. These rows add new *DataRow* objects to the table using the *Rows.Add* alternative syntax:

    ```
    CustomerAccounts.Rows.Add(new Object[] {1L, "Blue Yonder Airlines", true,
        500m, DateTime.Parse("1/1/2007")});
    CustomerAccounts.Rows.Add(new Object[] {2L, "Fourth Coffee", true, 350m,
        DateTime.Parse("7/25/2009")});
    CustomerAccounts.Rows.Add(new Object[] {3L, "Wingtip Toys", false});
    ```

Adding Rows to a *DataTable*: Visual Basic

1. Open the "Chapter 3 VB" project from the installed samples folder. The project includes two *Windows.Forms* classes: *AccountManager* and *AccountDetail*.

2. Open the source code view for the *AccountManager* form. Locate the *AccountManager_Load* event handler. This routine creates a custom *DataTable* instance with five columns: *ID* (a read-only, auto-generated long integer), *FullName* (a required 30-character unique string), *Active* (a Boolean), *AnnualFee* (an optional decimal), and *StartDate* (an optional date).

3. Add the following statements just after the "Build some sample data rows" comment. These rows add new *DataRow* objects to the table using the *Rows.Add* alternative syntax:

```
CustomerAccounts.Rows.Add({1&, "Blue Yonder Airlines", True, 500@, #1/1/2007#})
CustomerAccounts.Rows.Add({2&, "Fourth Coffee", True, 350@, #7/25/2009#})
CustomerAccounts.Rows.Add({3&, "Wingtip Toys", False})
```

Examining and Changing Data

After adding a data row to a table, you can process it as a table member. For instance, you can iterate through the table's *Rows* collection, examining the stored column values as you pass through each record. The following code adds up the sales tax for all records in the *allSales* table:

```
C#
decimal totalTax = 0m;
foreach (DataRow scanRow in someTable.Rows)
    if (!DBNull.Value.Equals(scanRow["SalesTax"]))
        totalTax += (decimal)scanRow["SalesTax"];
```

```
Visual Basic
Dim totalTax As Decimal = 0@
For Each scanRow As DataRow In someTable.Rows
    If (IsDBNull(scanRow!SalesTax) = False) Then _
        totalTax += CDec(scanRow!SalesTax)
Next scanRow
```

Because each row's collection of items is not strongly typed, you might need to cast or convert each field to the target data type before using it.

 Note ADO.NET does include extension methods that provide strongly typed access to each row's members. These methods were added to the system to support LINQ and its method of querying data within the context of the Visual Basic or C# language. Part IV of this book introduces LINQ and its use with ADO.NET data.

Because of this lack of strong typing, be careful when assigning new values to any row already included in a table. For example, code that assigns a string value to an integer column will compile without error, but will generate a runtime error.

Modifying Existing Rows in a *DataTable*: C#

 Note This exercise uses the "Chapter 3 CSharp" sample project and continues the preceding exercise in this chapter.

1. Open the source code view for the *AccountDetail* form. Locate the *AccountDetail_Load* routine.

2. Add the following code, which fills in the form's display fields with content from an existing *DataRow* instance:

```
if (AccountEntry != null)
{
    AccountID.Text = string.Format("{0:0}", AccountEntry["ID"]);
    ActiveAccount.Checked = (bool)AccountEntry["Active"];
    if (DBNull.Value.Equals(AccountEntry["FullName"]) == false)
        AccountName.Text = (string)AccountEntry["FullName"];
    if (DBNull.Value.Equals(AccountEntry["AnnualFee"]) == false)
        AnnualFee.Text = string.Format("{0:0.00}",
            (decimal)AccountEntry["AnnualFee"]);
    if (DBNull.Value.Equals(AccountEntry["StartDate"]) == false)
        StartDate.Text = string.Format("{0:d}",
            (DateTime)AccountEntry["StartDate"]);
}
```

3. Locate the *ActOK_Click* routine. In the *Try* block, just after the "Save the changes in the record" comment, you'll find the following code line:

```
workArea.BeginEdit();
```

Just after that line, add the following code, which updates an existing *DataRow* instance with the user's input:

```
workArea["Active"] = ActiveAccount.Checked;
if (AccountName.Text.Trim().Length == 0)
    workArea["FullName"] = DBNull.Value;
else
    workArea["FullName"] = AccountName.Text.Trim();
if (AnnualFee.Text.Trim().Length == 0)
    workArea["AnnualFee"] = DBNull.Value;
else
    workArea["AnnualFee"] = decimal.Parse(AnnualFee.Text);
if (StartDate.Text.Trim().Length == 0)
    workArea["StartDate"] = DBNull.Value;
else
    workArea["StartDate"] = DateTime.Parse(StartDate.Text);
```

Modifying Existing Rows in a *DataTable*: Visual Basic

> **Note** This exercise uses the "Chapter 3 VB" sample project and continues the preceding exercise in this chapter.

1. Open the source code view for the *AccountDetail* form. Locate the *AccountDetail_Load* routine.

2. Add the following code, which fills in the form's display fields with content from an existing *DataRow* instance:

```
If (AccountEntry IsNot Nothing) Then
    AccountID.Text = CStr(AccountEntry!ID)
    ActiveAccount.Checked = CBool(AccountEntry!Active)
    If (IsDBNull(AccountEntry!FullName) = False) Then _
        AccountName.Text = CStr(AccountEntry!FullName)
    If (IsDBNull(AccountEntry!AnnualFee) = False) Then _
        AnnualFee.Text = Format(CDec(AccountEntry!AnnualFee), "0.00")
    If (IsDBNull(AccountEntry!StartDate) = False) Then _
        StartDate.Text = Format(CDate(AccountEntry!StartDate), "Short Date")
End If
```

3. Locate the *ActOK_Click* routine. In the *Try* block, just after the "Save the changes in the record" comment, you'll find the following code line:

```
workArea.BeginEdit()
```

Just after that line, add the following code, which updates an existing *DataRow* instance with the user's input:

```
workArea!Active = ActiveAccount.Checked
If (AccountName.Text.Trim.Length = 0) _
    Then workArea!FullName = DBNull.Value _
    Else workArea!FullName = AccountName.Text.Trim
If (AnnualFee.Text.Trim.Length = 0) _
    Then workArea!AnnualFee = DBNull.Value _
    Else workArea!AnnualFee = CDec(AnnualFee.Text)
If (StartDate.Text.Trim.Length = 0) _
    Then workArea!StartDate = DBNull.Value _
    Else workArea!StartDate = CDate(StartDate.Text)
```

Removing Data

You remove *DataRow* objects from a table via the *DataTable.Rows* collection's *Remove* and *RemoveAt* methods. The *Remove* method accepts an instance of a row that is currently in the table.

```csharp
C#
DataRow oneRow = someTable.Rows[0];
someTable.Rows.Remove(oneRow);
```

Visual Basic
```vb
Dim oneRow As DataRow = someTable.Rows(0)
someTable.Rows.Remove(oneRow)
```

The *RemoveAt* method also removes a row, but you pass it the index position of the row to delete.

```csharp
C#
someTable.Rows.RemoveAt(0);
```

Visual Basic
```vb
someTable.Rows.RemoveAt(0)
```

If you have an instance of a data row available, but you want to call the *RemoveAt* method, you can obtain the index of the row from the *Rows* collection's *IndexOf* method.

```csharp
C#
int rowPosition = someTable.Rows.IndexOf(oneRow);
```

Visual Basic
```vb
Dim rowPosition As Integer = someTable.Rows.IndexOf(oneRow)
```

You can put any row you remove from a table right back into the *Rows* collection by using the standard *DataTable.Rows.Add* method. Another *Rows* method, *InsertAt*, adds a *DataRow* object to a table, but lets you indicate the zero-based position of the newly added row. (The *Add* method always puts new rows at the end of the collection.) The following code inserts a row as the first item in the collection:

```csharp
C#
someTable.Rows.InsertAt(oneRow, 0);
```

Visual Basic
```vb
someTable.Rows.InsertAt(oneRow, 0)
```

To remove all rows from a table at once, use the *DataTable.Rows* object's *Clear* method.

```
C#
someTable.Rows.Clear();
```

```
Visual Basic
someTable.Rows.Clear()
```

As convenient as *Remove*, *RemoveAt*, and *Clear* are, they come with some negative side effects. Because they fully remove a row and all evidence that it ever existed, these methods prevent ADO.NET from performing certain actions, including managing record removes within an external database. The next section, "Batch Processing," discusses a better method of removing data records from a *DataTable* instance.

Batch Processing

The features shown previously for adding, modifying, and removing data records within a *DataTable* all take immediate action on the content of the table. When you use the *Add* method to add a new row, it's included immediately. Any field-level changes made within rows are stored and considered part of the record—assuming that no data-specific exceptions get thrown during the updates. After you remove a row from a table, the table acts as if it never existed.

Although this type of instant data gratification is nice when using a *DataTable* as a simple data store, sometimes it is preferable to postpone data changes or make several changes at once, especially when you need to verify that changes occurring across multiple rows are collectively valid.

ADO.NET includes table and row-level features that let you set up "proposed" changes to be accepted or rejected en masse. When you connect data tables to their external database counterparts in later chapters, ADO.NET uses these features to ensure that updates to both the local copy of the data and the remote database copy retain their integrity. You can also use them for your own purposes, however, to monitor changes to independent *DataTable* instances.

Note In reality, ADO.NET always uses these batch processing monitoring tools when changes are made to any rows in a table, even changes such as those in this chapter's simple code samples. Fortunately, the Framework is designed so that you can safely ignore these monitoring features if you don't need them.

To use the batch system, simply start making changes. When you are ready to save or reject all changes made within a *DataTable*, call the table's *AcceptChanges* method to commit and approve all pending changes, or call the *RejectChanges* method to discard all unsaved changes. Each *DataRow* in the table also includes these methods. You can call the row-level methods directly, but the table-level methods automatically trigger the identically named methods in each modified row.

C#
```
someTable.AcceptChanges();  // Commit all row changes
someTable.RejectChanges();  // Reject changes since last commit
```
Visual Basic
```
someTable.AcceptChanges()  ' Commit all row changes
someTable.RejectChanges()  ' Reject changes since last commit
```

Row State

While making your row-level edits, ADO.NET keeps track of the original and proposed versions of all fields. It also monitors which rows have been added to or deleted from the table, and can revert to the original row values if necessary. The Framework accomplishes this by managing various state fields for each row. The main tracking field is the *DataRow.RowState* property, which uses the following enumerated values:

- ■ *DataRowState.Detached*   The default state for any row that has not yet been added to a *DataTable*.

- ■ *DataRowState.Added*   This is the state for rows added to a table when changes to the table have not yet been confirmed. If you use the *RejectChanges* method on the table, any added rows will be removed immediately.

- ■ *DataRowState.Unchanged*   The default state for any row that already appears in a table, but has not been changed since the last call to *AcceptChanges*. New rows created with the *NewRow* method use this state.

- ■ *DataRowState.Deleted*   Deleted rows aren't actually removed from the table until you call *AcceptChanges*. Instead, they are marked for deletion with this state setting. See the following discussion for the difference between "deleted" and "removed" rows.

- ■ *DataRowState.Modified*   Any row that has had its fields changed in any way is marked as modified.

Every time you add or modify a record, the data table updates the row state accordingly. However, removing records from a data table with the *Rows.Remove* and *Rows.RemoveAt* methods circumvents the row state tracking system, at least from the table's point of view.

To enable ADO.NET batch processing support on deleted rows, use the *DataRow* object's *Delete* method. This does not remove the row from the *DataTable.Rows* collection. Instead, it marks the row's state as deleted. The next time you use the table or row *AcceptChanges* method to confirm all updates, the row will be removed permanently from the table.

If you want to use the batch processing features, or if your *DataTable* instances are associated with a database table, even if that table is temporarily disconnected, you need to use the row-specific *Delete* method instead of *Remove* and *RemoveAt*.

```
C#
someTable.Rows.Remove(oneRow); // Removes row immediately
oneRow.Delete();               // Marks row for removal during approval
```
```
Visual Basic
someTable.Rows.Remove(oneRow) ' Removes row immediately
oneRow.Delete()               ' Marks row for removal during approval
```

If you retain a reference to a deleted row once it has been removed from the table, its *RowState* property will be set to *DataRowState.Detached*, just like a new row that has not yet been added to a table.

> **Note** When working with *DataTable* instances that are connected to true database tables, ADO.NET will still allow you to use the *Remove* and *RemoveAt* methods. However, these methods will not remove the row from the database-side copy. They remove only the local *DataTable.Rows* copy of the row. You must use the row's *Delete* method to ensure that the row gets removed from the database upon acceptance.

Row Versions

When you make changes to data within a data table's rows, ADO.NET keeps multiple copies of each changed value. Row version information applies to an entire row, even if only a single data column in the row has changed.

- **DataRowVersion.Original**   The starting value of the field before it was changed (the value that was in effect after the most recent use of *AcceptChanges* occurred).

- **DataRowVersion.Proposed**   The changed but unconfirmed field value. The *Proposed* version of a field doesn't exist until you begin to make edits to the field or row. When changes are accepted, the proposed value becomes the actual (*Original*) value of the field.

- *DataRowVersion.Current*   For fields with pending edits, this version is the same as *Proposed*. For fields with confirmed changes, the *Current* version is the same as the *Original* version.

- *DataRowVersion.Default*   For rows attached to a *DataTable*, this version is the same as *Current*. For detached rows, *Default* is the same as *Proposed*. The *Default* version of a row is not necessarily the same as the default values that might appear in newly created rows.

Depending on the current state of a row, some of these row versions might not exist. To determine whether a row version does exist, use the *DataRow.HasVersion* method. The following code block uses the *HasVersion* method and a special overload of the *Item* method to access various row versions:

```C#
if (oneRow.HasVersion(DataRowVersion.Proposed))
{
    if (oneRow.Item["Salary", DataRowVersion.Original] !=
            oneRow.Item["Salary", DataRowVersion.Proposed])
        MessageBox.Show("Proposed salary change.");
}
```

```Visual Basic
If (oneRow.HasVersion(DataRowVersion.Proposed) = True) Then
    If (oneRow.Item("Salary", DataRowVersion.Original) <>
            oneRow.Item("Salary", DataRowVersion.Proposed)) Then _
        MessageBox.Show("Proposed salary change.")
End If
```

The default row version returned by the *Item* property is the *Current* version.

Validating Changes

As mentioned earlier in the "Storing Rows in a Table" section on page 40, attempting to store data of the incorrect data type in a column will throw an exception. However, this will not prevent a user from entering invalid values, such as entering 7,437 into a *System.Int32* column that stores a person's age. Instead, you must add validation code to your data table to prevent such data range errors.

Exception-Based Errors

ADO.NET monitors some data errors on your behalf. These errors include the following:

- Assigning data of the wrong data type to a column value.

- Supplying string data to a column that exceeds the maximum length defined in the column's *DataColumn.MaxLength* property.

- Attempting to store a NULL value in a primary key column.

- Adding a duplicate value in a column that has its *Unique* property set.

- Taking data actions that violate one of the table's custom constraints. Constraints are discussed in Chapter 5, "Bringing Related Data Together."

When one of these data violations occurs, ADO.NET throws an exception in your code at the moment when the invalid assignment or data use happens. The following code block generates an exception because it attempts to assign a company name that is too long for a 20-character column:

```C#
DataColumn withRule = someTable.Columns.Add("FullName", typeof(string));
withRule.MaxLength = 20;
// ...later...
DataRow rowToUpdate = someTable.Rows[0];
rowToUpdate["FullName"] = "Graphic Design Institute"; // 24 characters
   // ----- Exception occurs with this assignment
```

```Visual Basic
Dim withRule As DataColumn = someTable.Columns.Add("FullName", GetType(String))
withRule.MaxLength = 20
' ...later...
Dim rowToUpdate As DataRow = someTable.Rows(0)
rowToUpdate!FullName = "Graphic Design Institute"  ' 24 characters
   ' ----- Exception occurs with this assignment
```

Naturally, you would want to enclose such assignments within exception handling blocks. However, there are times when adding this level of error monitoring around every field change is neither convenient nor feasible—not to mention the impact it has on performance when adding or updating large numbers of records. To simplify exception monitoring, the *DataRow* class includes the *BeginEdit* method. When used, any data checks normally done at assignment are postponed until you issue a matching *DataRow.EndEdit* call.

C#

```
rowToUpdate.BeginEdit();
rowToUpdate["FullName"] = "Graphic Design Institute"; // 24 characters
   // ----- No exception occurs
rowToUpdate["RevisionDate"] = DateTime.Today; // Other field changes as needed
rowToUpdate.EndEdit();
   // ----- Exception for FullName field occurs here
```

Visual Basic

```
rowToUpdate.BeginEdit()
rowToUpdate!FullName = "Graphic Design Institute"  ' 24 characters
   ' ----- No exception occurs
rowToUpdate!RevisionDate = Today  ' Other field changes as needed
rowToUpdate.EndEdit()
   ' ----- Exception for FullName field occurs here
```

To roll back any changes made to a row since using *BeginEdit*, use the *CancelEdit* method. Even when you complete a row's changes with the *EndEdit* method, the changes are not yet committed. It is still necessary to call the *AcceptChanges* method, either at the row or the table level.

The *DataTable.AcceptChanges* and *DataRow.AcceptChanges* methods, when used, automatically call *DataRow.EndEdit* on all rows with pending edits. Similarly, *DataTable.RejectChanges* and *DataRow.RejectChanges* automatically issue calls to *DataRow.CancelEdit* on all pending rows changes.

Validation-Based Errors

For data issues not monitored by ADO.NET, including business rule violations, you must set up the validation code yourself. Also, you must manually monitor the data table for such errors and refuse to confirm changes that would violate the custom validation rules.

Validation occurs in the various event handlers for the *DataTable* instance that contains the rows to monitor. Validation of single-column changes typically occurs in the *ColumnChanging* event. For validation rules based on the interaction between multiple fields in a data row, use the *RowChanging* event. The *RowDeleting* and *TableNewRow* events are useful for checking data across multiple rows or the entire table. You can also use any of the other table-level events (*ColumnChanged, RowChanged, RowDeleted, TableClearing, TableCleared*) to execute validation code that meets your specific needs.

Inside the validation event handlers, use the *Proposed* version of a row value to assess its preconfirmed value. When errors occur, use the row's *SetColumnError* method (with the name, position, or instance of the relevant column) to indicate the problem. For row-level errors, assign a description of the problem to the row's *RowError* property. The following code applies a column-level business rule to a numeric field, setting a column error if there is a problem:

C#
```csharp
private void Applicant_ColumnChanging(Object sender,
    System.Data.DataColumnChangeEventArgs e)
{
    // ----- Check the Age column for a valid range.
    if (e.Column.ColumnName == "Age")
    {
        if ((int)e.ProposedValue < 18 || (int)e.ProposedValue > 29)
            e.Row.SetColumnError(e.Column,
                "Applicant's age falls outside the allowed range.");
    }
}
```

Visual Basic
```vb
Private Sub Applicant_ColumnChanging(ByVal sender As Object,
        ByVal e As System.Data.DataColumnChangeEventArgs)
    ' ----- Check the Age column for a valid range.
    If (e.Column.ColumnName = "Age") Then
        If (CInt(e.ProposedValue) < 18) Or (CInt(e.ProposedValue) > 29) Then
            e.Row.SetColumnError(e.Column,
                "Applicant's age falls outside the allowed range.")
        End If
    End If
End Sub
```

Adding column or row-level errors sets both the *DataRow.HasErrors* and the *DataTable.HasErrors* properties to *True*, but that's not enough to trigger an exception. Instead, you need to monitor the *HasErrors* properties before confirming data to ensure that validation rules are properly applied. Another essential method, *ClearErrors*, removes any previous error notices from a row.

C#
```csharp
// ----- Row-level monitoring.
oneRow.ClearErrors();
oneRow.BeginEdit();
oneRow.FullName = "Tailspin Toys";  // Among other changes
if (oneRow.HasErrors)
{
    ShowFirstRowError(oneRow);
    oneRow.CancelEdit();
}
else
    oneRow.EndEdit();

// ----- Table-level monitoring. Perform row edits, then...
if (someTable.HasErrors)
{
    DataRow[] errorRows = someTable.GetErrors();
    ShowFirstRowError(errorRows[0]);
    someTable.RejectChanges();  // Or, let user make additional corrections
}
```

```
else
    someTable.AcceptChanges();
// ...later...
public void ShowFirstRowError(DataRow whichRow)
{
    // ----- Show first row-level or column-level error.
    string errorText = "No error";
    DataColumn[] errorColumns = whichRow.GetColumnsInError();
    if (errorColumns.Count > 0)
        errorText = whichRow.GetColumnError(errorColumns[0]);
    else if (whichRow.RowError.Length > 0)
        errorText = whichRow.RowError;
    if (errorText.Length == 0) errorText = "No error";
    MessageBox.Show(errorText);
}
```

Visual Basic

```
' ----- Row-level monitoring.
oneRow.ClearErrors()
oneRow.BeginEdit()
oneRow.FullName = "Tailspin Toys"  ' Among other changes
If (oneRow.HasErrors = True) Then
    ShowFirstRowError(oneRow)
    oneRow.CancelEdit()
Else
    oneRow.EndEdit()
End If


' ----- Table-level monitoring. Perform row edits, then...
If (someTable.HasErrors = True) Then
    Dim errorRows() As DataRow = someTable.GetErrors()
    ShowFirstRowError(errorRows(0))
    someTable.RejectChanges()  ' Or, let user make additional corrections
Else
    someTable.AcceptChanges()
End If


' ...later...

Public Sub ShowFirstRowError(ByVal whichRow As DataRow)
    ' ----- Show first column-level or row-level error.
    Dim errorText As String = ""
    Dim errorColumns() As DataColumn = whichRow.GetColumnsInError()

    If (errorColumns.Count > 0) Then
        errorText = whichRow.GetColumnError(errorColumns(0))
    ElseIf (whichRow.RowError.Length > 0) Then
        errorText = whichRow.RowError
    End If
    If (errorText.Length = 0) Then errorText = "No error"
    MessageBox.Show(errorText)
End Sub
```

Validating Content in a *DataRow*: C#

 Note This exercise uses the "Chapter 3 CSharp" sample project and continues the preceding exercise in this chapter.

1. Open the source code view for the *AccountManager* form.

2. Locate the *CustomerAccounts_ColumnChanging* event handler, which is called whenever a column value in a *CustomerAccounts* table row changes. Add the following code, which checks for valid data in two of the columns:

```csharp
if (e.Column.ColumnName == "AnnualFee")
{
    // ----- Annual fee may not be negative.
    if (DBNull.Value.Equals(e.ProposedValue) == false)
    {
        if ((decimal)e.ProposedValue < 0m)
            e.Row.SetColumnError(e.Column,
                "Annual fee may not be negative.");
    }
}
else if (e.Column.ColumnName == "StartDate")
{
    // ----- Start date must be on or before today.
    if (DBNull.Value.Equals(e.ProposedValue) == false)
    {
        if (((DateTime)e.ProposedValue).Date > DateTime.Today)
            e.Row.SetColumnError(e.Column,
                "Start date must occur on or before today.");
    }
}
```

3. Locate the *CustomerAccounts_RowChanging* event handler, which is called whenever any value in a row changes within the *CustomerAccounts* table. Add the following code, which checks for valid data involving multiple columns:

```csharp
if (e.Row.HasVersion(DataRowVersion.Proposed) == true)
{
    if (((bool)e.Row["Active", DataRowVersion.Proposed] == true) &&
            (DBNull.Value.Equals(e.Row["StartDate",
            DataRowVersion.Proposed]) == true))
        e.Row.RowError = "Active accounts must have a valid start date.";
}
```

4. Run the program. Use its features to create, edit, and delete data rows. When you attempt to provide invalid data—incorrect data types, violations of business rules, duplicate account names—the program provides the appropriate error messages.

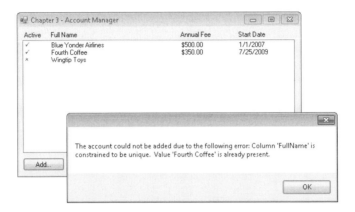

Validating Content in a *DataRow*: Visual Basic

 Note This exercise uses the "Chapter 3 VB" sample project and continues the preceding exercise in this chapter.

1. Open the source code view for the *AccountManager* form.

2. Locate the *CustomerAccounts_ColumnChanging* event handler, which is called whenever a column value in a *CustomerAccounts* table row changes. Add the following code, which checks for valid data in two of the columns:

```
If (e.Column.ColumnName = "AnnualFee") Then
    ' ----- Annual fee may not be negative.
    If (IsDBNull(e.ProposedValue) = False) Then
        If (CDec(e.ProposedValue) < 0@) Then _
            e.Row.SetColumnError(e.Column,
            "Annual fee may not be negative.")
    End If
ElseIf (e.Column.ColumnName = "StartDate") Then
    ' ----- Start date must be on or before today.
    If (IsDBNull(e.ProposedValue) = False) Then
        If (CDate(e.ProposedValue).Date > Today) Then _
            e.Row.SetColumnError(e.Column,
            "Start date must occur on or before today.")
    End If
End If
```

3. Locate the *CustomerAccounts_RowChanging* event handler, which is called whenever any value in a row changes within the *CustomerAccounts* table. Add the following code, which checks for valid data involving multiple columns:

```
If (e.Row.HasVersion(DataRowVersion.Proposed) = True) Then
    If (CBool(e.Row("Active", DataRowVersion.Proposed)) = True) And
            (IsDBNull(e.Row("StartDate",
            DataRowVersion.Proposed)) = True) Then
        e.Row.RowError = "Active accounts must have a valid start date."
    End If
End If
```

4. Run the program. Use its features to create, edit, and delete data rows. When you attempt to provide invalid data—incorrect data types, violations of business rules, duplicate account names—the program provides the appropriate error messages.

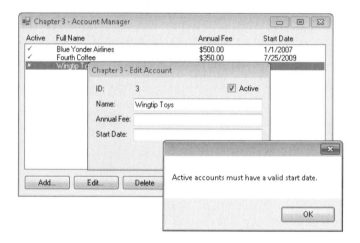

Summary

This chapter discussed the *DataRow* class, the final destination of all data in ADO.NET. With one instance created per data record, the *DataRow* class manages each individual columnar field. When used alone, its stored values use the generic *Object* data type, but when inserted into a *DataTable* object's *Rows* collection, all data type limitations and other constraints established for the table's columns act together to verify the row's content.

Beyond these column settings, you can add event handlers to the *DataTable* that apply custom business rules to the column and row data, providing an additional layer of validation—and ultimately, integrity—for the table's data.

Chapter 3 Quick Reference

To	Do This
Add a row to a *DataTable*	Use the *DataTable* object's *NewRow* method to obtain a *DataRow* instance.
	Update the *Item* values in the *DataRow* as needed.
	Add the row using the table's *Rows.Add* method.
Delete a row from a *DataTable*	Call the *DataRow* object's *Delete* method.
	Call the *DataTable* object's *AcceptChanges* method.
Check for data issues in new and modified *DataRow* objects	Create a *DataTable*.
	Add *DataColumn* definitions as needed.
	Add event handlers for the *DataTable* object's *ColumnChanging*, *RowChanging*, or other events.
	In the handlers, call the *DataRow* object's *SetColumnError* method or update its *RowError* property.
Temporarily suspend data validation while modifying a data row	Call the *DataRow* object's *BeginEdit* method.
	Update the *Item* values in the *DataRow* as needed.
	Call the *DataRow* object's *EndEdit* method.

Chapter 4
Accessing the Right Data Values

After completing this chapter, you will be able to:

- Find items in a *DataTable* by primary key

- Search for *DataRow* instances using standard query statements

- Obtain a set of *DataRow* objects sorted by one or more columns

- Add expression columns to a *DataTable* that present calculated values

Although adding records to a *DataTable* is important, the real value of ADO.NET lies in getting those records back out in a variety of ways. Fortunately, the data framework includes many different methods and tools to fulfill that very purpose.

This chapter introduces a few of the most basic tools, all of which appear in the *DataTable*, *DataColumn*, and *DataRow* classes you've already met. Each data table includes features that let you select just the records you need. These features are flexible enough to rival those you might find in traditional databases. The chapter also includes a discussion of "expression columns," a way to add useful values to each table row without adding any actual data.

> **Note** The exercises in this chapter all use the same sample project, a tool that queries data from a sample *DataTable*. Although you will be able to run the application after each exercise, the expected results for the full application might not appear until you complete all exercises in the chapter.
>
> Both forms in the sample application use the *DataGridView* control, one of the standard controls provided with Visual Studio. Chapter 21, "Binding Data with ADO.NET," discusses the ADO.NET-specific features of this control.

Querying and Sorting Data

In Chapter 3, "Storing Data in Memory," you learn how to iterate through all the records in a *DataTable* object's *Rows* collection. However, there are times when you need to access only specific rows, often based on applying search criteria to one or more of the table's columns. Although you can scan through every row in the table, checking each record as you encounter it to see whether it matches your search limits, the *DataTable* class already includes features that will let you select just those *DataRow* instances that match a selection rule.

Finding Rows by Primary Key

Each *DataTable* can include an optional primary key definition, a collection of *DataColumn* objects assigned to the table's *PrimaryKey* member. This key is often a unique value from a single column, but tables also support multicolumn keys. After you define a table's primary key, all rows added to that table must have a non-NULL, unique key.

To locate a row based on its primary key, use the table's *Rows.Find* method. For tables with single-column keys, pass this method a key value of the appropriate data type. For multi-column keys, pass the key components as an array. *Find* returns a single *DataRow* instance for the matching row.

```csharp
C#
// ----- Single-part key.
DataRow matchingRow = someTable.Rows.Find(searchValue);

// ----- Multi-part key.
DataRow matchingRow = someTable.Rows.Find(new Object[]
    {keyPart1, keyPart2, keyPart3});
```

```vb
Visual Basic
' ----- Single-part key.
Dim matchingRow As DataRow = someTable.Rows.Find(searchValue)

' ----- Multi-part key.
Dim matchingRow As DataRow = someTable.Rows.Find({keyPart1,
    keyPart2, keyPart3})
```

If no row matches the provided primary key, *Find* returns *Nothing* (in Visual Basic) or *null* (in C#). The method throws an exception if you apply it to tables with no defined primary key.

> **Note** It is possible to add two rows with the same primary key to a *DataTable* by disabling its constraints (as discussed in Chapter 5, "Bringing Related Data Together"). In such tables, the *Find* method returns only the first row with a matching primary key value.

Finding a Row by Primary Key: C#

1. Open the "Chapter 4 CSharp" project from the installed samples folder. The project includes two *Windows.Forms* classes: *TableExaminer* and *ResultsViewer*.

2. Open the source code view for the *TableExaminer* form. Locate the *ActPrimaryKey_Click* event handler. This routine obtains a long-integer value from the user and then uses it as the primary key lookup value in the application's sample *DataTable*. Most of the code exists to ensure that the user provides a valid ID.

3. Locate the *try...catch* statement just after the "Perform the lookup" comment. In the *try* block, add the following statement:

```
result = workTable.Rows.Find(usePrimaryKey);
```

This line performs the actual primary-key lookup, returning the *DataRow* of the matching record, or *null* when the key doesn't match any of the table's primary keys.

4. Run the program. On the Lookup By Primary Key tab, enter a value in the Primary Key field (try **2352**), and then click the Lookup button. The matching row appears in a separate window (not shown here).

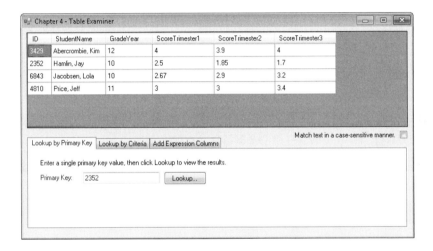

Finding a Row by Primary Key: Visual Basic

1. Open the "Chapter 4 VB" project from the installed samples folder. The project includes two *Windows.Forms* classes: *TableExaminer* and *ResultsViewer*.

2. Open the source code view for the *TableExaminer* form. Locate the *ActPrimaryKey_Click* event handler. This routine obtains a long-integer value from the user and then uses it as the primary key lookup value in the application's sample *DataTable*. Most of the code exists to ensure that the user provides a valid ID.

3. Locate the *Try...Catch* statement just after the "Perform the lookup" comment. In the *Try* block, add the following statement:

```
result = workTable.Rows.Find(usePrimaryKey)
```

This line performs the actual primary-key lookup, returning the *DataRow* of the matching record, or *Nothing* when the key doesn't match any of the table's primary keys.

4. Run the program. On the Lookup By Primary Key tab, enter a value in the Primary Key field (try **2352**), and then click Lookup. The matching row appears in a separate window, as shown here.

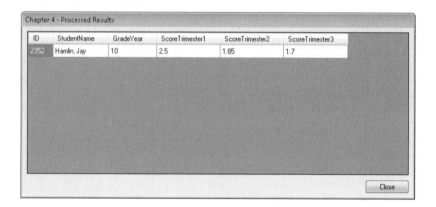

ID	StudentName	GradeYear	ScoreTrimester1	ScoreTrimester2	ScoreTrimester3
2352	Hamlin, Jay	10	2.5	1.85	1.7

Selecting Rows with a Search Criteria

The *Find* method is useful when you need to retrieve a single row based on a primary key lookup value, but useful data analysis typically involves searching across many of a table's columns and returning all possible matches. To provide this functionality, the *DataTable* class includes the *Select* method.

> **Note** When you anticipate issuing the same *Select* request on a table multiple times, it's more efficient to create a *DataView* that provides a limited presentation of the table's rows. Chapter 6, "Turning Data into Information," introduces the *DataView* class and its use in presenting content from a data table.

You pass the *Select* method a string that contains the selection criteria. When successful, the method returns an array of matching *DataRow* instances from the table.

C#
```csharp
DataRow[] matchingRows = someTable.Select(filterCriteria);
```

Visual Basic
```vb
Dim matchingRows() As DataRow = someTable.Select(filterCriteria)
```

> **Note** You can iterate through the returned array as your processing needs require. Although the rows come to you packaged in an array, they are still part of the original table. Any changes you make to these rows affect the underlying table.

The filter expression passed to the *Select* method uses a SQL-like syntax to build a Boolean statement that will either match or not match specific rows in the table. Any of the columns in your *DataTable* object is fair game for comparisons. As an example, the following expression will return all rows with a *Salary* column value of at least 100,000:

```
Salary >= 100000
```

Columns can be compared to each other and standard mathematical expressions can enhance the column elements.

```
Bonus > Salary * 0.15
```

You can string together multiple criteria using the Boolean operators *AND, OR,* and *NOT,* and use parentheses to force evaluation in a specific order.

```
Age >= 18 AND (InSchool = True OR LivingAtHome = True)
```

Table 4-1 lists the some of the elements you can use in filter expressions. To view the full documentation for filter expressions, access the Visual Studio online help entry for "DataColumn. Expression Property."

TABLE 4-1 Filter Expression Elements

Event Name	Triggering Action
Column names	Any of the column names from the *DataTable*. Surround column names that contain embedded space characters or other non-alphanumeric characters with a set of square brackets, as in *[Full Name]* for a column named *Full Name*.
<, >, <=, >=, <>, =	Use the standard comparison operators to compare columns to literal values, to each other, or to more complex expressions.
IN	Match from a collection of comma-delimited elements. `BillDenomination IN (5, 10, 20)`

LIKE	Match a string pattern. The pattern can include zero or more occurrences of the wildcard character ("*" or "%"), but at the ends of the pattern string only, not in the middle.
	
	`ProductClass = 'AA*'`
	
	or:
	
	`ProductClass = 'AA%'`

AND, OR, NOT	Use these Boolean operators to join multiple expressions together.
Parentheses	Force the order of expression evaluation with parentheses.

Event Name	Triggering Action
Literals	Literals include integers, decimals, numbers in scientific notation, strings in single quotes, and dates or times in # marks.
CONVERT	Convert an expression or column from one data type to another. CONVERT(*expression*, *new-type*) The list of allowed data types is pretty close to those allowed when creating data columns. There are also restrictions on which data types can be coerced into other types. See the Visual Studio online help for full details.
LEN	Returns the length of a string column or expression.
ISNULL	Returns an expression or a default expression if the first argument evaluates to NULL. Useful for ensuring that a NULL value does not appear in a calculation. For example, the following expression compares the *FamilyMembers* column to the value 2 when *FamilyMembers* is not NULL. However, if *FamilyMembers* evaluates to NULL, it defaults to 1 instead. ISNULL(FamilyMembers, 1) >= 2
IIF	The ternary conditional function, similar to the *If* and *IIf* operators in Visual Basic, and to the :? operator in C#. The operator contains three arguments. If the first argument evaluates to *true*, the function returns the second argument, the "true" part. Otherwise, it returns the third argument, the "false" part. IIF(Age >= 18, 'Adult', 'Minor')
TRIM	Trims whitespace from the ends of a string column or expression.
SUBSTRING	Returns a portion of a string column or expression, starting from a 1-based position and continuing on for a specific length count. SUBSTRING(PhoneNumber, 1, 3)

Sorting Search Results

By default, the *DataTable.Select* method returns *DataRow* objects in the order in which they were added to the table. To sort the results based on one or more columns in the returned rows, send a second string argument to the *Select* method that indicates the sort rules.

```
C#
DataRow[] sortedRows = someTable.Select(filterCriteria, sortRules);

Visual Basic
Dim sortedRows() As DataRow = someTable.Select(filterCriteria, sortRules)
```

The sort string contains a comma-delimited list of the columns to be used for sorting, from left to right. Each column can be optionally followed by **ASC** for an ascending sort on that column or **DESC** for a descending sort; ascending is the default. The following sort expression orders the returned rows by descending *OrderDate* and then by (ascending) customer name:

```
OrderDate DESC, CustomerName
```

A third argument to the *Select* method lets you limit the results based on the state of each row. In tables that have had row-level changes, but for which you haven't yet called *AcceptResults*, this feature can return just the deleted rows, or just the unchanged rows, among other options. See the Visual Studio online help entry "DataViewRowState Enumeration" for a complete list of available options.

Selecting and Sorting *DataRow* Objects: C#

> **Note** This exercise uses the "Chapter 4 CSharp" sample project and continues the previous exercise in this chapter.

1. Open the source code view for the *TableExaminer* form. Locate the *ActCriteria_Click* event handler. This routine collects user-supplied selection and sorting expressions; then uses them to obtain a set of *DataRow* instances from a *DataTable*. Most of the code exists to ensure that the user provides valid expressions.

2. Locate the *try...catch* statement just after the "Apply the filter and sorting list" comment. In the *try* block, add the following statement:

```
results = workTable.Select(CriteriaFilter.Text, CriteriaSorting.Text);
```

This line performs the actual row selection, returning the optionally sorted *DataRow* instances, or an empty array when the selection expression doesn't match any of the table's rows.

3. Run the program. On the Lookup By Criteria tab, provide expressions that will return a list of students with improving grades, sorted by name. Enter **ScoreTrimester3 > ScoreTrimester1 OR ScoreTrimester3 > ScoreTrimester2** in the Filter Criteria field, and **StudentName** in the Sorting List field. Click Lookup. The matching rows appear in a separate window.

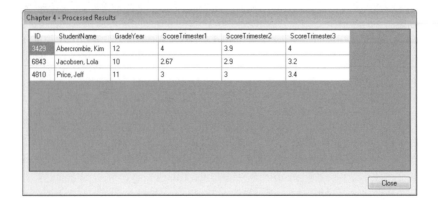

Selecting and Sorting *DataRow* Objects: Visual Basic

> **Note** This exercise uses the "Chapter 4 VB" sample project and continues the previous exercise in this chapter.

1. Open the source code view for the *TableExaminer* form. Locate the *ActCriteria_Click* event handler. This routine collects user-supplied selection and sorting expressions; then uses them to obtain a set of *DataRow* instances from a *DataTable*. Most of the code exists to ensure that the user provides valid expressions.

2. Locate the *Try...Catch* statement just after the "Apply the filter and sorting list" comment. In the *Try* block, add the following statement:

```
results = workTable.Select(CriteriaFilter.Text, CriteriaSorting.Text)
```

   This line performs the actual row selection, returning the optionally sorted *DataRow* instances or an empty array when the selection expression doesn't match any of the table's rows.

3. Run the program. On the Lookup By Criteria tab, provide expressions that will return a list of students with improving grades, sorted by name. Enter **ScoreTrimester3 > ScoreTrimester1 OR ScoreTrimester3 > ScoreTrimester2** in the Filter Criteria field, and **StudentName** in the Sorting List field. Click Lookup. The matching rows appear in a separate window.

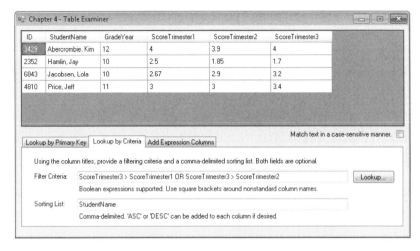

Performing Case-Sensitive Lookups

The *Select* method ignores character casing by default when comparing string values. For instance, the following expression will match joe, Joe, JOE, or any other mixed-case variation on the name:

```
FirstName = 'joe'
```

To enforce *case-sensitive* matches on all searches instead, set the table's *CaseSensitive* property.

C#
```csharp
someTable.CaseSensitive = true;
```

Visual Basic
```vbnet
someTable.CaseSensitive = True
```

Using Expression Columns

In Chapter 2, "Building Tables of Data," you learned how to add columns to a table that would each hold data values of a specific type. These *static columns* define the core data within a table. The *DataTable* class also supports *expression columns*, fields that expose a calculated result based on the data in other row columns. For instance, if your table of orders includes a *Subtotal* column and a *Tax* column, you could add an expression column named *Total* that calculated the sum of *Subtotal* and *Tax*.

To add an expression column to a table, create a standard *DataColumn* object, fill in its *ColumnName* and *DataType* properties, and then assign a string expression that performs the custom calculation to the *Expression* property.

```csharp
C#
// ----- Syntax using a DataColumn object.
DataColumn orderTotal = new DataColumn();
orderTotal.ColumnName = "Total";
orderTotal.DataType = typeof(decimal);
orderTotal.Expression = "Subtotal + ISNULL(Tax, 0)";
someTable.Columns.Add(orderTotal);

// ----- Syntax using Add arguments only.
someTable.Columns.Add("Total", typeof(decimal),
    "Subtotal + ISNULL(Tax, 0)");
```

```vbnet
Visual Basic
' ----- Syntax using a DataColumn object.
Dim orderTotal As New DataColumn
orderTotal.ColumnName = "Total"
orderTotal.DataType = GetType(Decimal)
orderTotal.Expression = "Subtotal + ISNULL(Tax, 0)"
someTable.Columns.Add(orderTotal)

' ----- Syntax using Add arguments only.
someTable.Columns.Add("Total", GetType(Decimal),
    "Subtotal + ISNULL(Tax, 0)")
```

The expression field uses the same elements from Table 4-1 that you used with the *DataTable.Select* method. To view the full documentation for this expression, access the Visual Studio online help entry for "DataColumn.Expression Property."

 Note The documentation for the *Expression* property discusses "aggregate functions." These are covered in Chapter 6.

After being added to your table, you can query expression columns in *Select* statements or examine them with standard ADO.NET code just like static columns. Expression columns are not calculated until you attempt to access them. If there is anything wrong with the expression, such as including references to non-existent columns, the code accessing the column will throw an exception.

Adding Expression Columns to a *DataTable*: C#

> **Note** This exercise uses the "Chapter 4 CSharp" sample project and continues the previous exercise in this chapter.

1. Open the source code view for the *TableExaminer* form. Locate the *ActExpression_Click* event handler. This routine defines up to three expression columns based on column names, data types, and calculation expressions supplied by the user. It then adds these columns to the application's sample *DataTable*. Most of the code exists to ensure that the user provides valid column definitions.

2. Locate the *try...catch* statement just after the "Add the expression column" comment. In the *try* block, add the following statement:

```
workTable.Columns.Add(nameField.Text.Trim(),
    Type.GetType("System." + typeField.SelectedItem.ToString()),
    expressionField.Text);
```

This code adds the expression columns to the sample table, passing the column name, the data type from the *System* namespace, and the field expression.

3. Run the program. On the Add Expression Columns tab, fill in the Name, Type, and Expression fields with the desired custom columns. To create a column that calculates the average annual score for each student, in the first row of fields, set Name to **YearAverage**, select **Decimal** in the Type field, and enter **(ScoreTrimester1 + ScoreTrimester2 + ScoreTrimester3) / 3** in the Expression field.

4. Expression columns can reference other expression columns. Create a column that calculates a letter grade for the *YearAverage* column. In the second row of fields, enter **LetterGrade** in the Name field, select **String** in the Type field, and enter **IIF(YearAverage >= 3.5, 'A', IIF(YearAverage >= 2.5, 'B', IIF(YearAverage >= 1.5, 'C', IIF(YearAverage >= 0.5, 'D', 'F'))))** in the Expression field. Click Build to see the results.

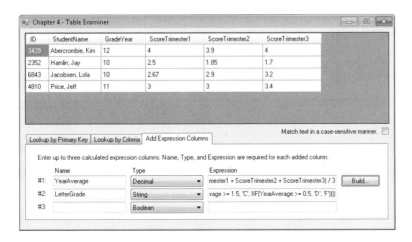

Adding Expression Columns to a *DataTable*: Visual Basic

> **Note** This exercise uses the "Chapter 4 VB" sample project and continues the previous exercise in this chapter.

1. Open the source code view for the *TableExaminer* form. Locate the *ActExpression_Click* event handler. This routine defines up to three expression columns based on column names, data types, and calculation expressions supplied by the user. It then adds these columns to the application's sample *DataTable*. Most of the code exists to ensure that the user provides valid column definitions.

2. Locate the *Try...Catch* statement just after the "Add the expression column" comment. In the *Try* block, add the following statement:

```
workTable.Columns.Add(nameField.Text.Trim,
    Type.GetType("System." & typeField.SelectedItem.ToString),
    expressionField.Text)
```

This code adds the expression columns to the sample table, passing the column name, the data type from the *System* namespace, and the field expression.

3. Run the program. On the Add Expression Columns tab, fill in the Name, Type, and Expression fields with the desired custom columns. To create a column that calculates the average annual score for each student, in the first row of fields, set Name to **YearAverage**, select **Decimal** in the Type field, and enter **(ScoreTrimester1 + ScoreTrimester2 + ScoreTrimester3) / 3** in the Expression field.

4. Expression columns can reference other expression columns. Create a column that calculates a letter grade for the *YearAverage* column. In the second row of fields, enter **LetterGrade** in the Name field, select **String** in the Type field, and enter **IIF(YearAverage >= 3.5, 'A', IIF(YearAverage >= 2.5, 'B', IIF(YearAverage >= 1.5, 'C', IIF(YearAverage >= 0.5, 'D', 'F'))))** in the Expression field. Click Build to see the results.

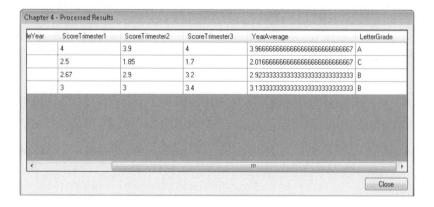

Summary

This chapter introduced different ways to access records previously added to a *DataTable* instance. The *DataTable.Rows.Find* method uses the table's primary key value(s) to return a single *DataRow* instance, similar to the way that .NET's *Generic.Dictionary* class returns an object based on a lookup key. The *DataTable.Select* method also performs a row lookup, but uses a SQL–like Boolean expression, expanding the search criteria to all columns in the table, not just the primary key. This method also provides a way to sort the results.

Expression columns let you add real-time calculated values to each *DataRow* in your table. Like the other columns in the table, expression columns are strongly typed. Because they are calculated only when accessed, their values refresh automatically whenever any of their dependent column values change.

Chapter 4 Quick Reference

To	Do This
Access a *DataRow* by its primary key	Add *DataColumn* instances to a *DataTable*.
	Add one or more of those *DataColumn* instances to the table's *PrimaryKey* property.
	Add relevant *DataRow* objects to the *DataTable*.
	Call the table's *Rows.Find* method, passing it the desired row's primary key value(s).
Locate *DataRow* objects with a SQL-like query	Add *DataColumn* instances to a *DataTable*.
	Add relevant *DataRow* objects to the *DataTable*.
	Build a query expression string (see the "DataColumn. Expression Property" entry in online help).
	Call the table's *Select* method, passing it the query expression.
Perform a case-sensitive or case-insensitive *DataRow* lookup	Set the *DataTable* object's *CaseSensitive* Boolean property.
	Call *Rows.Find* or *Select* methods with string search content.
Add calculated columns to a *DataTable*	Add standard *DataColumn* instances to a *DataTable*.
	Create a new *DataColumn* instance for the calculated column.
	Assign the *DataColumn* object's *ColumnName* and *DataType* fields.
	Build a column expression string (see "DataColumn. Expression Property" entry in online help).
	Set the *DataColumn* object's *Expression* property to the expression string.
	Add the *DataColumn* to the *DataTable*.

Chapter 5
Bringing Related Data Together

After completing this chapter, you will be able to:

- Join multiple *DataTable* instances into a *DataSet*

- Establish parent-child relationships between tables of data

- Understand the types of table constraints available in ADO.NET

- Build relationships that auto-correct linked rows when needed

The *DataTable* class provides ADO.NET's core data-management functionality. But many of the tools that build and interact with *DataTable* content do so through a higher level of abstraction: the *DataSet*. Instead of relying on a single table's worth of *DataRows*, a *DataSet* links multiple tables together, making it possible to generate data queries based on the relationships between the tables and their data.

In this chapter, the *DataSet* object takes center stage. You will discover how a *DataSet* becomes more than the sum of its *DataTable* parts. By combining data tables, relationship definitions between those tables, and column-specific constraints that help ensure data integrity between the tables, ADO.NET provides new views on data that would be complicated to achieve with solitary data tables.

 Note The exercises in this chapter all use the same sample project, a tool that shows the related records between two *DataTable* instances. Although you will be able to run the application after each exercise, the expected results for the full application might not appear until you complete all exercises in the chapter.

Collecting Tables into Sets

ADO.NET includes a *System.Data.DataSet* class that defines a collection of tables, their relationships, and related field constraints. To establish a data set in your program, create a new *DataSet* object, optionally passing it a set name.

```csharp
C#
DataSet someSet = new DataSet("SetName");
```

```vb
Visual Basic
Dim someSet As New DataSet("SetName")
```

Adding a name to a standalone *DataTable* instance might be inconsequential, but some table-related features in ADO.NET do enable access to a *DataTable* object by its table name. For example, the *DataSet* class includes a *Tables* property that, as expected, holds a collection of individual *DataTable* instances. You access tables within the collection either by name or by an index number. To add a new *DataTable* to a *DataSet*, write the following:

```
C#
someSet.Tables.Add(someTable);
```

Visual Basic
```
someSet.Tables.Add(someTable)
```

You can also pass a string to the *Add* method, which creates a new named table object without columns or rows. You can add as many data tables as you want to the *Tables* collection. At this point, they are still treated as individual tables; adding them to the collection of tables does not automatically endow them with relationship features.

> **Note** A *DataSet* can contain two tables with the same name as long as their namespace values differ. Chapter 7, "Saving and Restoring Data," discusses these namespaces. Also, if two tables share a common name (and namespace) but differ in the casing of those names ("CUSTOMERS" versus "customers"), the *DataSet* will treat them as distinct tables. When querying these tables, you must provide the same casing as the original table names, or else the query will fail. However, if a table name has no duplicate within a *DataSet*, its name in queries can be case-insensitive.

The *DataSet* includes some properties and methods that replicate the functionality of the contained tables. These features share identical names with their table counterparts. When used, these properties and methods work as if those same features had been used at the table level in all contained tables. Some of these members that you've seen before include the following:

- *Clear*
- *CaseSensitive*
- *AcceptChanges*
- *RejectChanges*
- *EnforceConstraints*
- *HasErrors*

Adding Tables to a *DataSet*: C#

1. Open the "Chapter 5 CSharp" project from the installed samples folder. The project in-cludes three *Windows.Forms* classes: *FlightInfo, FlightDetail,* and *LegDetail.*

2. Open the source code view for the *FlightInfo* form. Locate the *BuildSampleDataSet* function. This routine creates the main *DataSet* used in the application.

3. Just after the "Add the two tables to the data set" comment, add the following statements:

```
result = new DataSet("FlightSample");
parentTable = BuildFlightTable();
childTable = BuildLegTable();
result.Tables.Add(parentTable);
result.Tables.Add(childTable);
```

These lines create two tables that share a common value: the flight ID number. In the flight table the field is named *ID,* whereas it is called *FlightID* in the leg table. A later example in this chapter will establish the relationship between the two tables.

Adding Tables to a *DataSet*: Visual Basic

1. Open the "Chapter 5 VB" project from the installed samples folder. The project includes three *Windows.Forms* classes: *FlightInfo, FlightDetail,* and *LegDetail.*

2. Open the source code view for the *FlightInfo* form. Locate the *BuildSampleDataSet* function. This routine creates the main *DataSet* used in the application.

3. Just after the "Add the two tables to the data set" comment, add the following statements:

```
result = New DataSet("FlightSample")
parentTable = BuildFlightTable()
childTable = BuildLegTable()
result.Tables.Add(parentTable)
result.Tables.Add(childTable)
```

These lines create two tables that share a common value: the flight ID number. In the flight table the field is named *ID,* whereas it is called *FlightID* in the leg table. A later example in this chapter will establish the relationship between the two tables.

Establishing Relationships Between Tables

Before focusing on the relationship features of the *DataSet* class, it is essential to have a clear understanding of what it means for two tables to be related.

Understanding Table Relations

In relational database modeling, the term *cardinality* describes the type of relationship that two tables have. There are three main types of database model cardinality:

- **One-to-One**   A record in one table matches exactly one record in another table. This is commonly used to break a table with a large number of columns into two distinct tables for processing convenience.

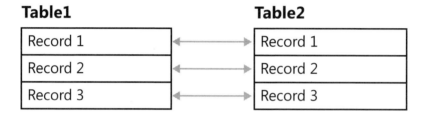

- **One-to-Many**   One record in a "parent" table has zero or more "child" records in another table. A typical use for the one-to-many relationship is in an ordering system in which a single customer record (the parent) will have none, one, or many order records (the children) on file. Likewise, a single order record will have multiple order line items. One-to-many relationships are the most common type of table link in relational databases.

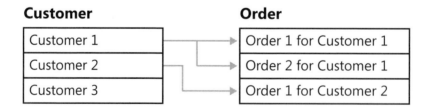

- **Many-to-Many**   In this third and most complex type of link, one record in the first table is associated with zero or more records in the second table, *and* each record in the second table can also be associated with zero or more records in the first table. Students taking classes is a typical real-world example of a many-to-many relationship. Each student can take multiple classes, and each class can have multiple students listed as class participants.

Student   **Class**

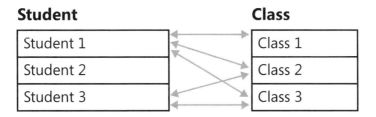

Fortunately, all three of these model relationships share a common physical implementation concept: the *foreign key*—the use of a table's identifying column(s) by another table. In a foreign-key relationship, both tables include a column (or multiple columns when the master table uses a multipart key) that uses an agreed-upon domain of values. When records in each table share a common value for that column, the records are related.

For example, in a customer-order relationship, the *Customer* table includes a customer identification column that uniquely defines each record. The associated *Order* table also includes a customer identification column. Each order that shares a customer identifier with a specific customer record belongs to that customer record. There might be multiple order records that include that customer's identifier, each of which is related to the same customer.

> **Note** The name given to the identifying column in the first table doesn't need to be the same as the name of the column in the second table. Only the data *relationships* are important, not the names given to the columns in those relationships.

Records in a one-to-one relationship work the same way, but there is never more than one occurrence of a specific identifier value in each table. If a record in one table always has a match in the second table, it doesn't matter which one is the parent and which is the child. If one table's records are optional, the table with the optional records is the child.

Many-to-many relationships also use the foreign-key concept, but they require a "go-between" table that indicates which two keys link up. Both primary tables are the parent; the interim table is the child.

Student   **StudentClassInterim**   **Class**

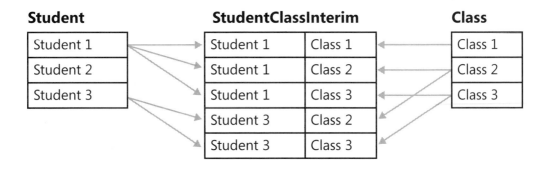

There are some expectations that come with these types of data relationships:

- The relationship column in the parent or master table must contain unique values; no duplicates are allowed. Also, NULL values are not allowed in this column.

- Any value that appears in the relationship column of the child *must* have a related parent record. If the child record has no related parent record, that child record must be deleted or its link-column value must be set to NULL.

In short, every parent must be unique, and every child requires a parent.

Creating Data Relations

The *DataRelation* class, found within the *System.Data* namespace, makes table joins within a *DataSet* possible. Each relationship includes a parent and a child. The *DataRelation* class even uses the terms "parent" and "child" in its defining members.

To create a relationship between two *DataSet* tables, first add the parent and child table to the data set. Then create a new *DataRelation* instance, passing its constructor the name of the new relationship, plus a reference to the linking columns in each table. The following code joins a *Customer* table with an *Order* table, linking the *Customer.ID* column as the parent with the related *Order.CustomerID* column as the child:

```csharp
C#
DataSet orderTracking = new DataSet("OrderTracking");
orderTracking.Tables.Add(customerTable);
orderTracking.Tables.Add(orderTable);
DataRelation customerOrder = new DataRelation("CustomerOrder",
    customerTable.Columns["ID"], orderTable.Columns["CustomerID"]);
orderTracking.Relations.Add(customerOrder);
```

```vbnet
Visual Basic
Dim orderTracking As New DataSet("OrderTracking")
orderTracking.Tables.Add(customerTable)
orderTracking.Tables.Add(orderTable)
Dim customerOrder As New DataRelation("CustomerOrder",
    customerTable.Columns!ID, orderTable.Columns!CustomerID)
orderTracking.Relations.Add(customerOrder)
```

For tables with multipart relational keys, the second and third arguments to the *DataRelation* constructor each accept an array of *DataColumn* objects.

Note Columns bound in a relationship must always be the same data type. In tables with multipart keys, each positional part between the tables must be the same data type.

Adding a Relationship Between Two Tables: C#

> **Note** This exercise uses the "Chapter 5 CSharp" sample project and continues the previous exercise in this chapter.

1. Open the source code view for the *FlightInfo* form. Locate the *BuildSampleDataSet* function.

2. Just after the "Build the relationship between the tables" comment, add the following statements:

```
tableLink = new DataRelation("FlightLeg", parentTable.Columns["ID"],
    childTable.Columns["FlightID"], true);
result.Relations.Add(tableLink);
```

These lines create a new *DataRelation* instance named "FlightLeg" using the matching *DataColumn* instances from the two tables. Adding the *DataRelation* to the *DataSet* completes the column-linking process

Adding a Relationship Between Two Tables: Visual Basic

> **Note** This exercise uses the "Chapter 5 VB" sample project and continues the previous exercise in this chapter.

1. Open the source code view for the *FlightInfo* form. Locate the *BuildSampleDataSet* function.

2. Just after the "Build the relationship between the tables" comment, add the following statements:

```
tableLink = New DataRelation("FlightLeg", parentTable.Columns("ID"),
    childTable.Columns("FlightID"), True)
result.Relations.Add(tableLink)
```

These lines create a new *DataRelation* instance named "FlightLeg" using the matching *DataColumn* instances from the two tables. Adding the *DataRelation* to the *DataSet* completes the column-linking process.

Locating Parent and Child Records

After you've established a parent-child relationship between two tables, it's easy to retrieve data that capitalizes on that relationship. The *DataRow* class includes two methods—*GetChildRows* and *GetParentRow*—that retrieve the relevant row(s) at the other end of a linked relationship. Because a column could be involved in multiple relationships, you must pass either the name or the instance of the relationship to the relevant method. The following statements retrieve the customer (parent) record given an order (child) record row, depending on the *DataRelation* with a name of "CustomerOrder":

```csharp
C#
DataRow customer = whichOrder.GetParentRow("CustomerOrder");
```

```vb
Visual Basic
Dim customer As DataRow = whichOrder.GetParentRow("CustomerOrder")
```

Getting the child records for a parent row uses nearly identical code. Because a parent can have multiple children, the *GetChildRows* method returns an array of *DataRow* matches.

```csharp
C#
DataRow[] orders = whichCustomer.GetChildRows("CustomerOrder");
```

```vb
Visual Basic
Dim orders() As DataRow = whichCustomer.GetChildRows("CustomerOrder")
```

The *DataRow* class also includes a variant of *GetParentRow* (named *GetParentRows*) that returns multiple parent rows for a single child record. This is useful for parent-child relationships that are linked on columns other than the parent's primary key. In the class-student example mentioned previously, consider a university that has multiple campuses within a city. If both students and classes are associated with a specific campus, a link can be established between the columns in each table that define the campus.

```csharp
C#
DataTable classTable = new DataTable("Class");
// Add columns, including...
classTable.Columns.Add("Campus", typeof(string));

DataTable studentTable = new DataTable("Student");
// Add columns, including...
studentTable.Columns.Add("Campus", typeof(string));

DataSet siteCourses = new DataSet("SiteCourses");
siteCourses.Tables.Add(classTable);
siteCourses.Tables.Add(studentTable);

DataRelation classStudent = new DataRelation("ClassStudent",
    classTable.Columns["Campus"], studentTable.Columns["Campus"], false);
siteCourses.Relations.Add(classStudent);

// ----- Later, get available classes for a student by campus.
DataRow[] availableClasses = whichStudent.GetParentRows("ClassStudent");
```

Visual Basic

```vb
Dim classTable As New DataTable("Class")
' Add columns, including...
classTable.Columns.Add("Campus", GetType(String))

Dim studentTable As New DataTable("Student")
' Add columns, including...
studentTable.Columns.Add("Campus", GetType(String))

Dim siteCourses As New DataSet("SiteCourses")
siteCourses.Tables.Add(classTable)
siteCourses.Tables.Add(studentTable)

Dim classStudent As New DataRelation("ClassStudent",
    classTable.Columns("Campus"), studentTable.Columns("Campus"), False)
siteCourses.Relations.Add(classStudent)

' ----- Later, get available classes for a student by campus.
Dim availableClasses() As DataRow = whichStudent.GetParentRows("ClassStudent")
```

Because the parent table can include duplicate values in its related column, this relationship doesn't follow the normal rules for a key-based, one-to-many relationship. It is instead a form of many-to-many cardinality, albeit one that does not involve either table's primary key. Normally, new *DataRelation* instances create special "constraint" objects that establish the relationship rules, such as the need for a unique primary key. (This next section, "Defining Table Constraints," discusses these constraints.) In this many-to-many relationship, such constraints would generate errors. Therefore, when creating the *DataRelation* instance, the code passed a fourth Boolean argument with a value of *False* to the constructor, telling it to dispense with the constraints.

Defining Table Constraints

As mentioned earlier in this chapter, data relationships come with certain expectations known as constraints, expressed through the *System.Data.Constraint* class. ADO.NET supports two types of constraints, both designed to maintain the integrity of each table's data: *unique column* (*System.Data.UniqueConstraint*) and *foreign key* (*System.Data.ForeignKeyConstraint*). As you would expect, the unique column constraint prevents duplicate values from showing up in a table column, a requirement for the parent column in a one-to-many relationship. Attempts to add a duplicate value to a unique column will result in a thrown exception.

The foreign-key constraint establishes similar limitations on the participating columns. Although the parent column might include values that do not appear in the child table's joined column, the reverse is not true. In a one-to-many relationship, any value in the child column must exist in the parent column as well. The *ForeignKeyConstraint* class enforces this rule. But unlike the *UniqueConstraint* class, which just throws an exception when you violate the rule, *ForeignKeyConstraint* gives you options for how ADO.NET should behave when data violates the foreign-key regulation. There are four rules that can be followed when a parent-column value is updated or deleted:

- The child rows can be automatically updated or deleted in the same manner.

- The child column values can be set to NULL.

- The child column values can be set to a default value, assuming that the value does not violate the foreign-key constraint.

- An exception can be thrown. This is the default.

You define these actions by setting the *DeleteRule* and *UpdateRule* properties in the *ForeignKeyConstraint* object as needed. Each field can be set to one of the following enumerated values:

- *System.Data.Rule.Cascade*

- *System.Data.Rule.SetNull*

- *System.Data.Rule.SetDefault*

- *System.Data.Rule.None*

By default, adding a *DataRelation* that links two tables in a *DataSet* adds both a unique constraint to the parent column and a foreign-key constraint to the child column. As shown previously, you can also pass an argument to the *DataRelation* constructor that prevents the creation of these constraints and add the constraints yourself as needed.

> **Note** If you choose to define the constraints for a relationship yourself, you must (1) add a *UniqueConstraint* to the parent column; (2) add a *ForeignKeyConstraint* to the child column; (3) update the appropriate properties in the *DataRelation* instance, including the *ChildKeyConstraint* and the *ParentKeyConstraint* properties; and (4) make various changes to properties in the *Constraint, DataTable,* and *DataRelation* instances so that they all reference each other. To ensure proper configuration between the fields, it is often best to let the *DataRelation* constructor fill in all these fields on your behalf.

To add a constraint manually, create and fill out an instance of either *UniqueConstraint* or *ForeignKeyConstraint*; you can't create an instance of the *Constraint* class directly. Then add the new instance to the *DataTable* object's *Constraints* collection.

C#

```csharp
Constraint exemptUnique = new UniqueConstraint(
    customers.Columns["TaxExemptID"]);
customers.Constraints.Add(exemptUnique);
```

Visual Basic

```vbnet
Dim exemptUnique As Constraint = New UniqueConstraint(
    customers.Columns!TaxExemptID)
customers.Constraints.Add(exemptUnique)
```

The second Boolean argument in the *UniqueConstraint* constructor can be set to *True* to indicate primary key columns. Other constructor variations let you name the constraint or associate it with multiple columns.

Implementing a many-to-many relationship based on primary keys—the multiple-students-in-multiple-classes scenario diagrammed earlier in this chapter—requires an interim table to join the two main tables. The interim table will have a two-part primary key, with each part hosting the primary key of one of the two main joined tables. Adding a multipart *UniqueConstraint* instance to the interim table prevents a pair of records between the tables from being joined twice to each other.

C#

```csharp
DataTable studentTable = new DataTable("Student");
// Add columns, including...
studentTable.Columns.Add("ID", typeof(long));

DataTable classTable = new DataTable("Class");
// Add columns, including...
classTable.Columns.Add("ID", typeof(long));

DataTable interimTable = new DataTable("StudentClassInterim");
// Add columns, including...
interimTable.Columns.Add("StudentID", typeof(long));
interimTable.Columns.Add("ClassID", typeof(long));

// ----- Make the linking fields unique.
Constraint interimKey = new UniqueConstraint(
    new DataColumn[] { interimTable.Columns["StudentID"],
    interimTable.Columns["ClassID"] }, true);
interimTable.Constraints.Add(interimKey);
```

```csharp
// ----- Relations exist within a data set context.
DataSet registration = new DataSet("Registration");
registration.Tables.Add(classTable);
registration.Tables.Add(studentTable);
registration.Tables.Add(interimTable);

// ----- Add standard joins between the core tables and the interim.
DataRelation joinPart = new DataRelation("ClassToStudent",
    classTable.Columns["ID"], interimTable.Columns["ClassID"], true);
registration.Relations.Add(joinPart);
joinPart = new DataRelation("StudentToClass",
    studentTable.Columns["ID"], interimTable.Columns["StudentID"], true);
registration.Relations.Add(joinPart);
```

Visual Basic

```vbnet
Dim studentTable As New DataTable("Student")
' Add columns, including...
studentTable.Columns.Add("ID", GetType(Long))

Dim classTable As New DataTable("Class")
' Add columns, including...
classTable.Columns.Add("ID", GetType(Long))

Dim interimTable As New DataTable("StudentClassInterim")
' Add columns, including...
interimTable.Columns.Add("StudentID", GetType(Long))
interimTable.Columns.Add("ClassID", GetType(Long))

' ----- Make the linking fields unique.
Dim interimKey As Constraint = New UniqueConstraint(
    { interimTable.Columns!StudentID, interimTable.Columns!ClassID }, True)
interimTable.Constraints.Add(interimKey)

' ----- Relations exist within a data set context.
Dim registration As New DataSet("Registration")
registration.Tables.Add(classTable)
registration.Tables.Add(studentTable)
registration.Tables.Add(interimTable)

' ----- Add standard joins between the core tables and the interim.
Dim joinPart As New DataRelation("ClassToStudent",
    classTable.Columns("ID"), interimTable.Columns("ClassID"), True)
registration.Relations.Add(joinPart)
joinPart = New DataRelation("StudentToClass",
    studentTable.Columns("ID"), interimTable.Columns("StudentID"), True)
registration.Relations.Add(joinPart)
```

Defining the Update and Delete Rules in a *DataRelation*: C#

> **Note** This exercise uses the "Chapter 5 CSharp" sample project and continues the previous exercise in this chapter.

1. Open the source code view for the *FlightInfo* form. Locate the *RefreshConstraints* method. The application lets the user alter the rules for adjusting the child table when changes are made to the parent table. The *RefreshConstraints* routine updates the relevant constraint with the user's rule choice.

2. Just after the "Alter its cascade rules" comment, add the following statements:

```
linkConstraint.DeleteRule = (System.Data.Rule)DeleteRule.SelectedItem;
linkConstraint.UpdateRule = (System.Data.Rule)UpdateRule.SelectedItem;
```

3. Run the program. The Update Rule and Delete Rule fields are both set to **None** by default. This prevents parent records (Flights) from being deleted or having their *ID* column values changed if related child rows (Legs) exist.

4. Test cascade updates. Set the Update Rule field to **Cascade**. Select the first row in the Flights field, the one with ID **834**. Click the (Flights) Edit button. Use the Edit Flight form that appears to alter the Flight ID value from **834** to another value, such as **759**. Click OK on that editor form.

5. Review the Flights and Legs fields. Not only did the first row in the Flights field have its ID value changed to **759** but the *FlightID* values for the related rows in the Legs field changed to **759** as well.

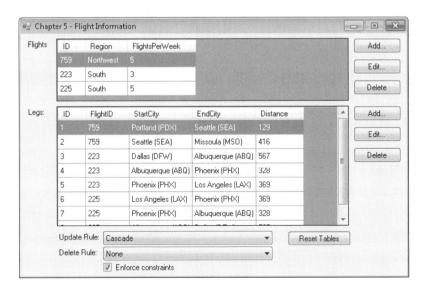

6. Test setting linked child fields to NULL when a parent record is deleted. Set the Delete Rule field to **SetNull**. Select the first row in the Flights field, the one with ID **759**. Click the (Flights) Delete button and confirm the delete action.

7. Review the Flights and Legs fields. Although the first row in the Flights field has been removed, its child records in the Legs field remain. However, their *FlightID* column values have been cleared and are set to NULL. Those records no longer have a parent row.

Defining the Update and Delete Rules in a *DataRelation*: Visual Basic

> **Note** This exercise uses the "Chapter 5 VB" sample project and continues the previous exercise in this chapter.

1. Open the source code view for the *FlightInfo* form. Locate the *RefreshConstraints* method. The application lets the user alter the rules for adjusting the child table when changes are made to the parent table. The *RefreshConstraints* routine updates the relevant constraint with the user's rule choice.

2. Just after the "Alter its cascade rules" comment, add the following statements:

```
linkConstraint.DeleteRule = CType(DeleteRule.SelectedItem, Data.Rule)
linkConstraint.UpdateRule = CType(UpdateRule.SelectedItem, Data.Rule)
```

3. Run the program. The Update Rule and Delete Rule fields are both set to **None** by default. This prevents parent records (Flights) from being deleted or having their *ID* column values changed if related child rows (Legs) exist.

4. Test cascade updates. Set the Update Rule field to **Cascade**. Select the first row in the Flights field, the one with ID **834**. Click the (Flights) Edit button. Use the *Edit Flight* form that appears to alter the *Flight ID* value from **834** to another value, such as **759**. Click OK on that editor form.

5. Review the Flights and Legs fields. Not only did the first row in the Flights field have its ID value changed to **759** but the *FlightID* values for the related rows in the Legs field changed to **759** as well.

6. Test setting linked child fields to NULL when a parent record is deleted. Set the Delete Rule field to **SetNull**. Select the first row in the Flights field, the one with ID **759**. Click the (Flights) Delete button and confirm the delete action.

7. Review the Flights and Legs fields. Although the first row in the Flights field has been removed, its child records in the Legs field remain. However, their *FlightID* column values have been cleared and are set to NULL. Those records no longer have a parent row.

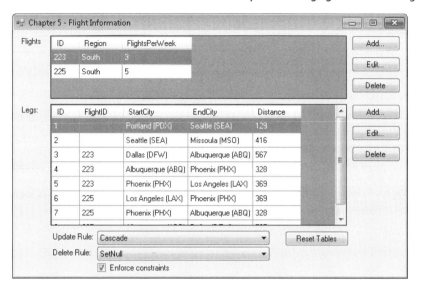

Summary

This chapter demonstrated how individual *DataTable* instances can be joined together in an ADO.NET *DataSet*. Each data table object includes many features that let you query and manipulate the data in its rows. By bringing distinct tables together in a data set, you gain additional features that affect multiple tables simultaneously and, if desired, automatically.

The *DataRelation* class defines the link between columns in two different tables. This class defines only the relationship; it doesn't enforce the rules of the relationship. *Constraint* objects, specifically the *UniqueConstraint* and *ForeignKeyConstraint* derived classes, impose the data requirements needed to ensure data integrity and data expectations between linked tables.

Chapter 5 Quick Reference

To	Do This
Add a table to a *DataSet*	Define a *DataSet* instance.
	Define a *DataTable* instance, adding columns and rows as needed.
	Call the *DataSet* object's *Tables.Add* method, passing it the instance of the *DataTable*.
Link two *DataTable* objects in a relationship	Define a *DataSet* instance.
	Define two *DataTable* instances, adding columns and rows as needed.
	Determine which columns from each table will form the relationship link.
	Add both tables to the *DataSet* using the *Tables.Add* method.
	Create a *DataRelation* instance, passing instances of the columns to be linked to its constructor.
	Call the *DataSet* object's *Relations.Add* method, passing it the instance of the *DataRelation*.
Enforce cascade deletes in a parent-child relationship	Locate the *DataRelation* instance that defines the link relationship.
	Set the *DataRelation* object's *DeleteRule* to *System.Data.Rule.Cascade*.
Locate the parent row for a child row	Ensure that the tables are linked with a *DataRelation*.
	Call the child DataRow object's *GetParentRow* method, passing it the name of the *DataRelation* that defines the link relationship.
Locate the child rows for a parent row	Ensure that the tables are linked with a *DataRelation*.
	Call the parent *DataRow* object's *GetChildRow* method, passing it the name of the *DataRelation* that defines the link relationship.

Chapter 6
Turning Data into Information

After completing this chapter, you will be able to:

- Return a value that aggregates data from a table column
- Add a column that aggregates data from a table, or from its parent or child table
- Build an index-based view of a table
- Generate a new table based on a projected view of the original table

After you have joined *DataTable* instances together in a *DataSet*, ADO.NET enables a few more features that let you use those table relationships to analyze and select data. These features build upon some of the single-table functions covered in earlier chapters.

This chapter introduces the data-aggregation features included in the ADO.NET Framework, expressions that summarize data across multiple table rows. Although not as powerful as the aggregation features found in relational database systems, the *DataTable* variations still provide quick access to multirow data summaries. The chapter ends with an introduction to the *DataView* class, which lets you establish row selection, filtering, and sorting standards for a *DataTable*.

 Note The exercises in this chapter all use the same sample project, a tool that demonstrates aggregate and data view features. Although you will be able to run the application after each exercise, the expected results for the full application might not appear until you complete all exercises in the chapter.

Aggregating Data

An *aggregation function* returns a single calculated value from a set of related values. Averages are one type of data aggregation; they calculate a single averaged value from an input of multiple source values. ADO.NET includes seven aggregation functions for use in expression columns and other *DataTable* features.

- **Sum** Calculates the total of a set of column values. The column being summed must be numeric, either integral or decimal.
- **Avg** Returns the average for a set of numbers in a column. This function also requires a numeric column.

- **Min**   Indicates the minimum value found within a set of column values. Numbers, strings, dates, and other types of data that can be placed in order are all valid for the target column.

- **Max**   Like *Min*, but returns the largest value from the available column values. As with the *Min* function, most column types will work.

- **Count**   Simply counts the number of rows included in the aggregation. You can pass any type of column to this function. As long as a row includes a non-NULL value in that column, it will be counted as 1.

- **StDev**   Determines the statistical standard deviation for a set of values, a common measure of variability within such a set. The indicated column must be numeric.

- **Var**   Calculates the statistical variance for a set of numbers, another measurement related to the standard deviation. Only numeric columns are supported.

These seven data aggregation features appear as functions within ADO.NET expressions. Expressions were introduced in the "Using Expression Columns" section of Chapter 4, "Accessing the Right Data Values." String expressions form the basis of custom expression columns and are also used in selecting subsets of *DataTable* rows. To aggregate data, use one of the following function formats as the expression string:

- *Sum(column-name)*

- *Avg(column-name)*

- *Min(column-name)*

- *Max(column-name)*

- *Count(column-name)*

- *StDev(column-name)*

- *Var(column-name)*

In ADO.NET, aggregates always summarize a single *DataTable* column. Each aggregate function considers only non-NULL column values. Rows that contain NULL values in the specified column are excluded from the aggregation. For example, if you take the average of a table column with 10 rows, but 3 of those rows contain NULL values in the column being averaged, the function will average only the 7 non-NULL values. This is especially useful with the *Count* function; it counts only the number of rows that have a non-NULL value for the passed column name. If all the column values are NULL, or if there are no rows to apply to the aggregation function, the result is NULL (*System.DBNull*).

Generating a Single Aggregate

To calculate the aggregate of a single table column, use the *DataTable* object's *Compute* method. Pass it an expression string that contains an aggregate function with a column-name argument.

```csharp
C#
DataTable employees = new DataTable("Employee");
employees.Columns.Add("ID", typeof(int));
employees.Columns.Add("Gender", typeof(string));
employees.Columns.Add("FullName", typeof(string));
employees.Columns.Add("Salary", typeof(decimal));

// ----- Add employee data to table, then...
decimal averageSalary = (decimal)employees.Compute("Avg(Salary)", "");
```

```vbnet
Visual Basic
Dim employees As New DataTable("Employee")
employees.Columns.Add("ID", GetType(Integer))
employees.Columns.Add("Gender", GetType(string))
employees.Columns.Add("FullName", GetType(String))
employees.Columns.Add("Salary", GetType(Decimal))

' ----- Add employee data to table, then...
Dim averageSalary As Decimal = CDec(employees.Compute("Avg(Salary)", ""))
```

In the preceding code, the *Compute* method calculates the average of the values in the *Salary* column. The second argument to *Compute* is a filter that limits the rows included in the calculation. It accepts a Boolean criteria expression similar to those used in the *DataTable. Select* method call.

```csharp
C#
int femalesInCompany = (int)employees.Compute("Count(ID)",
    "Gender = 'F'");
```

```vbnet
Visual Basic
Dim femalesInCompany As Integer = CInt(employees.Compute("Count(ID)",
    "Gender = 'F'"))
```

Computing an Aggregate Value: C#

1. Open the "Chapter 6 CSharp" project from the installed samples folder. The project includes three *Windows.Forms* classes: *Switchboard*, *Aggregates*, and *DataViews*.

2. Open the source code view for the *Aggregates* form. Locate the *ActCompute_Click* function. This routine computes an aggregate value for a single table column.

3. Just after the "Build the expression" comment, add the following statement:

```
expression = ComputeFunction.SelectedItem.ToString() + "(" +
    columnName + ")";
```

This code builds an expression string that combines one of the seven aggregate functions and a column name from the sample table.

4. Just after the "Process the expression" comment, add the following code:

```
try
{
    result = whichTable.Compute(expression, "");
}
catch (Exception ex)
{
    MessageBox.Show("Could not compute the column: " + ex.Message);
    return;
}
```

The code performs the calculation in a *try* block because the code that built the expression didn't bother to verify things such as allowing only numeric columns to be used with the *Sum* aggregate function. The *catch* block will capture such problems at runtime.

5. Just after the "Display the results" comment, add the following statements:

```
if (DBNull.Value.Equals(result))
    MessageBox.Show("NULL");
else
    MessageBox.Show(result.ToString());
```

Some aggregates may return a NULL result depending on the contents of the column. This code makes that distinction.

6. Run the program. When the *Switchboard* form appears, click Aggregate Functions. When the *Aggregates* form appears, use the fields to the right of the Compute label to generate the aggregate. For example, select **Sum** from the Aggregate Function field (the one just to the right of the Compute label), and choose **Child.Population2009** from the Column Name field (the one in parentheses). Then click Compute. The response of "307006550" comes from adding up all values in the child table's *Population2009* column.

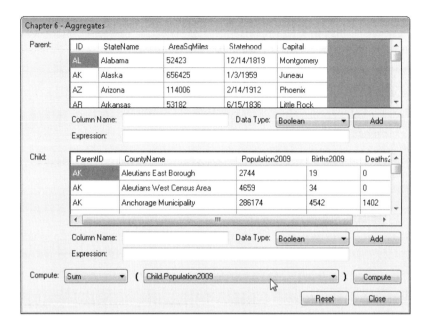

Note The "Child." prefix shown in the Column Name field is stripped out before the column name is inserted into the expression. The *Compute* method does not support the *Parent* and *Child* prefixes before column names.

Computing an Aggregate Value: Visual Basic

1. Open the "Chapter 6 VB" project from the installed samples folder. The project includes three *Windows.Forms* classes: *Switchboard, Aggregates,* and *DataViews.*

2. Open the source code view for the *Aggregates* form. Locate the *ActCompute_Click* function. This routine computes an aggregate value for a single table column.

3. Just after the "Build the expression" comment, add the following statement:

```
expression = ComputeFunction.SelectedItem.ToString() & "(" &
    columnName & ")"
```

This code builds an expression string that combines one of the seven aggregate functions and a column name from the sample table.

4. Just after the "Process the expression" comment, add the following code:

```
Try
    result = whichTable.Compute(expression, "")
Catch ex As Exception
    MessageBox.Show("Could not compute the column: " & ex.Message)
    Return
End Try
```

The code performs the calculation in a *Try* block because the code that built the expression didn't bother to verify things such as allowing only numeric columns to be used with the *Sum* aggregate function. The *Catch* block will capture such problems at runtime.

5. Just after the "Display the results" comment, add the following statements:

```
If (IsDBNull(result) = True) Then
    MessageBox.Show("NULL")
Else
    MessageBox.Show(result.ToString())
End If
```

Some aggregates may return a NULL result depending on the contents of the column. This code makes that distinction.

6. Run the program. When the *Switchboard* form appears, click Aggregate Functions. When the *Aggregates* form appears, use the fields to the right of the Compute label to generate the aggregate. For example, select **Sum** from the Aggregate Function field (the one just to the right of the Compute label), and choose **Child.Population2009** from the Column Name field (the one in parentheses). Then click Compute. The response of "307006550" comes from adding up all values in the child table's *Population2009* column.

Note In the example, the "Child." prefix shown in the Column Name field is stripped out before the column name is inserted into the expression. The *Compute* method does not support the *Parent* and *Child* prefixes before column names.

Adding an Aggregate Column

Expression columns typically compute a value based on other columns in the same row. You can also add an expression column to a table that generates an aggregate value. In the absence of a filtering expression, aggregates always compute their totals using all rows in a table. This is also true of aggregate expression columns. When you add such a column to a table, that column will contain the same value in every row, and that value will reflect the aggregation of all rows in the table.

C#

```csharp
DataTable sports = new DataTable("Sports");
sports.Columns.Add("SportName", typeof(string));
sports.Columns.Add("TeamPlayers", typeof(decimal));
sports.Columns.Add("AveragePlayers", typeof(decimal),
    "Avg(TeamPlayers)");

sports.Rows.Add(new Object[] {"Baseball", 9});
sports.Rows.Add(new Object[] {"Basketball", 5});
sports.Rows.Add(new Object[] {"Cricket", 11});

MessageBox.Show((string)sports.Rows[0]["AveragePlayers"]);  // Displays 8.3...
MessageBox.Show((string)sports.Rows[1]["AveragePlayers"]);  // Also 8.3...
```

Visual Basic

```vb
Dim sports As New DataTable("Sports")
sports.Columns.Add("SportName", GetType(String))
sports.Columns.Add("TeamPlayers", GetType(Decimal))
sports.Columns.Add("AveragePlayers", GetType(Decimal),
    "Avg(TeamPlayers)")

sports.Rows.Add({"Baseball", 9})
sports.Rows.Add({"Basketball", 5})
sports.Rows.Add({"Cricket", 11})

MessageBox.Show(CStr(sports.Rows(0)!AveragePlayers))  ' Displays 8.3...
MessageBox.Show(CStr(sports.Rows(1)!AveragePlayers))  ' Also 8.3...
```

Aggregating Data Across Related Tables

Adding aggregate functions to an expression column certainly gives you more data options, but as a calculation method it doesn't provide any benefit beyond the *DataTable.Compute* method. The real power of aggregate expression columns appears when working with related tables. By adding an aggregate function to a parent table that references the child table, you can generate summaries that are grouped by each parent row. This functionality is similar in purpose to the *GROUP BY* clause found in the SQL language.

To apply an aggregate to a table relationship, you first add both tables to a *DataSet* and then add the relevant *DataRelation* between the linked fields. After the tables are linked, you include the *Child* keyword with the aggregate function's column name reference.

```
function-name(Child.column-name)
```

As with single-table aggregation, the expression can reference any valid column in the child table, including other expression columns. Consider the following code, which calculates each customer's total orders and stores the result in an expression column in the customer (parent) table:

```csharp
C#
// ----- Build the parent table and add some data.
DataTable customers = new DataTable("Customer");
customers.Columns.Add("ID", typeof(int));
customers.Columns.Add("Name", typeof(string));
customers.Rows.Add(new Object[] {1, "Coho Winery"});
customers.Rows.Add(new Object[] {2, "Fourth Coffee"});

// ----- Build the child table and add some data. The "Total"
//       expression column adds sales tax to the subtotal.
DataTable orders = new DataTable("Order");
orders.Columns.Add("ID", typeof(int));
orders.Columns.Add("Customer", typeof(int));
orders.Columns.Add("Subtotal", typeof(decimal));
orders.Columns.Add("TaxRate", typeof(decimal));
orders.Columns.Add("Total", typeof(decimal), "Subtotal * (1 + TaxRate)");

// ----- Two sample orders for customer 1, 1 for customer 2.
orders.Rows.Add(new Object[] {1, 1, 35.24, 0.0875});  // Total = $38.32
orders.Rows.Add(new Object[] {2, 1, 56.21, 0.0875});  // Total = $61.13
orders.Rows.Add(new Object[] {3, 2, 14.94, 0.0925});  // Total = $16.32

// ----- Link the tables within a DataSet.
DataSet business = new DataSet();
business.Tables.Add(customers);
business.Tables.Add(orders);
business.Relations.Add(customers.Columns["ID"], orders.Columns["Customer"]);

// ----- Here is the aggregate expression column.
customers.Columns.Add("OrderTotals", typeof(decimal), "Sum(Child.Total)");

// ----- Display each customer's order total.
foreach (DataRow scanCustomer in customers.Rows)
{
    Console.WriteLine((string)scanCustomer["Name"] + ": " +
        string.Format("{0:c}", (decimal)scanCustomer["OrderTotals"]));
}
```

Visual Basic

```
' ----- Build the parent table and add some data.
Dim customers As New DataTable("Customer")
customers.Columns.Add("ID", GetType(Integer))
customers.Columns.Add("Name", GetType(String))
customers.Rows.Add({1, "Coho Winery"})
customers.Rows.Add({2, "Fourth Coffee"})

' ----- Build the child table and add some data. The "Total"
'       expression column adds sales tax to the subtotal.
Dim orders As New DataTable("Order")
orders.Columns.Add("ID", GetType(Integer))
orders.Columns.Add("Customer", GetType(Integer))
orders.Columns.Add("Subtotal", GetType(Decimal))
orders.Columns.Add("TaxRate", GetType(Decimal))
orders.Columns.Add("Total", GetType(Decimal), "Subtotal * (1 + TaxRate)")

' ----- Two sample orders for customer 1, 1 for customer 2.
orders.Rows.Add({1, 1, 35.24, 0.0875})  ' Total = $38.32
orders.Rows.Add({2, 1, 56.21, 0.0875})  ' Total = $61.13
orders.Rows.Add({3, 2, 14.94, 0.0925})  ' Total = $16.32

' ----- Link the tables within a DataSet.
Dim business As New DataSet
business.Tables.Add(customers)
business.Tables.Add(orders)
business.Relations.Add(customers.Columns!ID, orders.Columns!Customer)

' ----- Here is the aggregate expression column.
customers.Columns.Add("OrderTotals", GetType(Decimal), "Sum(Child.Total)")

' ----- Display each customer's order total.
For Each scanCustomer As DataRow In customers.Rows
    Console.WriteLine(CStr(scanCustomer!Name) & ": " &
        Format(scanCustomer!OrderTotals, "Currency"))
Next scanCustomer
```

This code generates the following output, correctly calculating the per-customer total of all child-record orders:

```
Coho Winery: $99.45
Fourth Coffee: $16.32
```

The code calculated these totals by adding up the *Child.Total* column values for only those child rows that were associated to the parent row through the defined *DataRelation*. Because the aggregate functions work only with a single named column, a more complex request such as *Sum(Child.SubTotal * (1 + Child.TaxRate))* would fail. The only way to generate totals from multiple child columns (or even multiple columns within the same table) is to first add an expression column to the child table and then apply the aggregate function to that new column.

Referencing Parent Fields in Expressions

Although ADO.NET query expressions support a "Parent" keyword, it can't be used with the aggregation functions. Instead you use it to add an expression column to a child table that references column data from the parent table. For instance, if you had Customer (parent) and Order (child) tables linked by a customer ID, and the parent table included the address for the customer, you could include the city name in the child table using an expression column.

```csharp
C#
orders.Columns.Add("CustomerCity", typeof(string), "Parent.City");
```
```vbnet
Visual Basic
orders.Columns.Add("CustomerCity", GetType(String), "Parent.City")
```

All standard expression operators that work with the local table's column data will also work with parent columns.

Setting Up Indexed Views

The *DataTable.Select* method lets you apply a selection query to a table, returning a subset of the available rows in the *DataTable*. It's convenient, but if you will run the same query against the table repeatedly, it's not the most efficient use of computing resources. Also, because it returns an array of *DataRow* instances instead of a new *DataTable*, some tools that expect a full table construct won't work with the returned results.

To overcome these issues, ADO.NET includes the *DataView* class. As with the *DataTable* class, each *DataView* exposes a set of *DataRow* objects. But unlike the *DataTable*, the *DataView* does not actually contain any *DataRow* instances. Instead, it contains an index that refers to rows in a true *DataTable*. It builds this index using the same query expressions used by the *DataTable.Select* method, with support for both a row selection component and a sorting component. Figure 6-1 shows the general relationship between a *DataView* and the *DataTable* it refers to.

Original *DataTable*

Row	ID	First Name	Birth Date
0	11	George	8/3/1985
1	96	Annette	2/12/2003
2	27	Toru	12/30/1948

DataView

Row
2
0
1

FIGURE 6-1   *DataView* entries referencing rows in a *DataTable*.

Note   The *DataView* does not actually reference a set of *DataRow* instances; instead, it refers to a set of *DataRowView* instances. ADO.NET uses the *DataRowView* class to manage the various versions of a row, especially when proposed changes have not yet been confirmed with the *DataTable.AcceptChanges* method. The *DataRowView.Row* property returns the actual row based on other settings in the *DataRowView* instance.

Creating a *DataView*

To create a *DataView* from a *DataTable*, pass the table to the *DataView* constructor.

C#
```csharp
DataView someView = new DataView(someTable);
```

Visual Basic
```vb
Dim someView As New DataView(someTable)
```

The new view includes all the rows in the original table, sorted in the order they appear in the *DataTable*. To alter the included rows, set the *DataView* object's *RowFilter* property. This property uses the same row-limiting query expression passed to the *DataTable.Select* method.

```
C#
DataView managersOnly = new DataView(employees);
managersOnly.RowFilter = "IsManager = true";
```

Visual Basic
```
Dim managersOnly As New DataView(employees)
managersOnly.RowFilter = "IsManager = True"
```

To sort the view's rows, set the *DataView.Sort* property, using the same sort-expression syntax from the *DataTable.Select* method.

```
C#
managersOnly.Sort = "HireDate DESC";
```

Visual Basic
```
managersOnly.Sort = "HireDate DESC"
```

You can also indicate which row state to expose through the view by setting the *DataView* instance's *RowStateFilter* property. By default, the view exposes all available rows that meet the *RowFilter* criteria. Setting *RowStateFilter* limits the expressed rows to just those in a specific edited state. It uses the following enumerated values:

- *DataViewRowState.None*   All rows, regardless of state.
- *DataViewRowState.Unchanged*   Only those rows with no data or state changes.
- *DataViewRowState.Added*   Only those rows added but not yet confirmed.
- *DataViewRowState.Deleted*   Only those rows deleted but not yet confirmed.
- *DataViewRowState.ModifiedCurrent*   Only those rows that have been modified. The exposed rows include the modified column values.
- *DataViewRowState.ModifiedOriginal*   Only those rows that have been modified. The exposed rows include the original column values, before changes were made.
- *DataViewRowState.OriginalRows*   Only rows that have not been changed, including deleted rows.
- *DataViewRowState.CurrentRows*   All nondeleted rows in their current state, including new rows.

Each time you modify the *RowFilter, Sort,* and *RowStateFilter* fields, the *DataView* rebuilds its index of the underlying *DataTable,* even if those properties were previously unset. To reduce the number of times that a *DataView* must rebuild the index, the class includes a constructor that accepts starting *RowFilter, Sort,* and *RowStateFilter* values.

C#
```
DataView someView = new DataView(table, filter-string, sort-string, rowState);
```

Visual Basic
```
Dim someView As New DataView(table, filter-string, sort-string, rowState)
```

The *DataView* class includes three Boolean properties that let you limit the operations that can be performed on rows through the view. The *AllowNew, AllowEdit,* and *AllowDelete* properties allow or prohibit new rows, changes to rows, and the removal of rows, respectively. Any attempt to carry out a prohibited action throws an exception. These limitations apply only to the view, not to the underlying table. If you set the view's *AllowDelete* property to *False,* you can still remove rows through the underlying *DataTable.Rows.Delete* method.

Using a *DataView*

The *DataView* class includes several features that return information about the in-view rows. The most basic is the *DataView.Count* property, which returns a count of the number of rows exposed by the *DataView* once its *RowFilter* and *RowStateFilter* properties have been applied.

C#
```
DataView managersOnly = new DataView(employees);
managersOnly.RowFilter = "IsManager = true";
MessageBox.Show("Total Managers: " + managersOnly.Count);
```

Visual Basic
```
Dim managersOnly As New DataView(employees)
managersOnly.RowFilter = "IsManager = True"
MessageBox.Show("Total Managers: " & managersOnly.Count)
```

The *DataView.FindRows* method returns an array of rows based on a matching "sort key" value. To use this method, you must have assigned an expression to the *DataView.Sort* property. The sort key must be for the column(s) identified in the *Sort* property, and must appear in the same order.

```csharp
C#
DataView playerView = new DataView(teamPlayers);
playerView.Sort = "Position, StartingYear DESC";
DataRowView[] newPitchers = playerView.FindRows(
    new Object[] {"Pitcher", DateTime.Today.Year});
```

Visual Basic
```vbnet
Dim playerView As New DataView(teamPlayers)
playerView.Sort = "Position, StartingYear DESC"
Dim newPitchers() As DataRowView =
    playerView.FindRows({"Pitcher", Today.Year})
```

FindRows returns an array of *DataRowView* instances, an ADO.NET class that manages the lifetime of a *DataRow* through its various data and state changes. To access the underlying row, use the instance's *Row* property.

Another *DataView* method, *Find*, carries out the same task as *FindRows*, but returns a zero-based index to the first matching row according to the view's defined sort order. If there are no matches, the method returns -1.

The *DataView.ToTable* method provides the most convenient way to generate a subset of table rows while at the same time selecting only a subset of columns. *ToTable* accepts an array of column names to build a new *DataTable* instance that includes only the filtered rows and only the specified data columns.

```csharp
C#
DataView playerView = new DataView(teamPlayers);
playerView.RowFilter = "LastActiveYear = " + DateTime.Today.Year;
DataTable currentTeam = playerView.ToTable(true,
    new string[] {"JerseyNumber", "PlayerName", "Position"});
```

Visual Basic
```vbnet
Dim playerView As New DataView(teamPlayers)
playerView.RowFilter = "LastActiveYear = " & Today.Year
Dim currentTeam As DataTable = playerView.ToTable(True,
    {"JerseyNumber", "PlayerName", "Position"})
```

The first argument to *ToTable* is the "distinct" flag. When *True*, only unique rows (based on all column values) get copied into the new table. When *False*, duplicate rows can appear in the resulting *DataTable*. Additional variations of the *ToTable* method let you supply a name for the new table, which is the same as the original table by default.

Note In addition to creating custom *DataView* instances, each *DataTable* can have its own default *DataView*. This data view, located at *DataTable.DefaultView*, not only exposes a filtered view of the table's rows but in certain situations it also imposes that view on the table, so that references to the table's collection of rows will express what the view itself expresses.

The *DefaultView* exists mainly to support data-binding situations. This book introduces data binding concepts in Chapter 21, "Binding Data with ADO.NET."

Generating a New *DataTable* from a *DataView*: C#

Note This exercise uses the "Chapter 6 CSharp" sample project and continues the previous exercise in this chapter.

1. Open the source code view for the *DataViews* form. Locate the *ActExtract_Click* event handler.

2. Just after the "Build a view that will generate the new table" comment, add the following statement:

```
interimView = new DataView(SampleData);
```

This line creates a new *DataView* instance, passing an existing *DataTable* object to the constructor.

3. Just after the "Apply the optional filter" comment, inside of the *try* block, add the following lines:

```
if (FilterExpression.Text.Trim().Length > 0)
    interimView.RowFilter = FilterExpression.Text.Trim();
```

You are not required to apply a *RowFilter* to a *DataView*. By default, all rows included in the view will appear in the generated table.

4. Just after the "Generate the new table" comment, inside of the *try* block, add the following lines:

```
generatedTable = interimView.ToTable(true,
    IncludedColumns.CheckedItems.Cast<string>().ToArray());
```

The *ToTable* method generates the new table. The first Boolean argument, when *true*, includes any rows that are duplicates in every column if they appear. The second argument is an array of column names to include in the new table.

5. Run the program. When the *Switchboard* form appears, click Data Views And Tables. When the Data Views form appears, use the Columns and Filter fields to indicate which columns and rows should appear in the generated table. (Filter accepts an ADO.NET *Select* filter expression.) Optionally, you can rearrange the columns using the Move Up and Move Down buttons. Click Extract to see the results. For example, select **StateName** and **AreaSqMiles** in the Column field, and enter **AreaSqMiles >= 100000** in the Filter field. Clicking Extract shows you the seven largest American states.

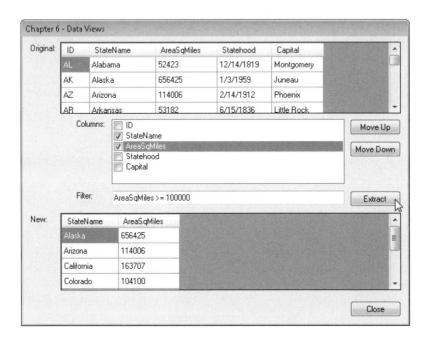

Generating a New *DataTable* from a *DataView*: Visual Basic

Note This exercise uses the "Chapter 6 VB" sample project and continues the previous exercise in this chapter.

1. Open the source code view for the *DataViews* form. Locate the *ActExtract_Click* event handler.

2. Just after the "Build a view that will generate the new table" comment, add the following statement:

```
interimView = New DataView(SampleData)
```

This line creates a new *DataView* instance, passing an existing *DataTable* object to the constructor.

3. Just after the "Apply the optional filter" comment, inside the *Try* block, add the following lines:

```
If (FilterExpression.Text.Trim.Length > 0) Then
    interimView.RowFilter = FilterExpression.Text.Trim
End If
```

You are not required to apply a *RowFilter* to a *DataView*. By default, all rows included in the view will appear in the generated table.

4. Just after the "Generate the new table" comment, inside the *Try* block, add the following lines:

```
generatedTable = interimView.ToTable(True,
    IncludedColumns.CheckedItems.Cast(Of String).ToArray())
```

The *ToTable* method generates the new table. The first Boolean argument, when *True*, includes any rows that are duplicates in every column if they appear. The second argument is an array of column names to include in the new table.

5. Run the program. When the *Switchboard* form appears, click Data Views And Tables. When the Data Views form appears, use the Columns and Filter fields to indicate which columns and rows should appear in the generated table. (Filter accepts an ADO.NET *Select* filter expression.) Optionally, you can rearrange the columns using the Move Up and Move Down buttons. Click Extract to see the results. For example, select **StateName** and **Statehood** in the Columns field, and enter **Statehood < #1/1/1791#** in the Filter field. Clicking Extract shows you the original 13 American colonies.

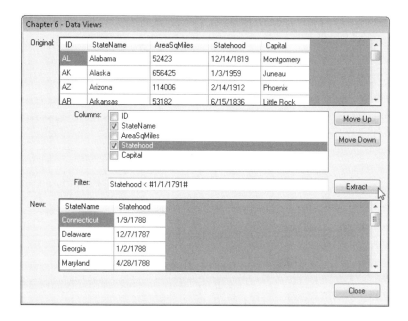

Summary

This chapter introduced two ADO.NET features that enhance its core functionality: aggregates and data views. *DataTable* objects support seven distinct aggregates that let you generate a single value based on computing results from a single table column. Each of these seven functions—*Sum, Avg, Min, Max, Count, StDev,* and *Var*—can be used in a standalone manner to calculate a single column's aggregate value. They can also be expressed through a table column, allowing for grouped summaries.

The *DataView* class rolls up sorting and filtering rules for a table in a single object that in some cases can be used much like the underlying *DataTable*. Containing no data, the *DataView* includes an indexed reference to each row in the linked *DataTable*. Changes made to the view are reflected in the table, and vice versa. Even more important, views allow you to have two unique expressions of a single table available at the same time.

Chapter 6 Quick Reference

To	Do This
Calculate the average of a column of data	Create a *DataTable* with valid columns and rows.
	Create a string containing the expression **Avg(*xxx*)**, where "xxx" is the name of the column to average.
	Call the *DataTable* object's *Compute* method, passing it the string expression.
Find the maximum value of a child-table column associated with each row in a parent table	Create parent and child *DataTable* objects.
	Add the tables to a *DataSet* instance.
	Link the tables with a *DataRelation* object.
	Create a string containing the expression **Child.Max(*xxx*)**, where "xxx" is the name of the child-table column in which to locate the maximum value.
	Create a new *DataColumn* of the same data type as the examined child column.
	Set the *DataColumn* object's *Expression* property to the string expression.
	Add the *DataColumn* to the parent *DataTable*.
Generate a *DataTable* from a *DataView*	Create the original *DataTable*.
	Create a new *DataView* instance, passing the *DataTable* object to its constructor.
	Set the *DataView* object's *RowFilter*, *Sort*, and *RowStateFilter* properties as needed.
	Call the *DataView* object's *ToTable* method, optionally indicating which columns to include.

Chapter 7
Saving and Restoring Data

After completing this chapter, you will be able to:

- Export a *DataSet* to a file in XML format
- Import a previously exported *DataSet* from XML format
- Define the structure of the exported XML content
- Access the XSD schema for a *DataSet* or *DataTable*

ADO.NET isn't the only popular format for managing data in .NET applications. XML—content crafted using the Extensible Markup Language—is another common format that provides standardized, cross-platform data management in a semi-human-readable format.

The *DataSet* class and the *DataTable* instances contained within it include features for moving data back and forth between ADO.NET and XML. This chapter demonstrates those features, focusing on the ability to serialize the contents of a *DataSet* for later use, either by loading it into another *DataSet* or by accessing the data directly through some other XML-enabled application. ADO.NET includes full schema definition support using Schema Definition Language (XSD).

 Note Before version 4, ADO.NET included an *XmlDataDocument* class that supported on-demand synchronization between the contents of a *DataSet* and an XML document. That class has since been deprecated. You can simulate some of the functionality formerly available through *XmlDataDocument* using the features discussed in this chapter. You can also use *DataSet*–focused LINQ queries, as discussed in Chapter 18, "Using LINQ to DataSet," as a substitute for the obsolete *XmlDataDocument* class.

Serializing *DataSet* and *DataTable* Objects

ADO.NET was designed with XML in mind, so generating XML content from a *DataSet* takes very little effort. Reading XML content into a *DataSet* is even easier because ADO.NET will guess at the correct structure of the data even if you don't provide table design guidance.

Writing XML

To generate XML for the data content of an existing *DataSet* instance, call its *WriteXml* method, passing an output file name.

```csharp
C#
DataSet infoSet = new DataSet();

// ----- Add tables, relations, and data, then call...
infoSet.WriteXml(@"c:\StorageFile.xml");
```

```vbnet
Visual Basic
Dim infoSet As New DataSet

' ----- Add tables, relations, and data, then call...
infoSet.WriteXml("c:\StorageFile.xml")
```

In addition to file names, various overloads of *WriteXml* accept a valid *Stream* instance, a *TextWriter* instance, or an *XmlWriter* instance as their first argument. The generated XML is straightforward, using table and column names to define each element tag. Here is some typical XML data content produced by *WriteXml*. This content includes three customer data rows, each with four fields: a string column (*BusinessName*), two numeric fields (*ID*, *AnnualFee*), and a date value (*ContractDate*) in UTC format with a time zone offset.

```xml
<CustomerDataSet>
  <Customer>
    <ID>1</ID>
    <BusinessName>City Power &amp; Light</BusinessName>
    <AnnualFee>500</AnnualFee>
    <ContractDate>2008-06-01T00:00:00-07:00</ContractDate>
  </Customer>
  <Customer>
    <ID>2</ID>
    <BusinessName>Lucerne Publishing</BusinessName>
    <AnnualFee>300</AnnualFee>
    <ContractDate>2008-01-01T00:00:00-08:00</ContractDate>
  </Customer>
  <Customer>
    <ID>3</ID>
    <BusinessName>Southridge Video</BusinessName>
    <AnnualFee>350</AnnualFee>
    <ContractDate>2010-02-15T00:00:00-08:00</ContractDate>
  </Customer>
</CustomerDataSet>
```

By default, *WriteXml* writes XML for only the data rows in each table; the method saves no information about the structure of the *DataSet*. To include the *DataSet* object's schema definition along with the data, add a second argument to the *WriteXml* method call, passing *XmlWriteMode.WriteSchema*.

```
C#
infoSet.WriteXml(targetFile, XmlWriteMode.WriteSchema);
```

Visual Basic
```
infoSet.WriteXml(targetFile, XmlWriteMode.WriteSchema)
```

Other *XmlWriteMode* enumeration members include *IgnoreSchema* (don't include the schema, which is the same as leaving off the second argument) and *DiffGram* (a special format that outputs differences between the *Original* and the *Current* versions of each *DataRow* within the *DataSet*).

If you want to output only the schema, use the *DataSet* object's *WriteXmlSchema* method, passing it a file name, a *Stream*, a *TextWriter*, or an *XmlWriter*.

```
C#
infoSet.WriteXmlSchema(targetSchemaFile);
```

Visual Basic
```
infoSet.WriteXmlSchema(targetSchemaFile)
```

The *DataTable* class also includes *WriteXml* and *WriteXmlSchema* methods that you can use to generate XML content on a table-by-table basis. In addition to the file/stream/writer target and the *XmlWriteMode* arguments, the *DataTable* versions of these methods accept an optional Boolean argument that indicates whether child tables linked via *DataRelation* objects should be sent to the output with the instantiating table's schema or data. You can use this Boolean argument either after or instead of the *XmlWriteMode* argument.

```
C#
// ----- Write the customer data AND the linked order data.
customers.WriteXml(targetFile, true);
```

Visual Basic
```
' ----- Write the customer data AND the linked order data.
customers.WriteXml(targetFile, True)
```

If you want to keep the XML content in the application, the *DataSet* class includes *GetXml* and *GetXmlSchema* methods that return string documents with content similar to the output of the *WriteXml* and *WriteXmlSchema* methods. The *DataTable.GetDataTableSchema* method returns the XSD for a table in plain string format.

Reading XML

Both the *DataSet* and *DataTable* classes include *ReadXml* and *ReadXmlSchema* counterparts to the XML-writing methods. To use them, create a new *DataSet* or *DataTable* instance; then call the appropriate method, passing a file name, a *Stream*, a *TextReader*, or an *XmlReader*.

```
C#
DataSet infoSet = new DataSet();

// ----- To read the schema, use...
infoSet.ReadXmlSchema(@"c:\StorageSchemaFile.xml");

// ----- To read the data, use...
infoSet.ReadXml(@"c:\StorageFile.xml");
```

```
Visual Basic
Dim infoSet As New DataSet

' ----- To read the schema, use...
infoSet.ReadXmlSchema("c:\StorageSchemaFile.xml")

' ----- To read the data, use...
infoSet.ReadXml("c:\StorageFile.xml")
```

A second argument to the *DataSet.ReadXml* method lets you indicate how the incoming content should be processed. It uses one of the following enumerated values:

- **XmlReadMode.Auto** Lets *ReadXml* figure out what to do with the incoming content automatically. If it detects a valid schema with the data, it processes the schema before loading the data. If it sees a *DiffGram*, it interprets it appropriately. This is the default option if you don't add the read-mode argument.

- **XmlReadMode.ReadSchema** Reconstructs the *DataTable* members of the *DataSet* without loading in the data.

- ■ ***XmlReadMode.IgnoreSchema***   Loads in the data, ignoring any schema that might be included in the XML. Instead, the existing *DataSet* structure is used.

- ■ ***XmlReadMode.InferSchema***   Builds a new schema based on the structure of the XML data alone, ignoring any included schema. If needed, any existing *DataSet* structure will be augmented with new schema information.

- ■ ***XmlReadMode.DiffGram***   Reads in the content previously written with the *WriteXml* method's *XmlWriteMode.DiffGram* mode.

- ■ ***XmlReadMode.Fragment***   Reads in and processes XML content that might be partial or incomplete.

- ■ ***XmlReadMode.InferTypedSchema***   Similar to the *InferSchema* mode, but *ReadXml* will go out of its way to figure out the data type of each incoming data column.

ReadXml or *ReadXmlSchema* support both inline and linked XSD structure definitions.

DataSet includes an additional *InferXmlSchema* method. It works just like the *ReadXmlSchema* method, but you can pass it an array of namespace names to exclude on import.

Guiding XML Generation

The *Read...* and *Write...* XML methods generate valid XML that can be used right away with any XML tools. Still, the default format might be insufficient for your processing needs. That's why ADO.NET includes features that let you guide and enhance the XML generation process. There are three main types of guidance you can provide to the XML content: namespace identification, child table nesting, and column management.

Identifying Namespaces

XML includes a namespace feature that lets you group content by purpose, even among tags that appear within the same parent element. Three ADO.NET classes—*DataSet, DataTable,* and *DataColumn*—include properties that let you assign both the namespace and the namespace prefix that will appear in the XML tags associated with the table and column values.

Each of these three classes includes a *Namespace* property, a string value containing the target XML namespace name. A second property, *Prefix*, defines the short prefix prepended to tag names that belong to the namespace. The following code sets the namespace and prefix for a *DataTable*; the process for setting these values in a *DataSet* or *DataColumn* is identical:

```
C#
DataTable customers = new DataTable("Customer");
customers.Namespace = "corporate";
customers.Prefix = "co";
```

```
Visual Basic
Dim customers As New DataTable("Customer")
customers.Namespace = "corporate"
customers.Prefix = "co"
```

The addition of the namespace and the prefix modifies the generated XML to include the necessary *xmlns* attributes and prefix components.

```
<co:Customer xmlns:co="corporate">
  <ID xmlns="corporate">1</ID>
  <BusinessName xmlns="corporate">City Power &amp; Light</BusinessName>
  ...
```

Setting only the *DataTable* (or *DataSet*) namespace values applies the *xmlns* tag to each contained column-related element. To change these column entries to prefix-bearing tags instead, set the *Namespace* and *Prefix* properties within each of the table's *DataColumn* objects.

The constructor for the *DataTable* class also includes a parameter that sets the *Namespace* property during object creation. Neither *DataSet* nor *DataColumn* includes such a parameter.

```
C#
DataTable customers = new DataTable("Customer", "corporate");
```

```
Visual Basic
Dim customers As New DataTable("Customer", "corporate")
```

The namespace and prefix settings are overridable. Setting these values at the *DataSet* level affects all tables within the data set except those that have their own distinct namespace values. Setting the *DataTable*-level fields affects its columns unless you override it by setting the two properties in the *DataColumn* object.

Nesting Child Tables

By default, each table within a *DataSet* has its rows output at the same element level. In a data set with *Customer* and *Order* tables, each row in the *Customer* table would appear within the data set's top-level XML element, followed by each row in the *Order* table at the same level as the *Customer* records. Sometimes it is better to have the child table records that belong to a parent record physically appear within their parent XML element. Sample code earlier in this chapter showed how adding an extra argument to the *DataTable.WriteXml* method would accomplish this. But when generating XML for an entire *DataSet*, you must indicate your desire to nest child tables by setting the *Nested* property in the relevant *DataRelation* object.

C#
```csharp
DataRelation customerOrder = new DataRelation(
    customers.Columns["ID"], orders.Columns["CustomerID"]);
customerOrder.Nested = true;
```

Visual Basic
```vb
Dim customerOrder As New DataRelation(
    customers.Columns!ID, orders.Columns!CustomerID)
customerOrder.Nested = True
```

Managing and Positioning Columns

As ADO.NET outputs the XML content for a *DataTable*, it first generates a tag for each row in the table, using the table's name as the containing tag. Within this row tag, each column gets its own tagged element. The data for each column appears as text within the column element. The following content shows a single row from the "Customer" table, with subordinate tag elements for each of the four columns in the row:

```xml
<Customer>
  <ID>1</ID>
  <BusinessName>City Power &amp; Light</BusinessName>
  <AnnualFee>500</AnnualFee>
  <ContractDate>2008-06-01T00:00:00-07:00</ContractDate>
</Customer>
```

Sometimes you might want one or more columns to appear as attributes for the row-level tag instead.

```xml
<Customer ID="1">
```

This is accomplished by setting the *DataColumn.ColumnMapping* property for the relevant column object. This property can be set to one of four enumerated values:

- **MappingType.Element** The column data appears within its own XML tag element. This is the default setting for all columns.

- **MappingType.Attribute** The column value is moved into the row's tag and stored as an XML attribute.

- **MappingType.SimpleContent** The data for this column becomes the entire content for the row's tag element. Only one column within a table can be designated as the *SimpleContent* column. All other columns must either be set as attributes or must be hidden.

> **Note** Setting a column's mapping type to *SimpleContent* will generate an exception if any other columns in the same table have a mapping type of *Element* or *SimpleContent*.

- **MappingType.Hidden** This column is excluded from the generated XML content.

In addition to setting the *ColumnMapping* property, the constructor for the *DataColumn* object lets you define the mapping type.

```csharp
C#
DataColumn orderID = new DataColumn("ID", typeof(int), MappingType.Attribute);
```

```vb
Visual Basic
Dim orderID As New DataColumn("ID", GetType(Integer), MappingType.Attribute)
```

Generating XML from a *DataSet*: C#

1. Open the "Chapter 7 CSharp" project from the installed samples folder. The project includes one *Windows.Forms* class named *Serialization*.

2. Open the source code view for the *Serialization* form. Locate the *ActGenerate_Click* function. This routine produces the XML content from a sample *DataSet* containing two tables: *Customer* and *Order*.

3. Just after the "Set the XML namespace" comment, add the following statements:

```
SampleDataSet.Tables["Customer"].Namespace = TableNamespace.Text.Trim();
SampleDataSet.Tables["Customer"].Prefix = TablePrefix.Text.Trim();
SampleDataSet.Tables["Order"].Namespace = TableNamespace.Text.Trim();
SampleDataSet.Tables["Order"].Prefix = TablePrefix.Text.Trim();
```

This code sets the namespace and prefix values for both of the sample tables.

Note   As mentioned in the chapter discussion, you can also define namespace and prefix values within each *DataColumn*. Although it is not included in the sample code, consider adding code that will loop through all columns in each of the two tables and add the user-specified namespace and prefix values.

4. Just after the "Indicate the relationship type" comment, add the following line:

```
SampleDataSet.Relations[0].Nested = NestChildRecords.Checked;
```

This statement determines whether the order rows for each customer record are contained within the *<Customer>* tag *(true)* or whether all *<Order>* tags appear after and at the same level as all the *<Customer>* tags in the XML *(false)*.

5. Just after the "Build a memory stream to hold the results" comment, add the following code:

```
holdBuffer = new MemoryStream(8192);
SampleDataSet.WriteXml(holdBuffer,
    (XmlWriteMode)OutputWriteMode.SelectedItem);
```

These lines perform the actual XML generation, sending the results to a stream, in this case a *MemoryStream* instance. The remaining code in the event handler moves the XML content from the stream to an on-form text box.

6. Run the program. Use the fields in the upper-right corner of the form to alter the XML content and then click Generate to produce the XML. As an example, set the XML Write Mode to **WriteSchema**, change the Mapping for both **Parent.ID** and **Child.ID** to **Attribute**, and set the Mapping for **Child.CustomerID** to **Hidden**. Click Generate. The XML will contain the XSD schema for the data set, followed by distinct *<Customer>* and *<Order>* elements.

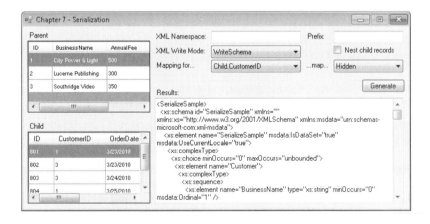

Generating XML from a *DataSet*: Visual Basic

1. Open the "Chapter 7 VB" project from the installed samples folder. The project includes one *Windows.Forms* class named *Serialization*.

2. Open the source code view for the *Serialization* form. Locate the *ActGenerate_Click* function. This routine produces the XML content from a sample *DataSet* containing two tables: *Customer* and *Order*.

3. Just after the "Set the XML namespace" comment, add the following statements:

```
SampleDataSet.Tables("Customer").Namespace = TableNamespace.Text.Trim
SampleDataSet.Tables("Customer").Prefix = TablePrefix.Text.Trim
SampleDataSet.Tables("Order").Namespace = TableNamespace.Text.Trim
SampleDataSet.Tables("Order").Prefix = TablePrefix.Text.Trim
```

This code sets the namespace and prefix values for both of the sample tables.

> **Note** As mentioned in the chapter discussion, you can also define namespace and prefix values within each *DataColumn*. Although it is not included in the sample code, consider adding code that will loop through all columns in each of the two tables and add the user-specified namespace and prefix values.

4. Just after the "Indicate the relationship type" comment, add the following line:

```
SampleDataSet.Relations(0).Nested = NestChildRecords.Checked
```

This statement determines whether the order rows for each customer record are contained within the *<Customer>* tag (*True*) or whether all *<Order>* tags appear after and at the same level as all the *<Customer>* tags in the XML (*False*).

5. Just after the "Build a memory stream to hold the results" comment, add the following code:

```
holdBuffer = New MemoryStream(8192)
SampleDataSet.WriteXml(holdBuffer,
    CType(OutputWriteMode.SelectedItem, XmlWriteMode))
```

These lines perform the actual XML generation, sending the results to a stream, in this case a *MemoryStream* instance. The remaining code in the event handler moves the XML content from the stream to an on-form text box.

6. Run the program. Use the fields in the upper-right corner of the form to alter the XML content and then click Generate to produce the XML. As an example, set the XML Write Mode to **IgnoreSchema**; select the Nest Child Records check box; change the Mapping for **Child.ID** to **Attribute**; change the Mapping for **Child.CustomerID**, **Child. OrderDate**, **Child.Subtotal**, and **Child.TaxRate** to **Hidden**; and finally change the Mapping for **Child.Total** to **SimpleContent**. Click Generate. The XML will contain a simple set of customer records, each containing one or more *<Order>* tags with an ID attribute, and with the order total set as the element content.

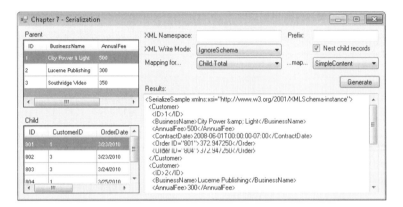

Summary

This chapter introduced the XML-specific features built into ADO.NET classes. These features exist primarily to assist in serializing static XML content for disk-based storage or for transfer to other applications that expect ADO.NET-generated XML content. The XML produced by these classes can define its own schema using embedded or external XSD and can build hierarchical XML elements based on the relationships in the original *DataSet*.

There are other ways to bring ADO.NET data and XML together in your applications. LINQ, a major language feature in both Visual Basic and C#, includes data-querying features for both ADO.NET and XML, features that can work in tandem. Chapters 17 through 20 in this book discuss various LINQ-related technologies. Although "LINQ to XML" is not specifically examined in this book, the general LINQ concepts outlined in those chapters are similar to those used when writing LINQ queries for XML data.

Chapter 7 Quick Reference

To	Do This
Export a *DataSet* to a file as XML	Create a *DataSet* instance. Add all relevant *DataTable, DataRelation,* and content objects. Call the *WriteXml* method of the *DataSet*, passing it the file name as an argument.
Import file-based XML into a new *DataSet*	Create a new *DataSet* instance. Call the *ReadXml* method of the *DataSet*, passing it the file name as an argument.
Generate hierarchical parent-child data	Create a *DataSet* instance. Add the relevant *DataTable* objects. Add a *DataRelation* instance that links the tables. Set the *DataRelation.Nested* property to *True*. Call *DataSet.WriteXml* to generate the XML content.
Store a *DataColumn* as an XML-based attribute	Set the *DataColumn.ColumnMapping* property to *MappingType.Attribute*.

Part II
Connecting to External Data Sources

Chapter 8: Establishing External Connections

Chapter 9: Querying Databases

Chapter 10: Adding Parameters to Queries

Chapter 11: Making External Data Available Locally

Chapter 12: Guaranteeing Data Integrity

Chapter 8
Establishing External Connections

After completing this chapter, you will be able to:

- Understand the components that make up connection strings

- Write code that connects to an external data source

- Identify the different data providers included in ADO.NET

The first seven chapters of this book demonstrated many ADO.NET features that let you work with data in a fully disconnected way. However, there are very few programs that depend on data created solely within the application itself. Most programs, especially those in a business environment, depend on content stored in a database or other source external to the application. This chapter examines ADO.NET data providers, the connection object, and other related features that make interactions between the Framework and data sources possible.

The examples in this chapter and in those that follow use the *StepSample* database mentioned in the book's Introduction. If you haven't yet installed that database, return to the Introduction and follow the steps listed there to prepare the sample SQL Server data. You might also want to review the "Connecting to External Data" section on page 8 of Chapter 1, for details on connecting to databases using Visual Studio's data access tools.

Using Connection Strings

The ADO.NET library provides generic access to many different external data platforms. These data sources include both local files in standardized formats and remote relational databases from a variety of vendors. To access these data stores, your application must tell ADO.NET how to locate the resources, tell which data format to expect, and supply the security credentials required for access. You communicate this information through *connection strings*: formatted text strings that document the relevant connection values.

A connection string contains multiple semicolon-delimited elements. Each element expresses a key-value pair that identifies one of the needed connection components or other relevant configuration settings. The connection string syntax looks like this:

```
key1=value1;key2=value2;key3=value3
```

Typical elements include the file-based or network-based location of the database, the user ID and password needed to access the data source, the timeout value used to limit the duration of exceptionally long-running queries, and other values needed to establish the connection and its configuration. The specific keys you must include depend on the target data platform or file format, the configuration of the data source, and the customizable features your application requires. This section focuses on the more common elements needed to communicate with a SQL Server database. For full details on other SQL Server elements, or on the elements needed by other platforms, see the "Connection String Syntax (ADO.NET)" page in the Visual Studio online help.

Note One popular web site, *http://www.connectionstrings.com*, includes sample connection strings for all major database platforms, as well as for some relatively unknown data sources. It also documents some of the more esoteric connection string keys that might be required for specific configurations. It is an independent site that is not sponsored or officially supported by Microsoft. But when you are struggling to construct a connection string for a complex or under-documented data environment, it is an invaluable resource.

SQL Server Connection Strings

In the "Creating a Data Source Using the Connection Wizard" example on page 8 in Chapter 1, step 12 briefly mentioned the connection string generated by the Data Source Connection Wizard. When creating the data source on the wizard's Choose Your Data Connection panel, the configured string appears in the Connection String field.

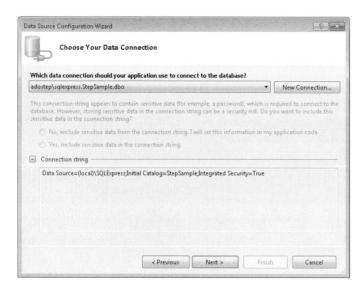

When following the steps in Chapter 1 on my own system, that connection string contained three key-value pairs.

```
Data Source=(local)\SQLEXPRESS;Initial Catalog=StepSample;
    Integrated Security=True
```

The wizard might create a slightly different string on your system. This particular connection string establishes a connection to a SQL Server 2008 Express Edition database engine. The three keys provide the information ADO.NET needs to establish the connection.

- The *Data Source* key indicates which server to access. In this case, the *(local)\ SQLEXPRESS* value refers to the SQL Server 2008 Express Edition installation on the local workstation.

- The *Initial Catalog* key tells the connection which database within the hosted database engine to use as the default. In this sample string, *StepSample* is the name of the default database catalog to use. You must have the appropriate security credentials to access this database.

- The *Integrated Security* key with a value of *True* tells ADO.NET to use your existing Microsoft Windows security credentials to access the database.

So far, you've seen the typical basic format of a SQL Server 2008 connection string when using your Microsoft Windows security credentials; however, a few additional keys are commonly included in SQL Server connection strings.

- As shown above, the *Data Source* key indicates the source database engine. The special value of *"(local)"* tells ADO.NET to access the SQL Server instance running on the local workstation. More commonly, *(local)* will be replaced with the name of the server that hosts the database.

- If you prefer to use SQL Server's own security system, set the *Integrated Security* key to *False* (or you can just omit it from the connection string; *False* is the default value). Then add two additional keys: *User ID* (with its value set of the SQL Server user name) and *Password* (with its value set to the password of the specified user).

- The *Application Name* key is optional though useful. A user with appropriate security access can obtain from the SQL Server database engine a list of all connected users, a list that includes this *Application Name* setting. If you have users running multiple versions of multiple applications, setting this value to the name and version number of the connecting application can simplify application use reporting.

- The *AttachDBFilename* key lets you attach a SQL Server Express Edition .mdf data file by referring to its filename.

- The *Connection Timeout* key specifies the number of seconds to wait before terminating long-running queries or updates. The default is 15 seconds.

- The *MultipleActiveResultSets* key defaults to *False*. If you set it to *True*, SQL Server will allow you to have multiple simultaneous *SELECT* queries open to the database, or will allow you to run *INSERT, UPDATE,* or *DELETE* commands even when a *SELECT* query is active.

- The *Encrypt* and *TrustServerCertificate* keys work together to enable encrypted database sessions.

Note While you've seen the most common connection string keys, be aware that these comprise only a portion of the keys available with SQL Server connections. Some keys also have synonyms, including the *Server* synonym that is used in place of the *Data Source* key. See the "SqlConnection.ConnectionString Property" page in the Visual Studio documentation for additional key values.

OLE DB and ODBC Connection Strings

ADO.NET provides generic access to many data platforms through the older OLE DB and ODBC data access layers. The .NET classes for this type of access are wrappers that provide a .NET-friendly interface to the underlying data libraries.

Connection strings for both OLE DB and ODBC data sources are conceptually identical to their SQL Server counterparts. They differ only in the specific keys and values included in each string. For example, you can connect to Microsoft Access databases (.mdb files) using the OLE DB interface.

```
Provider=Microsoft.Jet.OLEDB.4.0;
    Data Source=C:\MyDataFolder\MyDatabase.mdb;
    User Id=admin;Password=
```

For additional examples or details on the keys needed to connect to OLE DB or ODBC data sources, see the "OleDbConnection.ConnectionString Property" and "OdbcConnection.ConnectionString Property" pages in the Visual Studio online help, or reference the documentation for your specific data source platform.

Connection String Builders

Building connection string content by hand is never an exciting proposition, and can sometimes involve security risks. If you allow users to provide portions of the connection string to your application, you open your program up to malicious code injection attacks. Consider the following SQL Server connection string:

```
Source=ServerName;Initial Catalog=SalesData;User ID=xxx;Password=yyy
```

If a user provides the user ID (*xxx*) and password (*yyy*) values, a password that includes its own semicolon-delimited value can alter the intent of the string.

```
...;Password=abc!123;Initial Catalog=master
```

Because the rightmost element of a connection string takes priority, the user-supplied *Initial Catalog=master* element would override the earlier key, directing the user to the master database.

To prevent such attacks and make connection string building a more programmer-friendly activity, ADO.NET includes *connection string builders*, platform-specific classes that expose strongly typed properties associated with the keys normally included in the connection string.

The connection string builder class for SQL Server is located at *System.Data.SqlClient. SqlConnectionStringBuilder*. To use it, create a new instance of the class, set its properties as needed, and then access the object's *ConnectionString* property to obtain the ready-to-use connection string. The following code builds the wizard-generated connection string shown earlier in this chapter:

```
C#
SqlClient.SqlConnectionStringBuilder builder =
    new SqlClient.SqlConnectionStringBuilder();
builder.DataSource = @"(local)\SQLEXPRESS";
builder.InitialCatalog = "StepSample";
builder.IntegratedSecurity = true;
return builder.ConnectionString;
```

```
Visual Basic
Dim builder As New SqlClient.SqlConnectionStringBuilder
builder.DataSource = "(local)\SQLEXPRESS"
builder.InitialCatalog = "StepSample"
builder.IntegratedSecurity = True
Return builder.ConnectionString
```

The .NET Framework also includes string builders for OLE DB (*System.Data.OleDb.OleDb ConnectionStringBuilder*) and ODBC (*System.Data.Odbc.OdbcConnectionStringBuilder*) connections. As with connection strings, the builders include a large number of platform-specific properties used to set the supported keys and values. See the Visual Studio documentation of each string builder class for specific property lists.

Storing Connection Strings

Because they are standard text strings, how or where you store the connection strings used in your applications is up to you. The Data Source Connection Wizard, demonstrated in Chapter 1, offers to store its generated connection string in your application's settings file. As mentioned in that chapter, storing the string in the "user" settings file makes it possible to modify this string within the application, perhaps based on user-updated values. Storing the string in the "application" settings file provides consistent access to the connection string, but it can't be modified by the application itself.

Wherever you store the string, be sure to weigh the risks of storing a plain-text key into the database system's locking mechanism. If your connection string includes the *Password* element, you might want to encrypt the entire string before storing it in a disk file or registry entry.

Understanding Data Providers

ADO.NET provides a generic interface to many different types of data stores, including SQL Server, Microsoft Access file-based databases, comma-delimited text files, and Excel spreadsheets, among others. To link these varied data sources with the common *DataSet* model, ADO.NET includes *providers*, class libraries that understand how to interact with a specific data platform such as SQL Server, or a common data layer such as OLE DB. Other vendors offer additional providers beyond those included with Visual Studio that enable access to more third-party database systems and file formats.

The ADO.NET Framework comes with three providers:

- The Microsoft SQL Server provider, expressed through the *System.Data.SqlClient* namespace.

- The OLE DB provider, expressed through the *System.Data.OleDb* namespace.

- The ODBC provider, expressed through the *System.Data.Odbc* namespace.

Although all providers are conceptually identical, classes that expose similar functionality between the providers sometimes have different names. For instance, the SQL Server provider class that establishes a connection to a database is called *SqlConnection*. The equivalent class in the OLE DB provider is called *OleDbConnection*. (They both derive from the *System.Data. Common.DbConnection* class.) Each provider also includes many classes that are specific to its provider experience. The *SqlClient* namespace includes *SqlBulkCopy*, a class that provides access to SQL Server's bulk copy features, and that has no counterpart in either the OLE DB or ODBC providers. This book focuses on the most commonly used classes found in the *System. Data.SqlClient* namespace.

> **Note** Prior to version 4 of ADO.NET, Microsoft also included a functional Oracle provider with the .NET Framework. This provider, stored in the *System.Data.OracleClient* namespace, still ships with Visual Studio. However, its classes have been marked as deprecated and obsolete. Microsoft will likely remove the provider completely in a future release and recommends that Oracle users obtain a third-party provider.

Providers exist to transport data between proprietary data platforms and the generic ADO.NET data layer. They include platform-specific classes that access data resources through connection strings, establish communications with those data sources, pass query and data modification commands from the application to the data store, and return data records back to the application in a form understood by a *DataSet* and its related classes. The connection string builder classes discussed earlier in this chapter exist within the provider-specific namespaces.

The key classes within each provider (with their SQL Server provider-specific class names) include *Command* (*SqlCommand*), *Connection* (*SqlConnection*), *DataAdapter* (*SqlDataAdapter*), and *DataReader* (*SqlDataReader*). The chapters in this section of the book discuss these classes plus a few others that form the basis of data management between ADO.NET and external data sources.

> **Note** ADO.NET includes an "Entity Client" provider that enables provider-like functionality to the new ADO.NET Entity Framework system. It does not communicate with databases directly, but piggybacks on other ADO.NET providers to enable access to external data. Chapter 15, "Querying Data in the Framework," discusses this provider.

Connecting to SQL Server via a Data Provider

Connecting to a SQL Server database with ADO.NET requires three components: an active SQL Server database, an instance of *SqlClient.SqlConnection*, and a valid connection string.

Creating and Opening Connections

To create a new database connection, pass a valid SQL Server connection string to the *SqlConnection* constructor. After the instance exists, your code must specifically open and close and dispose of the connection.

C#
```
SqlConnectionStringBuilder builder = new SqlConnectionStringBuilder();
// ----- Fill in the builder properties as needed, then...
SqlConnection linkToDB = new SqlConnection(builder.ConnectionString);
linkToDB.Open();
// ------ Do various database activities, then...
linkToDB.Close();
linkToDB.Dispose();
```

Visual Basic
```
Dim builder As New SqlConnectionStringBuilder
' ----- Fill in the builder properties as needed, then...
Dim linkToDB As New SqlConnection(builder.ConnectionString)
linkToDB.Open()
' ------ Do various database activities, then...
linkToDB.Close()
linkToDB.Dispose()
```

Again, you must close and dispose of the connection when you are finished with it. Letting the connection object go out of scope will *not* automatically close the database connection; you must close it manually.

> **Note** Calling the connection's *Dispose* method will automatically call *Close* (if you haven't done so already). Calling *Close* will not automatically call *Dispose*.

To simplify the process, employ a *using/Using* block to automatically dispose of the connection object.

C#
```
using (SqlConnection linkToDB =
    new SqlConnection(builder.ConnectionString))
{
    linkToDB.Open();
    // ----- Additional code here.
}
```

Visual Basic

```
Using linkToDB As New SqlConnection(builder.ConnectionString)
    linkToDB.Open()
    ' ----- Additional code here.
End Using
```

For effective connection pooling (discussed later in this chapter), it is best to open the connection as late as you can, and close it again as soon as you can after that.

Opening a Database Connection: C#

1. Open the "Chapter 8 CSharp" project from the installed samples folder. The project includes a single *Windows.Forms* class: *ConnectionTest*.

2. Open the source code view for the *ConnectionTest* form. Locate the *BuildConnection* function. This routine creates a *SqlConnectionStringBuilder* instance based on the user-specified connection settings.

3. Just after the "Add the server name" comment, add the following code:

```
if (LocalServer.Checked == true)
    connection.DataSource = "(local)";
else
    connection.DataSource = ServerName.Text;
if (IsExpressEdition.Checked == true)
    connection.DataSource += @"\SQLEXPRESS";
```

This code defines the main SQL Server data source. The code differentiates between the Express Edition (and its default name extension) and standard instances.

4. Just after the "Add the authentication" comment, add the following code:

```
if (AuthenticateWindows.Checked == true)
    connection.IntegratedSecurity = true;
else
{
    connection.IntegratedSecurity = false;
    connection.UserID = UserName.Text;
    connection.Password = UserPassword.Text;
}
```

This conditional code supports two types of authentication: integrated security based on the current Windows login and SQL Server user-based security.

5. Locate the *ActTest_Click* event handler. This routine attempts the connection with the configured data source. Just after the "Test the connection" comment, add the following statements:

```
testLink = new SqlConnection(connection.ConnectionString);
testLink.Open();
```

6. Run the program. Use the fields on the form to test your local configuration of SQL Server. For my test setup, I selected the Local Server option, selected the SQL Server Express Installation field, entered **StepSample** in the Initial Catalog field, and left the other fields at their default settings. Then I clicked Test, which ran successfully. If you installed the sample database described in the book's Introduction, your settings will be similar, although you should set the Server Name field to your own server's name for nonlocal databases.

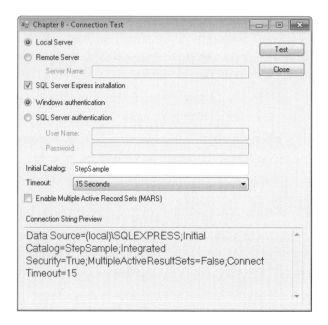

Opening a Database Connection: Visual Basic

1. Open the "Chapter 8 VB" project from the installed samples folder. The project includes a single *Windows.Forms* class: *ConnectionTest*.

2. Open the source code view for the *ConnectionTest* form. Locate the *BuildConnection* function. This routine creates a *SqlConnectionStringBuilder* instance based on the user-specified connection settings.

3. Just after the "Add the server name" comment, add the following code:

```
If (LocalServer.Checked = True) Then
    connection.DataSource = "(local)"
Else
    connection.DataSource = ServerName.Text
End If
If (IsExpressEdition.Checked = True) Then
    connection.DataSource &= "\SQLEXPRESS"
```

This code defines the main SQL Server data source. The code differentiates between the Express Edition (and its default name extension) and standard instances.

4. Just after the "Add the authentication" comment, add the following code:

```
If (AuthenticateWindows.Checked = True) Then
    connection.IntegratedSecurity = True
Else
    connection.IntegratedSecurity = False
    connection.UserID = UserName.Text
    connection.Password = UserPassword.Text
End If
```

This conditional code supports two types of authentication: integrated security based on the current Windows login and SQL Server user-based security.

5. Locate the *ActTest_Click* event handler. This routine attempts the connection with the configured data source. Just after the "Test the connection" comment, add the following statements:

```
testLink = New SqlConnection(connection.ConnectionString)
testLink.Open()
```

6. Run the program. Use the fields on the form to test your local configuration of SQL Server. For my test setup, I selected the Local Server option, selected the SQL Server Express Installation field, entered **StepSample** in the Initial Catalog field, and left the other fields at their default settings. Then I clicked Test, which ran successfully. If you installed the sample database described in the book's Introduction, your settings will be similar, although you should set the Server Name field to your own server's name for nonlocal databases.

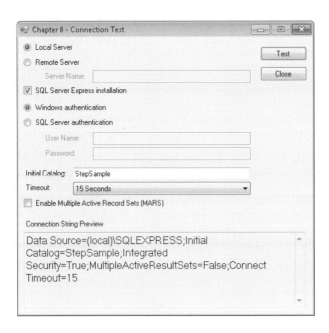

Connection Pooling

Traditional client-server applications typically established a connection to a database when the program started up, maintaining the data link until the user exited the application. The introduction of ADO.NET and a drive toward multitier development challenged that always-on connection preference with their disconnected models. Yet even a fully disconnected, web-based, data-centric application might execute multiple queries and updates against a database during a single server-side page processing event. An important question in designing database applications is this: How long should the connection to the database remain open?

The answer is this: It depends. If you are still writing client-server desktop applications, it's not unheard of to open a connection object and keep it open during the lifetime of the application, although both ADO.NET and the wider programming community discourage this practice. More common, especially in web-centric apps, is to open a connection and keep it open just long enough to process the database operations needed during a single event handler call. Some developers prefer to open a new connection for each distinct database operation. These developers still at times need to keep a connection open through multiple queries. For example, if you execute a query that creates local temporary tables (those SQL Server tables that begin with a single "#" symbol), you must maintain an active connection to use the tables across multiple queries. Also, committable multiupdate database transactions require a consistent connection experience to work properly.

Even if you choose to limit your connection length to the minimum time required to carry out your database operations, the SQL Server provider might maintain the underlying connection for a much longer time. That's because the provider uses *connection pooling*—the reuse of identical connection objects to reduce the time needed to establish new connections. Creating a database connection is somewhat time-consuming because it involves the overhead of network-level handshaking and security credentialing for each new connection request. Connection pooling reduces these repetitive activities by keeping prior connections around in case they are needed again by a new *SqlConnection* object.

The SQL Server provider maintains separate pools based on different connection strings and other factors that make shared connections impossible. A single connection pool can include more than one active connection, each waiting for your code to issue a new *Open* method call on a *SqlConnection* object.

You can turn off pooling for a specific connection by including the **Pooling=false** key-value pair in your connection string. The *SqlConnection* class also includes two methods—*ClearPool* and *ClearAllPools*—that let you clear its associated pool or all pools currently managed by the provider within your application respectively.

Summary

This chapter began the transition from using ADO.NET with purely internal data to engaging in data communications with external content sources. Platform-specific providers play the pseudo-role of device drivers, enabling the generic *DataSet* and its family of objects to communicate seamlessly with disparate data sources. Within each provider, the connection object (known as *SqlConnection* in the SQL Server provider) contains the information that initiates a relationship between your application and the external data.

Connection strings provide a simple text-based medium for defining which database or other content store your application should access. Although the content of these strings can vary widely from platform to platform, ADO.NET assists you on its supported platforms by including connection string builder objects: classes that wrap the crafting of connection strings within the familiar class-based model.

Chapter 8 Quick Reference

To	Do This
Build a SQL Server connection string using a class	Create an instance of *SqlClient.SqlConnectionStringBuilder.* Set its properties as needed. Access the object's *ConnectionString* property.
Establish a connection to a SQL Server database	Build a connection string to the database. Create an instance of *SqlClient.SqlConnection*, passing the connection string to the constructor. Call the *SqlConnection* instance's *Open* method.
Connect to a Microsoft Access database using an OLE DB connection	Build a connection string that includes the *Data Source* key with a value of the Access file path. Create an instance of *OleDb.OleDbConnection*, passing the connection string to the constructor. Call the *OleDbConnection* instance's *Open* method.
Disable connection pooling for a database connection	Add the *Pooling=false* key-value pair to the connection string before opening the connection.

Chapter 9
Querying Databases

After completing this chapter, you will be able to:

- Issue data-modifying queries on external data sources

- Retrieve a table of records from a SQL Server database

- Return the primary key value for a newly inserted database record

Despite its capability to work with data generated completely within an application, ADO.NET's main purpose is to access and manipulate data in external data stores. To enable this query-and-update functionality on the source data platform, ADO.NET includes a "command" object, a wrapper around a platform-specific query that updates, inserts, or deletes target data; or returns single or multiple values from the data source.

This chapter introduces this command wrapper, and demonstrates how to process records returned from a data query. ADO.NET does not impose any limits on the content of the query statements because they are simply passed on to the data platform. However, the results that come back might require special handling depending on the structure of the returned data.

 Note This chapter focuses on the SQL Server provider and its implementation of command-related processing features. The OLE DB and ODBC providers include conceptually identical features, although some of the class names and processing details might differ. For complete information on these providers, refer to the Visual Studio online help.

Processing SQL Queries

SQL is the *lingua franca* of relational database processing. Although most database systems include specialized tools that let you organize data values and the table constructs that contain them, you can manage most essential features by crafting queries in SQL. From table creation to multitable data queries, SQL includes data definition and manipulation commands that give those with sufficient security rights complete control over the database and its content.

In SQL Server databases, the SQL language includes different types of statements, including the following:

- **SQL query statements**   Selection queries that return data results
- **Data manipulation statements**   Statements that modify or change data content
- **Data definition statements**   Commands that modify tables and other structures that support the data content
- **Stored procedures**   Named blocks of processing logic

ADO.NET lets you process any of these statement types through instances of the *System. Data.SqlClient.SqlCommand* class. This class encapsulates one or more SQL statements and includes methods that request processing of the statement(s) on a SQL Server connection, optionally returning query results.

 Note In the OLE DB provider, the equivalent command class is located at *System.Data. OleDb.OleDbCommand*, whereas the ODBC provider version is found at *System.Data.Odbc. OdbcCommand*. These two classes and the *SqlCommand* class in the SQL Server provider all derive from *System.Data.Common.DbCommand*.

Creating Command Objects

Using the *SqlCommand* class is a straightforward procedure:

1. Create an instance of *SqlCommand*.
2. Assign a valid SQL statement to the object's *CommandText* property.
3. Set the object's *Connection* property to an open *SqlConnection* instance.
4. Assign other optional properties as needed.
5. Call one of the object's many synchronous or asynchronous "execute" methods.

The *SqlCommand* object's constructor has various overloaded versions that let you specify the SQL statement text and the ADO.NET connection as arguments.

C#

```csharp
SqlConnection linkToDB = new SqlConnection(connectionString);
linkToDB.Open();
string sqlText = @"UPDATE WorkTable SET ProcessedOn = GETDATE()
    WHERE ProcessedOn IS NULL";
SqlCommand dataAction = new SqlCommand(sqlText, linkToDB);
```

Visual Basic

```vbnet
Dim linkToDB As New SqlConnection(connectionString)
linkToDB.Open()
Dim sqlText As String = "UPDATE WorkTable SET ProcessedOn = GETDATE() " &
    "WHERE ProcessedOn IS NULL"
Dim dataAction As New SqlCommand(sqlText, linkToDB)
```

The *SqlCommand.CommandText* field accepts two types of string data:

- **Standard SQL statements**   This is the default type. Normally, only a single SQL statement appears in this field. However, you can include multiple semicolon-delimited statements within a single command instance. Information on retrieving the results of multiple *SELECT* statements from a single command appears later in this chapter.

- **Stored procedures** The command text field contains the stored procedure name. Set the *SqlCommand.CommandType* property to *CommandType.StoredProcedure*. You add any "in" or "out" arguments to the command through distinct parameters. See Chapter 10, "Adding Parameters to Queries," for details on using parameters. If you want to include the arguments within the command text itself (as is commonly done through SQL Server's Management Studio tool), treat the text as a standard SQL statement, setting the *CommandType* property to *CommandType.Text*.

> **Note** The *SqlCommand.CommandType* property also accepts a value of *CommandType.TableDirect*, which indicates that the *CommandText* field contains nothing more than a table name to be used for row retrieval and management. The SQL Server provider does not support this command variation.

Processing Queries

The command object works for queries that return data values from the data source, and also for statements that take some action on the database but that return no stored data. These "nonquery" actions are typical when adding, updating, or removing records from the database; or when processing Data Definition Language commands, such as SQL Server's *CREATE TABLE* statement.

To run a nonquery, create a new *SqlCommand* object and set its command text to the server-side SQL statement. Then call the object's *ExecuteNonQuery* method.

C#

```csharp
string sqlText = "DELETE FROM WorkTable WHERE Obsolete - 1";
SqlCommand dataAction = new SqlCommand(sqlText, linkToDB);
try
{
    dataAction.ExecuteNonQuery();
}
catch (Exception ex)
{
    MessageBox.Show("Failure: " + ex.Message);
}
```

Visual Basic

```vb
Dim sqlText As String = "DELETE FROM WorkTable WHERE Obsolete = 1"
Dim dataAction As New SqlCommand(sqlText, linkToDB)
Try
    dataAction.ExecuteNonQuery()
Catch ex As Exception
    MessageBox.Show("Failure: " & ex.Message)
End Try
```

ExecuteNonQuery sends the command text to the data source through the previously opened connection. Any processing errors, including those generated by the data source, throw an exception.

Calls to stored procedures work the same way.

C#

```csharp
string sqlText = "dbo.CancelOrder " + orderID;
SqlCommand dataAction = new SqlCommand(sqlText, linkToDB);
dataAction.ExecuteNonQuery();
```

Visual Basic

```vb
Dim sqlText As String = "dbo.CancelOrder " & orderID
Dim dataAction As New SqlCommand(sqlText, linkToDB)
dataAction.ExecuteNonQuery()
```

Note Building SQL statements through string concatenation, especially with user-supplied components, can be risky. Chapter 10, "Adding Standards to Queries," introduces command parameters, which can reduce or eliminate these risks. Parameters also let your code retrieve data from stored procedure "out" parameters.

Processing Asynchronously

The *ExecuteNonQuery* method is synchronous; your application will block until the database operation completes successfully or aborts with an error or connection timeout. If your application is single threaded, it will cease to function (or at least appear that way) until the method returns.

The command object also supports asynchronous processing of nonqueries. It includes a pair of methods—*BeginExecuteNonQuery* and *EndExecuteNonQuery*—that bracket the operation. The *BeginExecuteNonQuery* method returns an object with the interface *System.IAsyncResult* that sets its *IsCompleted* property to *True* when processing ends. At that point, your code must call the *EndExecuteNonQuery* method to complete the process.

```csharp
C#
SqlCommand dataAction = new SqlCommand(sqlText, linkToDB);
IAsyncResult pending = dataAction.BeginExecuteNonQuery();
while (pending.IsCompleted == false)
{
    // ----- Do work as needed, or...
    Threading.Thread.Sleep(100);
}
dataAction.EndExecuteNonQuery(pending);
```

```vbnet
Visual Basic
Dim dataAction As New SqlCommand(sqlText, linkToDB);
Dim pending As IAsyncResult = dataAction.BeginExecuteNonQuery()
Do While (pending.IsCompleted = False)
    ' ----- Do work as needed, or...
    Threading.Thread.Sleep(100)
Loop
dataAction.EndExecuteNonQuery(pending)
```

A variation of the *BeginExecuteNonQuery* method lets you specify a callback method and an optional object that will be passed to the callback method when the operation completes. You must still call *EndExecuteNonQuery*, although you can call it from within the callback code. *Passing the SqlCommand* object as the optional argument simplifies this process.

C#

```csharp
SqlCommand dataAction = new SqlCommand(sqlText, linkToDB);
AsyncCallback callback = new AsyncCallback(WhenFinished);
dataAction.BeginExecuteNonQuery(callback, dataAction);

// ----- Elsewhere...
private void WhenFinished(IAsyncResult e)
{
    // ----- The IAsyncResult.AsyncState property contains the
    //       optional object sent in by BeginExecuteNonQuery.
    SqlCommand dataAction = (SqlCommand)e.AsyncState;

    // ----- Finish processing.
    dataAction.EndExecuteNonQuery(e);
}
```

Visual Basic

```vb
Dim dataAction As New SqlCommand(sqlText, linkToDB)
Dim callback As New AsyncCallback(AddressOf WhenFinished)
dataAction.BeginExecuteNonQuery(callback, dataAction)

' ----- Elsewhere...
Private Sub WhenFinished(ByVal e As IAsyncResult)
    ' ----- The IAsyncResult.AsyncState property contains the
    '       optional object sent in by BeginExecuteNonQuery.
    Dim dataAction As SqlCommand = CType(e.AsyncState, SqlCommand)

    ' ----- Finish processing.
    dataAction.EndExecuteNonQuery(e)
End Sub
```

The connection used by the command must remain open during processing. If you want to halt execution of the command before it completes, call the *SqlCommand* object's *Cancel* method. Be aware that—depending on the state of processing—the *Cancel* method might or might not cancel the execution in time.

Returning Query Results

Sending commands to a database is useful; getting data back is also essential for data-centric applications. The command object includes several methods that return both single values and multiple rows of tabular data.

Returning a Single Value

The *SqlCommand* object's *ExecuteScalar* method sends a SQL command or stored procedure request to the database, just like the *ExecuteNonQuery* method, but it also returns a single value produced by the query. This method is useful with *SELECT* queries that return a simple result.

```csharp
C#
string sqlText = "SELECT COUNT(*) FROM WorkTable";
SqlCommand dataAction = new SqlCommand(sqlText, linkToDB);
int totalItems = (int)dataAction.ExecuteScalar();
```

```vb
Visual Basic
Dim sqlText As String = "SELECT COUNT(*) FROM WorkTable"
Dim dataAction As New SqlCommand(sqlText, linkToDB)
Dim totalItems As Integer = CInt(dataAction.ExecuteScalar())
```

Because *ExecuteScalar* returns data of type *System.Object*, you must coerce it into the expected data type. The method can return *System.DBNull* for nondata results.

SQL Server 2005 introduced a new *OUTPUT* keyword on *INSERT* statements that returns a specified field (typically the primary key) from the newly inserted data row. Before this change, programmers often had to issue two statements to obtain this new key value: the first to insert the record and the second to retrieve the primary key through a new *SELECT* statement. By combining the *OUTPUT* keyword with the *ExecuteScalar* method, it's easy to obtain the primary key in a single command.

```csharp
C#
// ----- Pretend the ...'s represent actual fields, and that
//       WorkTable.ID is the name of the primary key.
string sqlText = @"INSERT INTO WorkTable (...)
    OUTPUT INSERTED.ID VALUES (...)";
SqlCommand dataAction = new SqlCommand(sqlText, linkToDB);
int newID = (int)dataAction.ExecuteScalar();
```

```vb
Visual Basic
' ----- Pretend the ...'s represent actual fields, and that
'       WorkTable.ID is the name of the primary key.
Dim sqlText As String = "INSERT INTO WorkTable (...) " &
    "OUTPUT INSERTED.ID VALUES (...)"
Dim dataAction As New SqlCommand(sqlText, linkToDB)
Dim newID As Integer = CInt(dataAction.ExecuteScalar())
```

Stored procedures that return a single value are identical in concept.

Returning Data Rows

To process one or more rows returned from a SELECT query or row-producing stored procedure, use the *SqlCommand* object's *ExecuteReader* method. This method returns an object of type *System.Data.SqlClient.SqlDataReader*, which lets you scan through the returned rows once, examining the columnar data values in each row. The data reader is fast and lightweight, providing no-nonsense access to each row's values.

 Note *ExecuteReader* accesses the database in a synchronous manner. *SqlCommand* also includes a *BeginExecuteReader* and *EndExecuteReader* method pair that enables asynchronous access to the data. The discussion of asynchronous processing earlier in this chapter also applies to these methods.

To create the reader, add the relevant command text and connection to a *SqlCommand*, and call its *ExecuteReader* method to return the new *SqlDataReader* instance.

```csharp
C#
string sqlText = "SELECT ID, FullName, ZipCode FROM Customer";
SqlCommand dataAction = new SqlCommand(sqlText, linkToDB);
SqlDataReader scanCustomer = dataAction.ExecuteReader();
```

```vbnet
Visual Basic
Dim sqlText As String = "SELECT ID, FullName, ZipCode FROM Customer"
Dim dataAction As New SqlCommand(sqlText, linkToDB)
Dim scanCustomer As SqlDataReader = dataAction.ExecuteReader()
```

SqlDataReader exposes exactly one data row at a time as a collection of column values. The reader returned by *ExecuteReader* doesn't yet point to a data row. You must call the reader's *Read* method to access the first row, calling it again for subsequent rows. *Read* returns *False* when there are no more rows available. The *HasRows* property indicates whether any rows were returned from the query.

```csharp
C#
SqlDataReader scanCustomer = dataAction.ExecuteReader();
if (scanCustomer.HasRows)
    while (scanCustomer.Read())
    {
        // ----- Perform row processing here.
    }
scanCustomer.Close();
```

Visual Basic

```vb
Dim scanCustomer As SqlDataReader = dataAction.ExecuteReader()
If (scanCustomer.HasRows = True) Then
    Do While scanCustomer.Read()
        ' ----- Perform row processing here.
    Loop
End If
scanCustomer.Close()
```

Always call the reader's *Close* or *Dispose* method when finished. By default, SQL Server will permit only a single reader to be open at once. To open another reader, you must close the previous one. This also applies to other types of queries. Statements issued through the *SqlCommand.ExecuteNonQuery* method will also fail if a *SqlDataReader* is open and in use.

> **Note** If you include the *MultipleActiveRecordSets=True* key-value pair in the SQL Server connection string used to access the database, you will be able to open multiple readers at once and process other commands while a reader is open. However, be careful when using this feature because you won't get a warning if you inadvertently leave a reader open.

When you close the data reader, the associated connection remains open for your further use, until you specifically close the connection. Passing *CommandBehavior.CloseConnection* as an argument to *ExecuteReader* tells the reader to close the connection when the reader closes.

C#

```csharp
SqlDataReader scanCustomer =
    dataAction.ExecuteReader(CommandBehavior.CloseConnection);
// ----- Scan through the reader, then...
scanCustomer.Close();
// ----- The connection closes as well.
```

Visual Basic

```vb
Dim scanCustomer As SqlDataReader =
    dataAction.ExecuteReader(CommandBehavior.CloseConnection)
' ----- Scan through the reader, then...
scanCustomer.Close()
' ----- The connection closes as well.
```

SqlDataReader is a unidirectional, read-once construct. After you scan through all the available rows using the *Read* method, that's it. You cannot return to the beginning of the set and scan through again; to do that, you'd need to generate a new data reader from a new command object. The reader's forward-only, read-once limitation helps keep it speedy and memory-friendly.

Accessing Field Values

Accessing each field in a *SqlDataReader* is similar to the process used with a *DataRow* instance. Both objects include a default *Item* collection that exposes column values by zero-based position or by name. (If two fields share a common name that differs only by case, the name lookup is case-sensitive.)

```
C#
result = scanCustomer[0];      // By position
result = scanCustomer["ID"];   // By name
```

```
Visual Basic
result = scanCustomer(0)    ' By position
result = scanCustomer!ID    ' By name
```

The official documentation for the *SqlDataReader* class says that this method returns data in its "native format." In essence, it returns a *System.Object* instance. You need to cast the data to the appropriate data type. NULL data fields contain *DBNull.Value*. The reader's *IsDBNull* method indicates whether a column at a specific ordinal position contains *DBNull*.

For strongly typed access to fields, the data reader exposes a seemingly endless number of data-returning methods with names that indicate the format of the resulting value. For example, the *SqlDataReader.GetDecimal* method returns a *System.Decimal* value from one of the row's fields. These methods accept only an ordinal position; if you want to use them with a field name, you must convert the name to its position using the *GetOrdinal* method.

```
C#
rowID = scanCustomer.GetInt64(scanCustomer.GetOrdinal("ID"));
```

```
Visual Basic
rowID = scanCustomer.GetInt64(scanCustomer.GetOrdinal("ID"))
```

Naturally, you must use the appropriate function for a specific column. For example, using the *GetInt32* method on a non-numeric text column will fail. Table 9-1 lists these typed methods and the data types they return.

TABLE 9-1 Typed Data Access Methods on *SqlDataReader* Class

Method Name	Returned Data Type
GetBoolean	*System.Boolean*
GetByte	*System.Byte*
GetBytes	Array of *System.Byte*. This method reads a specified portion of a field into a preallocated *Byte* array. Arguments to the method indicate the starting positions in both the source and target buffers, and the length of the data to copy. This method is useful for retrieving binary large objects (BLOBs) from a database.
GetChar	*System.Char*
GetChars	Array of *System.Char*. This method is similar to the *GetBytes* method, but it copies data as *Char* instead of *Byte*.
GetDateTime	*System.DateTime*
GetDateTimeOffset	*System.DateTimeOffset*
GetDouble	*System.Double*
GetFloat	*System.Single*
GetGuid	*System.Guid*
GetInt16	*System.Int16*
GetInt32	*System.Int32*
GetInt64	*System.Int64*
GetString	*System.String*
GetTimeSpan	*System.TimeSpan*

In addition to these standard data types, *SqlDataReader* also includes methods that return data fields in a format more in line with their true SQL Server counterparts. All these methods return data for types found in the *System.Data.SqlTypes* namespace. For example, *SqlDataReader.GetSqlMoney* returns a value of type *System.Data.SqlTypes.SqlMoney*. These types are similar to the standard .NET types, but support NULL values as well. The methods include *GetSqlBinary, GetSqlBoolean, GetSqlByte, GetSqlBytes, GetSqlChars, GetSqlDateTime, GetSqlDecimal, GetSqlDouble, GetSqlGuid, GetSqlInt16, GetSqlInt32, GetSqlInt64, GetSqlMoney, GetSqlSingle, GetSqlString*, and *GetSqlXml*.

A few additional methods including *GetName, GetDataTypeName, GetFieldType, GetValue* (and others), and the *FieldCount* property provide more generic access to the fields in a reader row. These features are handy for retrieving data from a query for which the code does not expect any specific set of fields. A test program that displays the tabular results of any user-supplied query might use these methods.

Along those same generic lines, the *SqlDataReader* object's *GetSchemaTable* method returns a *DataTable* instance that describes the structure of the queried data. The new table's content includes columns such as *ColumnName*, *IsKey*, and *DataTypeName*, plus about two dozen more that you can use to understand the makeup of the incoming data. See the Visual Studio online help entry for "SqlDataReader.GetSchemaTable Method" for more information about this method.

Processing More Complicated Results

SQL Server supports returning multiple record sets in a single query. You can generate them by sending a batch of two or more semicolon-delimited *SELECT* statements within a single *SqlCommand* object's command text, or by executing a stored procedure that generates multiple selections.

When retrieving multiple record sets, the returned *SqlDataReader* initially refers to the first set of records. To access the second set, call the reader's *NextResult* method. The method returns *False* after it passes the final results set. Just as with the reader's view of individual data rows, *SqlDataReader* cannot return to an earlier results set.

> **Note** The OLE DB and ODBC providers also support nested results, where a single row might contain subordinate data rows. The SQL Server provider does not support nested sets.

If you prefer to process the data returned from the query as XML, use the *SqlCommand* object's *ExecuteXmlReader* method (or the asynchronous *BeginExecuteXmlReader* and *EndExecuteXmlReader* methods), which returns a *System.Xml.XmlReader* instance. Your query must include the appropriate XML-specific keywords (such as *FOR XML*), or it must return valid XML content, such as from a table field.

Processing Database Queries: C#

1. Open the "Chapter 9 CSharp" project from the installed samples folder. The project includes a *Windows.Forms* class named *StateBuilder* and a sealed class named *General*.

2. Open the code for the *General* class. This class centralizes much of the database functionality for the sample application. Locate the *GetConnectionString* function, a routine that uses a *SqlConnectionStringBuilder* to create a valid connection string to the sample database. It currently includes the following statements:

```
builder.DataSource = @"(local)\SQLExpress";
builder.InitialCatalog = "StepSample";
builder.IntegratedSecurity = true;
```

Adjust these statements as needed to provide access to your own test database.

3. Locate the *ExecuteSQL* method. This routine processes a SQL statement (*sqlText*) on a connected database (*linkToDB*), expecting no returned results. Within the *try* block, add the following code:

```
SqlCommand commandWrapper = new SqlCommand(sqlText, linkToDB);
commandWrapper.ExecuteNonQuery();
```

4. Locate the *ExecuteSQLReturn* method. This routine processes a SQL statement (*sqlText*) on a connected database (*linkToDB*), collecting a single return value from the database and returning it to the calling code. Within the *try* block, add the following statements:

```
SqlCommand commandWrapper = new SqlCommand(sqlText, linkToDB);
return commandWrapper.ExecuteScalar();
```

5. Locate the *OpenReader* method. This function processes a SQL statement (*sqlText*) on a connected database (*linkToDB*), creating a *SqlDataReader* object to process the returned data rows. Within the *try* block, add the following lines:

```
SqlCommand commandWrapper = new SqlCommand(sqlText, linkToDB);
return commandWrapper.ExecuteReader();
```

6. Open the source code view for the *StateBuilder* form. Locate the *RefreshEverything* routine. Just after the "See if a custom state already exists" comment, add the following code:

```
sqlText = "SELECT * FROM StateRegion WHERE RegionType = 99";
stateReader = General.OpenReader(sqlText, linkToDB);
if ((stateReader != null) && (stateReader.HasRows == true))
{
    // ----- Existing custom state record.
    stateReader.Read();
    ActiveStateID = (long)(int)stateReader["ID"];

    AddName.Text = (string)stateReader["FullName"];
    AddAbbreviation.Text = (string)stateReader["Abbreviation"];
}
else
{
    // ----- No custom state record.
    AddName.Clear();
    AddAbbreviation.Clear();
}
if (stateReader != null) stateReader.Close();
```

This code uses the *General.OpenReader* function from step 5 to obtain a *SqlDataReader* instance built from a SQL statement (*sqlText*) and a connection (*linkToDB*). If the reader contains at least one row, the code accesses specific fields in that first row to populate various internal and onscreen values.

7. Run the program, a simple database application that lets you create, modify, and re-move a single "state" record. On the Add A State tab, enter **New C Sharp** in the New State Name field and add **CS** in the New Abbreviation field. The SQL statement that will add the new record to the *StateRegion* table appears just below the edit fields. Click Add to create the record.

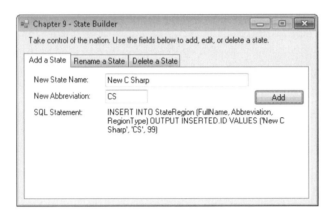

8. Use the Rename A State tab to make changes to the test record. When you are finished with the record, use the Delete A State tab to remove the test record.

Processing Database Queries: Visual Basic

1. Open the "Chapter 9 VB" project from the installed samples folder. The project includes a *Windows.Forms* class named *StateBuilder* and a module named *General*.

2. Open the code for the *General* module. This file centralizes much of the database func-tionality for the sample application. Locate the *GetConnectionString* function, a routine that uses a *SqlConnectionStringBuilder* to create a valid connection string to the sample database. It currently includes the following statements:

```
builder.DataSource = "(local)\SQLExpress"
builder.InitialCatalog = "StepSample"
builder.IntegratedSecurity = True
```

Adjust these statements as needed to provide access to your own test database.

3. Locate the *ExecuteSQL* method. This routine processes a SQL statement (*sqlText*) on a connected database (*linkToDB*), expecting no returned results. Within the *Try* block, add the following code:

```
Dim commandWrapper As New SqlCommand(sqlText, linkToDB)
commandWrapper.ExecuteNonQuery()
```

4. Locate the *ExecuteSQLReturn* method. This routine processes a SQL statement (*sqlText*) on a connected database (*linkToDB*), collecting a single return value from the database and returning it to the calling code. Within the *Try* block, add the following statements:

```
Dim commandWrapper As New SqlCommand(sqlText, linkToDB)
Return commandWrapper.ExecuteScalar()
```

5. Locate the *OpenReader* method. This function processes a SQL statement (*sqlText*) on a connected database (*linkToDB*), creating a *SqlDataReader* object to process the returned data rows. Within the *Try* block, add the following lines:

```
Dim commandWrapper As New SqlCommand(sqlText, linkToDB)
Return commandWrapper.ExecuteReader()
```

6. Open the source code view for the *StateBuilder* form. Locate the *RefreshEverything* routine. Just after the "See if a custom state already exists" comment, add the following code:

```
sqlText = "SELECT * FROM StateRegion WHERE RegionType = 99"
stateReader = OpenReader(sqlText, linkToDB)
If (stateReader IsNot Nothing) AndAlso (stateReader.HasRows = True) Then
    ' ----- Existing custom state record.
    stateReader.Read()
    ActiveStateID = CLng(stateReader!ID)


    AddName.Text = CStr(stateReader!FullName)
    AddAbbreviation.Text = CStr(stateReader!Abbreviation)
Else
    ' ----- No custom state record.
    AddName.Clear()
    AddAbbreviation.Clear()
End If
If (stateReader IsNot Nothing) Then stateReader.Close()
```

This code uses the *OpenReader* function from step 5 to obtain a *SqlDataReader* instance built from a SQL statement (*sqlText*) and a connection (*linkToDB*). If the reader contains at least one row, the code accesses specific fields in that first row to populate various internal and onscreen values.

7. Run the program, a simple database application that lets you create, modify, and remove a single "state" record. On the Add A State tab, enter **North Visual Basic** in the New State Name field and add **VB** in the New Abbreviation field. The SQL statement that will add the new record to the *StateRegion* table appears just below the edit fields. Click Add to create the record.

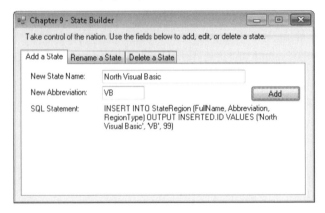

8. Use the Rename A State tab to make changes to the test record. When you are finished with the record, use the Delete A State tab to remove the test record.

Summary

This chapter introduced methods for issuing commands to an ADO.NET connected database, and using those commands to retrieve individual or tabular results. The core of this functionality is the *SqlClient.SqlCommand* class, a wrapper for SQL Server queries. It includes a variety of methods that process the contained query, optionally returning either a single value or a set of data rows.

The *SqlDataReader* class provides the row-scanning functionality for results retrieved as a data reader. Use the reader's various *Get...* methods or the default *Item* property to retrieve field values on each scanned row. When finished with a *SqlDataReader*, always call its *Close* or *Dispose* method.

Chapter 9 Quick Reference

To	Do This
Run a SQL query over an ADO.NET connection	Create a *SqlCommand* instance.
	Set its *CommandText* property to the SQL statement.
	Set its *Connection* property to a valid *SqlConnection* instance.
	Call the command object's *ExecuteNonQuery* method.
Call a SQL Server stored procedure that returns a single static result	Create a *SqlCommand* instance.
	Set its *CommandText* property to the stored procedure name, followed by space-delimited arguments if needed.
	Set its *Connection* property to a valid *SqlConnection* instance.
	Call the command object's *ExecuteScalar* method, capturing the return value.
Retrieve two sets of data rows from a SQL Server batch query	Create a *SqlCommand* instance.
	Set its *CommandText* property to the semicolon-delimited SQL statements.
	Set its *Connection* property to a valid *SqlConnection* instance.
	Call the command object's *ExecuteReader* method, assigning the return value to a *SqlDataReader* variable.
	Use the reader's *Read* method to access rows in the batch's first set of rows.
	Call the reader's *NextResult* method to access additional results sets.

Chapter 10
Adding Standards to Queries

After completing this chapter, you will be able to:

- Understand why parameters are important in queries

- Add parameters to standard selection and data update queries

- Call stored procedures that include both in and out parameters

In ADO.NET, queries pass to external data sources as strings. These strings include not only essential command keywords and syntactical elements but also the data values used to limit and fulfill each query. Building command strings is an art long practiced by developers in many programming languages, but it's quite different from .NET's promise of strongly typed data management. Why store values as distinct data types at all if you are eventually going to convert everything to ASCII text?

To push aside these and other deficiencies that stem from inserting all types of data values into SQL statements, ADO.NET includes the *parameter*, an object that bridges the gap between the text-based needs of the external data source's command processing system and the intelligent data type system that epitomizes .NET development. This chapter demonstrates query parameters and their uses in SQL Server database queries.

 Note This chapter focuses on parameters as implemented in the SQL Server provider. Although the OLE DB and ODBC providers also implement parameters, there are some minor differences that will be pointed out within the chapter.

The exercises in this chapter all use the same sample project, a tool that uses parameters to retrieve and update database values. Although you can run the application after each exercise, the expected results for the full application might not appear until you complete all exercises in the chapter.

Developing Parameterized Queries

In the SQL Server provider, parameters appear as the *System.Data.SqlClient.SqlParameter* class. By creating relevant parameters and attaching them to *SqlCommand* instances, ordinary text queries become parameterized queries.

> **Note** In the OLE DB provider, the parameter class appears as *System.Data.OleDb.OleDbParameter*. The ODBC equivalent is *System.Data.Odbc.OdbcParameter*. Both of these classes and the *SqlParameter* class in the SQL Server provider derive from *System.Data.Common.DbParameter*.

Understanding the Need for Parameters

As mentioned in the "Connection String Builders" section on page 124 of Chapter 8, "Establishing External Connections," there are certain risks involved in building SQL statements and related string elements. A key risk is the SQL injection attack, in which a user can inadvertently or deliberately alter the intent of a SQL statement by supplying corrupted content. Consider the following statement, which modifies the *Employee.Salary* value for a specific employee record:

```
UPDATE Employee SET Salary = XXX WHERE ID = 5;
```

It works well if the user provides **50000** or a similar number as the value of *XXX*. But what if resourceful employee John Doe replaces *XXX* with the following SQL fragments?

```
150000 WHERE FirstName = 'John' AND LastName = 'Doe';
    UPDATE Employee SET Salary = 50000
```

The user-supplied content includes a semicolon, effectively turning one statement into a batch of two statements. Most programmers design their code to avoid such scenarios, but this type of situation still manages to show up from time to time. Parameters help reduce such issues by using typed substitution placeholders instead of unchecked plain-text gaps in SQL strings. Parameters understand how to properly format their replacement values so that SQL injection attacks and other mishaps don't occur.

Parameters solve these problems by making changes to both the SQL statement and the data destined for that statement. Instead of piecing together workable SQL statements from a combination of programmer and user-supplied parts, parameterized query statements exist in a standardized form, free of unknown and unsafe user data. Portions of the statement that require user input exist as named placeholders, *@name* elements that get replaced with the final type-specific data values after they have been transmitted to the database.

This process provides for a more generic command text, and a logical separation between the command and its data.

Removing ever-changing data values from SQL statements also increases performance within SQL Server. Like many advanced relational database systems, SQL Server compiles each statement into an internal format, one that doesn't require it to constantly parse a text string to determine its actions. If SQL Server encounters the same SQL statement twice, it doesn't need to go through the time-consuming compilation process again. For example, the following three SQL statements are different in the compiler's view:

```
UPDATE Employee SET Salary = 50000 WHERE ID = 5;
UPDATE Employee SET Salary = 56000 WHERE ID = 12;
UPDATE Employee SET Salary = 52000 WHERE ID = 8;
```

Parameterized queries replace these three instance-specific versions with a generic version of the statement, free of the varying data portions. Removing dynamic data values from what would otherwise be standard SQL command structures allows applications to send a much more limited number of queries to SQL Server, queries that show up again and again, and that don't need to be recompiled every time.

Implementing Standard Queries

The *UPDATE* statement shown previously modifies the salary for an employee record based on that record's primary key.

```
UPDATE Employee SET Salary = 50000 WHERE ID = 25;
```

To prepare the statement for parameters, all elements destined for substitution by the parameter values get replaced with "@" identifiers.

```
UPDATE Employee SET Salary = @NewSalary WHERE ID = @EmployeeID;
```

In standard SQL statements (all statements other than stored procedures), the names you provide are up to you, so being descriptive is best. Each placeholder must begin with the @ sign followed by a unique name. Parameter names are not case-sensitive.

As with nonparameterized queries, this enhanced statement gets wrapped up in a *SqlCommand* object:

```
C#
string sqlText = @"UPDATE Employee SET Salary = @NewSalary
    WHERE ID = @EmployeeID";
SqlCommand salaryUpdate = new SqlCommand(sqlText, linkToDB);
```

```
Visual Basic
Dim sqlText As String =
    "UPDATE Employee SET Salary = @NewSalary WHERE ID = @EmployeeID"
Dim salaryUpdate = New SqlCommand(sqlText, linkToDB)
```

The *SqlCommand* class includes a *Parameters* collection to which you add the specific replacement values for each placeholder. You wrap up each parameter in an instance of *SqlParameter*, setting its properties as needed, and adding it to the *SqlCommand.Parameters* collection. When you execute the command, ADO.NET passes both the placeholder-laden SQL text and the parameter collection to the database for evaluation.

Each parameter includes the elements you would expect: the parameter name (which must match a placeholder name in the SQL statement), the data type along with any data type-specific settings (such as the length of string parameters), the actual data content to be included in the processed command, and a few other generic settings. To add a parameter to a command, create a *SqlParameter* instance and add it to the *SqlCommand* object.

```
C#
SqlParameter paramValue = new SqlParameter("@NewSalary", SqlDbType.Money);
paramValue.Value = 50000m;
salaryUpdate.Parameters.Add(paramValue);


paramValue = new SqlParameter("@EmployeeID", SqlDbType.BigInt);
paramValue.Value = 25L;
salaryUpdate.Parameters.Add(paramValue);
```

```
Visual Basic
Dim paramValue As New SqlParameter("@NewSalary", SqlDbType.Money)
paramValue.Value = 50000@
salaryUpdate.Parameters.Add(paramValue)


paramValue = New SqlParameter("@EmployeeID", SqlDbType.BigInt)
paramValue.Value = 25&
salaryUpdate.Parameters.Add(paramValue)
```

SqlParameter includes lots of constructor options for setting the data type of the passed data, plus other settings. Or you can go the traditional route and update the object's individual properties directly, including the following:

- **ParameterName**   The name of the parameter; that is, the placeholder. Don't forget to include the @ sign at the start of the name.

- **DbType** or **SqlDbType**   One of the *System.Data.SqlDbType* enumeration values, which all parallel the available data types in SQL Server. For example, *SqlDbType.VarChar* maps to SQL Server's *varchar* column type. Both *DbType* and *SqlDbType* refer to the same property; update either one as needed.

- **IsNullable**   Indicates whether the parameter accepts NULL values.

- **Precision** and **Scale**   Some of SQL Server's numeric data types require specific precision and scale values. Use these properties to configure the data from ADO.NET's point of view.

- **Size**   Similar to *Precision* and *Scale*, *Size* is commonly used for text and binary data types. It affects only the amount of data sent to SQL Server with a query. If your query sends data back through a parameter (described below), it ignores this *Size* setting.

- **Value** and **SqlValue**   The actual value that will replace the placeholder in the SQL statement. Use *Value* to work with data defined using the standard .NET data types. Use the *SqlValue* property instead to work with data in a format that more closely resembles SQL Server's data types, and as expressed through the classes in the *System.Data.SqlTypes* namespace.

If your data needs are simple, you can let the *SqlCommand.Parameters* collection define the data type of your parameters for you. The collection's *AddWithValue* method accepts the parameter name and the intended value and adds a new *SqlParameter* instance to the command using the specified settings.

C#
```csharp
salaryUpdate.Parameters.AddWithValue("@NewSalary", 50000m);
salaryUpdate.Parameters.AddWithValue("@EmployeeID", 25L);
```

Visual Basic
```vb
salaryUpdate.Parameters.AddWithValue("@NewSalary", 50000@)
salaryUpdate.Parameters.AddWithValue("@EmployeeID", 25&)
```

Once the parameters are all in place, calling one of the command's *Execute* methods processes the command on the database, and returns any results as with nonparameterized queries.

C#

```
salaryUpdate.ExecuteNonQuery();
```

Visual Basic

```
salaryUpdate.ExecuteNonQuery()
```

Updating Data with Parameters: C#

1. Open the "Chapter 10 CSharp" project from the installed samples folder. The project includes multiple *Windows.Forms* classes and a sealed class named *General*.

2. Open the code for the *General* class. This class centralizes much of the database functionality for the sample application. Locate the *GetConnectionString* function, a routine that uses a *SqlConnectionStringBuilder* to create a valid connection string to the sample database. It currently includes the following statements:

```
builder.DataSource = @"(local)\SQLExpress";
builder.InitialCatalog = "StepSample";
builder.IntegratedSecurity = true;
```

   Adjust these statements as needed to provide access to your own test database.

3. Open the code for the *RenameCustomer* form. This form lets the user modify the *FullName* value for a single record in the *Customer* database table. Locate the *ActOK_Click* event handler. This routine does the actual update of the record. Just after the "Save the new name" comment, add the following code:

```
sqlText = "UPDATE Customer SET FullName = @NewName WHERE ID = @CustID";
commandWrapper = new SqlCommand(sqlText);
commandWrapper.Parameters.AddWithValue("@NewName", NewName.Text.Trim());
commandWrapper.Parameters.AddWithValue("@CustID", ActiveCustomerID);
try
{
    General.ExecuteSQL(commandWrapper);
}
catch (Exception ex)
{
    MessageBox.Show("Error occurred updating customer name: " +
        ex.Message);
    return;
}
```

   These statements create a *SqlCommand* object with a SQL statement that includes two placeholders: *@NewName* and *@CustID*. The code then adds two matching parameters to the command and sends it to the database for processing.

4. Run the program. On the *Customer Management* form, select a customer from the list of customers and then click Rename Customer. When the *Rename Customer* form appears, enter a new value in the New Name field and then click OK. This process updates the database using the newly added code.

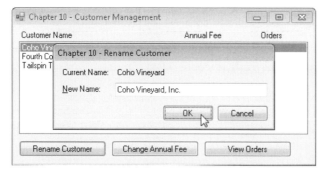

Updating Data with Parameters: Visual Basic

1. Open the "Chapter 10 VB" project from the installed samples folder. The project includes multiple *Windows.Forms* classes and a module named *General*.

2. Open the code for the *General* module. This file centralizes much of the database functionality for the sample application. Locate the *GetConnectionString* function, a routine that uses a *SqlConnectionStringBuilder* to create a valid connection string to the sample database. It currently includes the following statements:

```
builder.DataSource = "(local)\SQLExpress"
builder.InitialCatalog = "StepSample"
builder.IntegratedSecurity = True
```

Adjust these statements as needed to provide access to your own test database.

3. Open the code for the *RenameCustomer* form. This form lets the user modify the *FullName* value for a single record in the *Customer* database table. Locate the *ActOK_ Click* event handler. This routine does the actual update of the record. Just after the "Save the new name" comment, add the following code:

```
sqlText = "UPDATE Customer SET FullName = @NewName WHERE ID = @CustID"
commandWrapper = New SqlCommand(sqlText)
commandWrapper.Parameters.AddWithValue("@NewName", NewName.Text.Trim)
commandWrapper.Parameters.AddWithValue("@CustID", ActiveCustomerID)
Try
    ExecuteSQL(commandWrapper)
Catch ex As Exception
    MessageBox.Show("Error occurred updating customer name: " &
        ex.Message)
    Return
End Try
```

These statements create a *SqlCommand* object with a SQL statement that includes two placeholders: *@NewName* and *@CustID*. The code then adds two matching parameters to the command and sends it to the database for processing.

4. Run the program. On the *Customer Management* form, select a customer from the list of customers and then click Rename Customer. When the *Rename Customer* form appears, enter a new value in the New Name field and then click OK. This process updates the database using the newly added code.

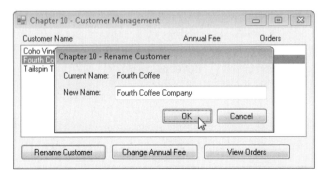

Using Parameters with Other Providers

The OLE DB and ODBC providers also include support for parameterized queries. However, the definitions of both the command text and the associated parameters vary somewhat from the SQL Server implementation. Instead of including placeholder names prefixed with @ signs, each replaceable element appears as a nameless question mark (?) in the command text. Parameters added to the associated *OleDbCommand* or *OdbcCommand* instance must be added in the order indicated by the placeholders. Although the command text does not include parameter names, each added *OleDbParameter* or *OdbcParameter* instance should still include @-prefixed names.

C#
```csharp
string sqlText = @"UPDATE Employee SET Salary = ? WHERE ID = ?";
SqlCommand salaryUpdate = new SqlCommand(sqlText, linkToDB);
salaryUpdate.Parameters.AddWithValue("@NewSalary", 50000m);
salaryUpdate.Parameters.AddWithValue("@EmployeeID", 25L);
```

Visual Basic
```vb
Dim sqlText As String = "UPDATE Employee SET Salary = ? WHERE ID = ?"
Dim salaryUpdate = New SqlCommand(sqlText, linkToDB)
salaryUpdate.Parameters.AddWithValue("@NewSalary", 50000@)
salaryUpdate.Parameters.AddWithValue("@EmployeeID", 25&)
```

Using Parameters in Stored Procedures

Calls to stored procedures with parameterized queries vary only slightly from those to standard statements. There are four main differences you need to consider when accessing stored procedures. The first is simple: Make sure you set the *SqlCommand* object's *CommandType* property to *CommandType.StoredProcedure*.

The second difference is equally simple: The command object's *CommandText* property should include only the name of the stored procedure. Exclude any arguments or query elements.

The third difference is in how you name the parameters. As with standard queries, each parameter includes an @-prefixed name and a data type, plus other optional settings you might want to configure. Unlike standard queries, you have no flexibility in how you define the parameter names. They must match precisely the parameter names used when the stored procedure was defined within SQL Server.

The last difference has to do with the direction of a parameter. The *SqlParameter* class includes a *Direction* property that tells ADO.NET which way data flows from your query's data value to the stored procedure. There are four available *System.Data.ParameterDirection* options:

- ■ *ParameterDirection.Input*   The parameter value is considered input, flowing from the application to the stored procedure. This is the default for all parameters.

- ■ *ParameterDirection.Output*   The parameter is used to retrieve data back from the stored procedure, much like a *ByRef* (Visual Basic) or *out* (C#) function argument.

- ■ *ParameterDirection.InputOutput*   A combination of the input and output directions. Your application provides an input value that can be modified and returned by the stored procedure.

- ■ *ParameterDirection.ReturnValue*   For stored procedures or other database features that sport a return value, this parameter type lets you collect that value.

Parameters added to standard query commands also support the *Direction* property, but in most cases the default of *ParameterDirection.Input* is the right choice.

The following SQL Server stored procedure includes an input value (*@locationName*), an output value (*@newID*), and a return value (*@@ROWCOUNT*):

```
CREATE PROCEDURE AddLocation (@locationName varchar(50), @newID bigint OUT)
AS
BEGIN
    INSERT INTO BuildingLocation (Name) VALUES (@locationName);
    SET @newID = SCOPE_IDENTITY();
    RETURN @@ROWCOUNT;
END
```

The following code calls the *AddLocation* stored procedure, passing it the name of a new location and returning the new ID value:

C#

```csharp
// ----- Use a stored procedure to add a new building location.
string sqlText = "dbo.AddLocation";
SqlCommand locationCommand = new SqlCommand(sqlText, linkToDB);
locationCommand.CommandType = CommandType.StoredProcedure;

// ----- Add the input parameter: locationName.
SqlParameter workParameter = locationCommand.Parameters.AddWithValue(
    "@locationName", LocationNameField.Text.Trim());
workParameter.Size = 50;

// ----- Add the output parameter: newID.
workParameter = locationCommand.Parameters.Add("@newID", SqlDbType.BigInt);
workParameter.Direction = ParameterDirection.Output;

// ----- Add the return value parameter. The name is not important.
workParameter = locationCommand.Parameters.Add("@returnValue", SqlDbType.Int);
workParameter.Direction = ParameterDirection.ReturnValue;

// ----- Add the location.
locationCommand.ExecuteNonQuery();

// ----- Access returned values as:
//         locationCommand.Parameters["@newID"].Value
//         locationCommand.Parameters["@returnValue"].Value
```

Visual Basic

```vbnet
' ----- Use a stored procedure to add a new building location.
Dim sqlText As String = "dbo.AddLocation"
Dim locationCommand As New SqlCommand(sqlText, linkToDB)
locationCommand.CommandType = CommandType.StoredProcedure

' ----- Add the input parameter: locationName.
Dim workParameter As SqlParameter =
    locationCommand.Parameters.AddWithValue(
    "@locationName", LocationNameField.Text.Trim)
workParameter.Size = 50
```

```
' ----- Add the output parameter: newID.
workParameter = locationCommand.Parameters.Add("@newID", SqlDbType.BigInt)
workParameter.Direction = ParameterDirection.Output

' ----- Add the return value parameter. The name is not important.
workParameter = locationCommand.Parameters.Add("@returnValue", SqlDbType.Int)
workParameter.Direction = ParameterDirection.ReturnValue

' ----- Add the location.
locationCommand.ExecuteNonQuery()

' ----- Access returned values as:
'           locationCommand.Parameters("@newID").Value
'           locationCommand.Parameters("@returnValue").Value
```

The return value will be 1 if the code was successful, or 0 if the insert failed (along with a thrown error).

Calling a Stored Procedure with Parameters: C#

> **Note** This exercise uses the "Chapter 10 CSharp" sample project and continues from where the previous exercise in this chapter left off.

1. Open the code for the *ViewOrders* form. This form processes data from a stored procedure that returns two distinct sets of records. The stored procedure *GetCustomerOrders* has the following definition:

```
CREATE PROCEDURE dbo.GetCustomerOrders(@customerID bigint) AS
BEGIN
  SELECT * FROM Customer WHERE ID = @customerID;
  SELECT * FROM OrderEntry WHERE Customer = @customerID
    ORDER BY OrderDate;
END;
```

2. Locate the *ViewOrders_Load* event handler. This routine calls the stored procedure and processes the returned records. In the *try* block, just after the "Process the query..." comment, add the following statements:

```
sqlText = "dbo.GetCustomerOrders";
commandWrapper = new SqlCommand(sqlText, linkToDB);
commandWrapper.CommandType = CommandType.StoredProcedure;
commandWrapper.Parameters.AddWithValue("@customerID", ActiveCustomerID);
customerReader = commandWrapper.ExecuteReader();
```

These lines add the @*customerID* parameter to the stored procedure command. The @*customerID* parameter name must match the @*customerID* parameter as defined in the original stored procedure.

3. Just after the "First read the customer record" comment, add the following code:

```
customerReader.Read();
CustomerName.Text = (string)customerReader["FullName"];
AnnualFee.Text = string.Format("{0:c}",
    (decimal)customerReader["AnnualFee"]);
```

These statements process the first set of results from the stored procedure, the *SELECT* statement for the *Customer* table.

4. Just after the "Read the next set, which contains the orders" comment, add the following code:

```
customerReader.NextResult();
while (customerReader.Read())
{
    oneOrder = new OrderInfo();
    oneOrder.ID = (long)customerReader["ID"];
    oneOrder.OrderDate = (DateTime)customerReader["OrderDate"];
    oneOrder.OrderTotal = (decimal)customerReader["Total"];
    AllOrders.Items.Add(oneOrder);
}
```

This code accesses the records in the second set of results, the *SELECT* statement for the *OrderEntry* table, via the *NextResult* method call.

5. Run the program. On the *Customer Management* form, select a customer from the list of customers and then click View Orders. When the *View Orders* form appears, it includes content from both *SELECT* statements as returned by the stored procedure.

Calling a Stored Procedure with Parameters: Visual Basic

> **Note** This exercise uses the "Chapter 10 VB" sample project and continues from where the previous exercise in this chapter left off.

1. Open the code for the *ViewOrders* form. This form processes data from a stored procedure that returns two distinct sets of records. The stored procedure *GetCustomerOrders* has the following definition:

```
CREATE PROCEDURE dbo.GetCustomerOrders(@customerID bigint) AS
BEGIN
  SELECT * FROM Customer WHERE ID = @customerID;
  SELECT * FROM OrderEntry WHERE Customer = @customerID
    ORDER BY OrderDate;
END;
```

2. Locate the *ViewOrders_Load* event handler. This routine calls the stored procedure and processes the returned records. In the *Try* block, just after the "Process the query..." comment, add the following statements:

```
sqlText = "dbo.GetCustomerOrders"
commandWrapper = New SqlCommand(sqlText, linkToDB)
commandWrapper.CommandType = CommandType.StoredProcedure
commandWrapper.Parameters.AddWithValue("@customerID", ActiveCustomerID)
customerReader = commandWrapper.ExecuteReader()
```

These lines add the *@customerID* parameter to the stored procedure command. The *@customerID* parameter name must match the *@customerID* parameter as defined in the original stored procedure.

3. Just after the "First read the customer record" comment, add the following code:

```
customerReader.Read()
CustomerName.Text = CStr(customerReader!FullName)
AnnualFee.Text = Format(CDec(customerReader!AnnualFee), "Currency")
```

These statements process the first set of results from the stored procedure, the *SELECT* statement for the *Customer* table.

4. Just after the "Read the next set, which contains the orders" comment, add the following code:

```
customerReader.NextResult()
Do While (customerReader.Read = True)
    oneOrder = New OrderInfo
    oneOrder.ID = CLng(customerReader!ID)
    oneOrder.OrderDate = CDate(customerReader!OrderDate)
    oneOrder.OrderTotal = CDec(customerReader!Total)
    AllOrders.Items.Add(oneOrder)
Loop
```

This code accesses the records in the second set of results, the *SELECT* statement for the *OrderEntry* table, via the *NextResult* method call.

5. Run the program. On the *Customer Management* form, select a customer from the list of customers and then click View Orders. When the *View Orders* form appears, it includes content from both *SELECT* statements returned by the stored procedure.

Summary

This chapter discussed parameters, which are data value objects that help ensure the accuracy and safety of the data being sent to and returned from external data sources. Parameterized queries use special SQL statements that include placeholders for each parameter. Each *SqlParameter* instance defines the name of the parameter, its data type, and its value.

Parameters work with either standard SQL commands or with stored procedures. When using them with stored procedures, you can create both input and output stored procedures, supporting two-way communications with these custom database functions.

Chapter 10 Quick Reference

To	Do This
Create a parameterized query for SQL Server	Create a SQL query string that includes @-prefixed placeholders.
	Create a *SqlCommand* instance.
	Assign the SQL query to the *SqlCommand* object's *CommandText* property.
	Create *SqlParameter* objects, one for each placeholder in the query, and add them to the command object's *Parameters* collection.
	Set the *SqlCommand.Connection* property.
	Call one of the command object's *Execute* methods.
Create a parameterized query for an OLE DB data source	Create a SQL query string that includes question marks (?) for placeholders.
	Create an *OleDbCommand* instance.
	Assign the SQL query to the *OleDbCommand* object's *CommandText* property.
	Create *OleDbParameter* objects, one for each placeholder in the query, and add them to the command object's *Parameters* collection.
	Set the *OleDbCommand.Connection* property.
	Call one of the command object's *Execute* methods.
Create an "out" parameter for a stored procedure	Create a *SqlParameter* instance, setting its fields as needed.
	Set the *SqlParameter.Direction* property to *ParameterDirection.Output*.

Chapter 11
Making External Data Available Locally

After completing this chapter, you will be able to:

- Load external data into a *DataTable* or *DataSet*

- Return updated *DataSet* content to an external source

- Use SQL statements and stored procedures to manage *DataSet* content

The disconnected data experience provided by ADO.NET revolves around the *DataSet* class and its supporting objects. The last few chapters have introduced ways to access external data with ADO.NET, but none of those features took advantage of the disconnected aspects of the framework. Still, part of the promise of ADO.NET is its ability to manage external data in a disconnected and table-focused way.

This chapter introduces the *DataAdapter* class—the class that fulfills that core data promise. The *DataAdapter* bridges the simple data connectedness exhibited by the *DataReader* and joins it with the advanced data management features found in the *DataSet*. By creating a few simple objects and crafting a minimum number of SQL statements, you can safely give your *DataSet* the tools needed to keep it and its associated external data source in sync.

Understanding Data Adapters

Data adapters link your external database tables and your local *DataSet*-managed tables by issuing SQL statements. Anytime you need to get data from the database into a *DataSet*, the adapter must perform a "Fill" operation, issuing a *SELECT* statement and moving the results into local *DataTable* instances. You can then update the values in those *DataTable* instances. When it's time to return changes stored in the *DataSet* to the database, the data adapter's "Update" operation sends the relevant *INSERT, UPDATE,* and *DELETE* statements to the database to bring the external data store into line with local changes. Figure 11-1 shows these components working on a single database table, *Customer.*

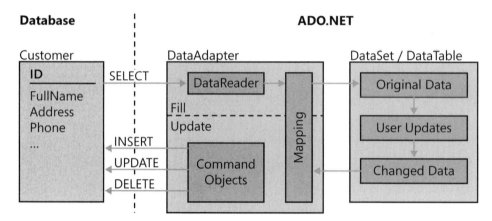

FIGURE 11-1 The data adapter in action.

As Figure 11-1 makes clear, the *DataAdapter* manages a lot of complex activity between the database and a *DataSet* or *DataTable*. It is no exaggeration to say that the *DataAdapter* is possibly the most complex part of ADO.NET, especially when you take advantage of all the flexibility it provides. All the classes introduced so far in this book—from *DataSet* to *SqlParameter*, from *DataRow* to *DataReader*—come into play when creating instances of a data adapter class.

The *System.Data.SqlClient.SqlDataAdapter* class exposes the SQL Server provider implementation of the adapter. You can also find OLE DB and ODBC variations of the data adapter in the classes *System.Data.OleDb.OleDbDataAdapter* and *System.Data.Odbc.OdbcDataAdapter*, respectively. All these classes derive from *System.Data.Common.DbDataAdapter*, which in turn derives from *System.Data.Common.DataAdapter*.

 Note Although the information in this chapter applies generally to all data adapter implementations, this chapter's code samples and examples focus specifically on the SQL Server provider version.

SqlDataAdapter provides three general support features in your application:

- **Record retrieval** Populating a *DataTable* with database records represents the minimal functionality of the data adapter. Internally, the *SqlDataAdapter* uses a *DataReader* instance to retrieve records out of the database, so you must provide it with a *SELECT* statement and a connection string. Stored procedures that return data rows also work; the adapter will correctly process multiple record sets returned by the query.

- **Record updating**   Moving modified data back to external storage is a little more involved. Although the "fill" from the database requires only a basic *SELECT* statement, the "update" operation requires distinct *INSERT, UPDATE,* and *DELETE* statements to complete its work. You can write these by hand or use a "command builder" to automatically generate these statements based on the original *SELECT* query.

- **Table and column name mapping**   The naming needs of your database tables and columns may not always mesh with the needs of your application. Each data adapter includes a mapping layer that automatically renames tables and columns as needed while data is passed between local and remote storage areas.

The remainder of this chapter elaborates on these three data adapter features.

Moving Data from Source to Memory

The *SqlDataAdapter.Fill* method requests data from SQL Server using a valid *SELECT* statement or a data-selection stored procedure. After it accesses the data through an internal *SqlDataReader*, it moves the records into the *DataTable* or *DataSet* of your choice.

Moving Data into a *DataTable*

To move data from a database table into a *DataTable* instance, set up a new *SqlDataAdapter* object and call its *Fill* method, passing it the instance of the *DataTable*.

```
C#
DataTable targetTable = new DataTable();
SqlDataAdapter workAdapter = new SqlDataAdapter(
    "SELECT * FROM Customer ORDER BY LastName", connectionString);
workAdapter.Fill(targetTable);
```

```
Visual Basic
Dim targetTable As New DataTable
Dim workAdapter As New SqlDataAdapter(
    "SELECT * FROM Customer ORDER BY LastName", connectionString)
workAdapter.Fill(targetTable)
```

The data adapter uses the constructor arguments to create a new *SqlCommand* instance. It then assigns this instance to its *SelectCommand* property, a property that must be set before the *SqlDataAdapter* can do its data retrieval work.

In addition to the two-string constructor variation shown previously, overloaded versions let you pass in a configured *SqlCommand* instance, pass in a SQL string and *SqlConnection* pair, or just leave off the arguments altogether. The *SqlDataAdapter* class has no connection string or connection properties, so if you don't provide them with the constructor, you need to include them with a *SqlCommand* instance that you assign to the *SqlDataAdapter. SelectCommand* property directly, as shown here:

```csharp
C#
DataTable targetTable = new DataTable();
using (SqlConnection linkToDB = new SqlConnection(connectionString))
{
    SqlDataAdapter workAdapter = new SqlDataAdapter();
    workAdapter.SelectCommand = new SqlCommand(
        "SELECT * FROM Customer ORDER BY LastName", linkToDB);
    workAdapter.Fill(targetTable);
}
```

```vbnet
Visual Basic
Dim targetTable As New DataTable
Using linkToDB As New SqlConnection(builder.ConnectionString)
    Dim workAdapter As New SqlDataAdapter
    workAdapter.SelectCommand = New SqlCommand(
        "SELECT * FROM Customer ORDER BY LastName", linkToDB)
    workAdapter.Fill(targetTable)
End Using
```

Neither of the preceding examples opened the connection explicitly. If the command's connection isn't open yet, the *Fill* method opens it for you—and closes it when the operation completes.

As the data adapter reads the incoming data, it examines the schema of that data and builds the columns and properties of the *DataTable* instance as needed. If the *DataTable* already has matching columns (names and data types), they are used as is. Any new columns are created alongside the preexisting columns.

> **Note** You can alter this default behavior, as described in this chapter's "Table and Column Mapping" section on page 186.

The *DataTable.TableName* property will be set to "Table," even if you selected records from a specific table with a different name. To alter the target table's name, modify its *TableName* property after the data load or use the table mapping features discussed later in this chapter.

Because the *SqlDataAdapter.SelectCommand* property is a standard *SqlCommand* instance, you can use any of that command object's features to access the remote data. This includes adding one or more *SqlParameter* objects for @-prefixed placeholders embedded in the SQL statement. Configuring the *SqlCommand* instance as a stored procedure with associated parameters also works.

C#
```csharp
// ----- Call the GetCustomerOrders stored procedure with a
//       single 'customer ID' argument.
string sqlText = "dbo.GetOrdersForCustomer";
SqlCommand commandWrapper = new SqlCommand(sqlText, linkToDB);
commandWrapper.CommandType = CommandType.StoredProcedure;
commandWrapper.Parameters.AddWithValue("@customerID", ActiveCustomerID);


// ----- Retrieve the data.
SqlDataAdapter workAdapter = new SqlDataAdapter(commandWrapper);
DataTable orders = new DataTable();
workAdapter.Fill(orders);
```

Visual Basic
```vb
' ----- Call the GetCustomerOrders stored procedure with a
'       single 'customer ID' argument.
Dim sqlText As String = "dbo.GetOrdersForCustomer"
Dim commandWrapper As New SqlCommand(sqlText, linkToDB)
commandWrapper.CommandType = CommandType.StoredProcedure
commandWrapper.Parameters.AddWithValue("@customerID", ActiveCustomerID)


' ----- Retrieve the data.
Dim workAdapter As New SqlDataAdapter(commandWrapper)
Dim orders As New DataTable
workAdapter.Fill(orders)
```

Moving Data into a *DataSet*

Moving external data into a waiting *DataSet* instance is as easy as filling a *DataTable*. To import the data into a *DataSet*, call the *SqlDataAdapter.Fill* method, passing it an instance of *DataSet*.

C#
```csharp
DataSet targetSet = new DataSet();
SqlDataAdapter workAdapter = new SqlDataAdapter(
    "SELECT * FROM Customer ORDER BY LastName", connectionString);
workAdapter.Fill(targetSet);
```

Visual Basic
```vb
Dim targetSet As New DataSet
Dim workAdapter As New SqlDataAdapter(
    "SELECT * FROM Customer ORDER BY LastName", connectionString)
workAdapter.Fill(targetSet)
```

As with a *DataTable* load, the *DataSet* version of *Fill* will auto-build the schema for you. If you want to preconfigure the *DataSet* schema, you can build its table by hand or call the *SqlDataAdapter.FillSchema* method just before you call the *Fill* method.

C#
```csharp
// ----- First build the schema using the structure defined
//       in the data source.
workAdapter.FillSchema(targetSet, SchemaType.Source);

// ----- Then load the data.
workAdapter.Fill(targetSet);
```

Visual Basic
```vb
' ----- First build the schema using the structure defined
'       in the data source.
workAdapter.FillSchema(targetSet, SchemaType.Source)

' ----- Then load the data.
workAdapter.Fill(targetSet)
```

> **Note** Passing *SchemaType.Mapped* as the second argument to *FillSchema* enables a "mapped" schema build. Schema mapping is discussed on page 186 in the "Table and Column Mapping" section of this chapter.

Fill names the first created table in the data set "Table," as is done when filling a *DataTable* directly. To alter this default name, specify the new name as a second argument to the *Fill* method.

C#
```
workAdapter.Fill(targetSet, "Customer");
```

Visual Basic
```
workAdapter.Fill(targetSet, "Customer")
```

The *Fill(DataSet)* method will import multiple tables if its *SelectCommand* includes a batch of *SELECT* statements or a stored procedure that returns multiple result sets. The first table created is still named "Table" (by default). Subsequent tables are named numerically, with the second table given the name "Table1," the third table "Table2," and so on. Duplicate column names found in any table are treated the same way. The first duplicate column is given a "1" suffix, the second has a "2" suffix, and so on.

> **Note** When retrieving multiple tables of data, a call to *SqlDataAdapter.FillSchema* examines only the schema of the *first* result set. The schemas of subsequent sets can be imported only as a side effect of the *Fill* method.

Moving Data from Memory to Source

After imported data has been modified within a *DataTable* (with or without a surrounding *DataSet*), the same *SqlDataAdapter* that brought the data in can move the changes back out to the source. Setting up the adapter to accomplish that feat is a little more involved than just crafting a *SELECT* statement but still not overwhelmingly difficult. Configuring the data adapter for the return data trip requires setting up the appropriate data manipulation statements and calling the *SqlDataAdapter.Update* method.

Configuring the Update Commands

The *SqlDataAdapter.SelectCommand* property manages the movement of data only from the external source to the local *DataSet* or *DataTable*. To move data in the other direction or delete data, you need to set up three distinct properties: *InsertCommand, UpdateCommand*, and *DeleteCommand*. Like *SelectCommand*, these three properties are *SqlCommand* instances, each containing a SQL statement (or stored procedure), a *SqlConnection* reference, and parameters. Although parameters are optional in the *SelectCommand* instance, they are an essential part of the three update commands.

The following code sets up selection and data modification properties for a simple table, *UnitOfMeasure*, which includes an identity field, *ID*; and two text fields, *ShortName* and *FullName*:

C#

```csharp
// ----- Build the selection query.
SqlDataAdapter unitAdapter = new SqlDataAdapter();
SqlCommand unitCommand = new SqlCommand(
    "SELECT * FROM UnitOfMeasure", linkToDB);
unitAdapter.SelectCommand = unitCommand;

// ----- Build the insertion query.
unitCommand = new SqlCommand(
    @"INSERT INTO UnitOfMeasure (ShortName, FullName)
    VALUES (@ShortName, @FullName); SET @ID = @@IDENTITY;", linkToDB);
unitCommand.Parameters.Add("@ShortName", SqlDbType.VarChar, 15, "ShortName");
unitCommand.Parameters.Add("@FullName", SqlDbType.VarChar, 50, "FullName");
SqlParameter param =
    unitCommand.Parameters.Add("@ID", SqlDbType.BigInt, 0, "ID");
param.Direction = ParameterDirection.Output;
unitAdapter.InsertCommand = unitCommand;

// ----- Build the revision query.
unitCommand = new SqlCommand(
    @"UPDATE UnitOfMeasure SET ShortName = @ShortName,
    FullName = @FullName WHERE ID = @ID", linkToDB);
unitCommand.Parameters.Add("@ShortName", SqlDbType.VarChar, 15, "ShortName");
unitCommand.Parameters.Add("@FullName", SqlDbType.VarChar, 50, "FullName");
param = unitCommand.Parameters.Add("@ID", SqlDbType.BigInt, 0, "ID");
param.SourceVersion = DataRowVersion.Original;
unitAdapter.UpdateCommand = unitCommand;

// ----- Build the deletion query.
unitCommand = new SqlCommand(
    "DELETE FROM UnitOfMeasure WHERE ID = @ID", linkToDB);
param = unitCommand.Parameters.Add("@ID", SqlDbType.BigInt, 0, "ID");
param.SourceVersion = DataRowVersion.Original;
unitAdapter.DeleteCommand = unitCommand;
```

Visual Basic

```vb
' ----- Build the selection query.
Dim unitAdapter As New SqlDataAdapter
Dim unitCommand As New SqlCommand(
    "SELECT * FROM UnitOfMeasure", linkToDB)
unitAdapter.SelectCommand = unitCommand


' ----- Build the insertion query.
unitCommand = New SqlCommand(
    "INSERT INTO UnitOfMeasure (ShortName, FullName) " &
    "VALUES (@ShortName, @FullName); SET @ID = @@IDENTITY;", linkToDB)
unitCommand.Parameters.Add("@ShortName", SqlDbType.VarChar, 15, "ShortName")
unitCommand.Parameters.Add("@FullName", SqlDbType.VarChar, 50, "FullName")
With unitCommand.Parameters.Add("@ID", SqlDbType.BigInt, 0, "ID")
    .Direction = ParameterDirection.Output
End With
unitAdapter.InsertCommand = unitCommand


' ----- Build the revision query.
unitCommand = New SqlCommand(
    "UPDATE UnitOfMeasure SET ShortName = @ShortName, " &
    "FullName = @FullName WHERE ID = @ID", linkToDB)
unitCommand.Parameters.Add("@ShortName", SqlDbType.VarChar, 15, "ShortName")
unitCommand.Parameters.Add("@FullName", SqlDbType.VarChar, 50, "FullName")
With unitCommand.Parameters.Add("@ID", SqlDbType.BigInt, 0, "ID")
    .SourceVersion = DataRowVersion.Original
End With
unitAdapter.UpdateCommand = unitCommand


' ----- Build the deletion query.
unitCommand = New SqlCommand(
    "DELETE FROM UnitOfMeasure WHERE ID = @ID", linkToDB)
With unitCommand.Parameters.Add("@ID", SqlDbType.BigInt, 0, "ID")
    .SourceVersion = DataRowVersion.Original
End With
unitAdapter.DeleteCommand = unitCommand
```

This code is more complex than the earlier retrieval code, which makes sense given its increased responsibilities. Besides the increase in the quantity of code, there are three main enhancements that make this code different from the retrieval-only use of the data adapter.

- **Parameter column designation**   You might have noticed a final column-name argument added to each of the *SqlParameter* instances created for use with the @-prefixed placeholders. For example, in the insertion portion of the Visual Basic sample code, the *@ShortName* placeholder uses this parameter definition.

```
unitCommand.Parameters.Add("@ShortName", SqlDbType.VarChar, 15, "ShortName")
```

  The ending "ShortName" argument indicates the name of the column as referenced in an associated *DataTable*. This allows the three data update commands to associate the parameter with specific columns in the local *DataTable* version of the content. ADO.NET needs to know this to make data updates at the source possible.

- **Key retrieval on insertion**   In the example code shown previously, the SQL statement for the *InsertCommand* portion of the data adapter is actually a two-statement batch.

```
INSERT INTO UnitOfMeasure (ShortName, FullName)
    VALUES (@ShortName, @FullName);
SET @ID = @@IDENTITY;
```

  The first statement performs the insert of a new record; the second statement retrieves the primary key of the new record, a column tied to a SQL Server *IDENTITY* constraint. The goal is to retrieve the new record identifier so that the local *DataTable* copy of the record can be properly refreshed with this ID. The associated *SqlParameter* instance for the *@ID* placeholder has its *Direction* property set to *Output*, as shown in the following C# code line:

```
param.Direction = ParameterDirection.Output;
```

  As long as the parameter is configured to retrieve the key value, the data adapter will correctly propagate the new ID value to the *DataTable* record. If you plan to update the data source only once and then immediately destroy the associated *DataTable*, retrieving the key value is not strictly required. But if there is any chance that your code will allow further update and delete operations on the newly inserted record, you will need that ID.

- **Use of original image on update and delete**   The SQL statement for the *DeleteCommand* portion of the code references the record ID as a parameter.

```
DELETE FROM UnitOfMeasure WHERE ID = @ID
```

The code adds a *SqlParameter* instance for the *@ID* placeholder, shown here as Visual Basic code:

```
unitCommand.Parameters.Add("@ID", SqlDbType.BigInt, 0, "ID")
```

The problem is that by the time the update occurs, the "current" view of the record in the *DataTable* has already been deleted. There is no current record from which the adapter can obtain the ID column value. To locate the ID, the code must tell the adapter to access the "original" version of the deleted record, using the ID as it existed when the table was imported or since the last *AcceptChanges* method call. Setting the *SqlParameter.SourceVersion* property to *DataRowVersion.Original* provides that instruction to the *SqlDataAdapter*, as shown in this Visual Basic code:

```
With unitCommand.Parameters.Add("@ID", SqlDbType.BigInt, 0, "ID")
    .SourceVersion = DataRowVersion.Original
End With
```

The *UpdateCommand* portion includes similar code for cases where the identifying fields may have been modified in the *DataTable*.

The code shown previously defines the actions the data adapter will perform to move modified data from the local *DataSet* or *DataTable* to the external data store. Note that instead of specific SQL statements, you can define some or all of the four *SqlCommand* objects tied to the *SqlDataAdapter* using parameterized stored procedures. Whether you use SQL statements or SQL Server stored procedures to modify the external data is up to you. The *SqlDataAdapter* will work as long as the statements and the linked *SqlParameter* objects match up correctly.

Performing the Update

With the data modification statements in place, after you have updated records in the local *DataTable* copy of your *SqlDataAdapter*-linked content, you simply call the adapter's *Update* method to move those changes into the external database. You must identify which local source the *Update* method is to use for the update, which can be either a *DataSet* (which updates all tables included in that set), a *DataTable*, or an array of *DataRow* objects. This lets you manage the granularity of the data you want to send back to external storage.

C#
```
workAdapter.Update(localTable);
```

Visual Basic
```
workAdapter.Update(localTable)
```

The *Update* method examines each row in the specified *DataSet, DataTable,* or array of *DataRow* objects, deciding which rows require an *INSERT, UPDATE,* or *DELETE* action; or no action at all. For each row that needs updating, the adapter raises its own *OnRowUpdating* event just before issuing the SQL command; then raises the related *OnRowUpdated* event after the row has been changed in the database. These events give you an opportunity to monitor each row as update processing occurs, or even skip or modify the update plan for specific rows. For instance, in the *OnRowUpdating* event handler, the event argument passed into the handler exposes a *Status* property. Setting this property to *UpdateStatus. SkipCurrentRow* abandons the update for a given row.

Normally, any errors that occur during the update process cause an exception to be thrown. You can tell the adapter to suppress such exceptions by setting the *SqlDataAdapter. ContinueUpdateOnError* property to *True.* When doing this, be sure to monitor the *OnRowUpdated* event to manually handle any errors reported by the database.

Generating Update Commands Automatically

Normally, you will provide each of the four selection and data modification commands to the *SqlDataAdapter.* However, there may be instances, such as when the selection command is generated by an automated process, where supplying the *INSERT, UPDATE,* and *DELETE* commands may be difficult or impossible. For such situations, ADO.NET includes a *command builder,* a provider-specific class that will write the data modification commands on your behalf.

The command builder for SQL Server is located at *System.Data.SqlClient.SqlCommandBuilder.* To use it, create your data adapter, providing at least the *SelectCommand.* Then create a new instance of *SqlCommandBuilder,* passing the data adapter to it.

```
C#
SqlDataAdapter workAdapter = new SqlDataAdapter(
    "SELECT * FROM Customer ORDER BY LastName", connectionString);
SqlCommandBuilder customerBuilder = new SqlCommandBuilder(workAdapter);
```

```
Visual Basic
Dim workAdapter As New SqlDataAdapter(
    "SELECT * FROM Customer ORDER BY LastName", connectionString)
Dim customerBuilder As New SqlCommandBuilder(workAdapter)
```

The builder generates the appropriate *INSERT, UPDATE,* and *DELETE* statements to parallel the content of the *SELECT* statement. It does this by running the *SELECT* query and examining the schema of the records that come back from the data source. (This occurs in addition to running the query during the *Fill* operation.) If your *SELECT* query takes a long time to run, this may not be the most efficient way of creating the data modification statements.

After you associate the builder with a *SqlDataAdapter*, if you examine the adapter, you'll see no new *SqlCommand* instances for the *InsertCommand, UpdateCommand,* or *DeleteCommand* properties. Instead, *SqlCommandBuilder* monitors the update phase of the adapter, and volunteers to hand-craft data modification statements as needed for each row.

There are a few limitations when using command builders:

- *SqlCommandBuilder* can be used only with single-table queries. You should not use it with joined-table queries.

- The schema of the selected records must include at least one primary key or unique-value column. Tables defined without primary keys or unique columns will not work with command builders.

- If for any reason you modify the *SelectCommand* associated with the data adapter, you must call the *SqlCommandBuilder.RefreshSchema* method to adjust the generated queries.

- The command builder will generate commands only for those actions that do not already have defined actions in the *SqlDataAdapter*. For example, if your adapter defines both a *SelectCommand* and an *InsertCommand* but not the other two commands, the builder will manage only *UpdateCommand* and *DeleteCommand* processing.

- The command builder doesn't work well with external tables or columns that have non-standard names. If your field names include space characters, you will need to craft the update statements yourself.

Syncing Data with a *SqlDataAdapter*: C#

1. Open the "Chapter 11 CSharp" project from the installed samples folder. The project includes a *Windows.Forms* class named *UnitEditor*, a simple database table editor.

2. Open the source code view for the *UnitEditor* form. Locate the *GetConnectionString* function, a routine that uses a *SqlConnectionStringBuilder* to create a valid connection string to the sample database. It currently includes the following statements:

```
builder.DataSource = @"(local)\SQLExpress";
builder.InitialCatalog = "StepSample";
builder.IntegratedSecurity = true;
```

Adjust these statements as needed to provide access to your own test database.

3. Locate the *UnitEditor_Load* event handler. This routine configures the main *SqlDataAdapter* used by the program to edit the *UnitOfMeasure* table from the sample database. Just after the "Build the selection query" comment, add the following statements:

```
unitCommand = new SqlCommand(
    "SELECT * FROM UnitOfMeasure ORDER BY ID", linkToDB);
UnitAdapter.SelectCommand = unitCommand;
```

This code adds the required *SELECT* command to the adapter, extracting records (and indirectly, the schema) from the *UnitOfMeasure* table.

4. Just after the "Build the insertion query" comment, add the following code:

```
unitCommand = new SqlCommand(
    @"INSERT INTO UnitOfMeasure (ShortName, FullName)
    VALUES (@ShortName, @FullName); SET @ID = @@IDENTITY;", linkToDB);
unitCommand.Parameters.Add(
    "@ShortName", SqlDbType.VarChar, 15, "ShortName");
unitCommand.Parameters.Add(
    "@FullName", SqlDbType.VarChar, 50, "FullName");
SqlParameter param = unitCommand.Parameters.Add(
    "@ID", SqlDbType.BigInt, 0, "ID");
param.Direction = ParameterDirection.Output;
UnitAdapter.InsertCommand = unitCommand;
```

This block adds the *INSERT* portion of the query set. The three parameters transfer the table content, with two parameters (*@ShortName* and *@FullName*) included for data returning to the database, and the third parameter (*@ID*) coming back.

5. Just after the "Build the revision query" comment, add the following lines:

```
unitCommand = new SqlCommand(
    @"UPDATE UnitOfMeasure SET ShortName = @ShortName,
    FullName = @FullName WHERE ID = @ID", linkToDB);
unitCommand.Parameters.Add(
    "@ShortName", SqlDbType.VarChar, 15, "ShortName");
unitCommand.Parameters.Add(
    "@FullName", SqlDbType.VarChar, 50, "FullName");
param = unitCommand.Parameters.Add("@ID", SqlDbType.BigInt, 0, "ID");
param.SourceVersion = DataRowVersion.Original;
UnitAdapter.UpdateCommand = unitCommand;
```

This *UPDATE* query is much like the *INSERT* query added in the previous step, but it also uses data from the original version of the edited *DataSet* row to help locate the matching record in the database.

6. Just after the "Build the deletion query" comment, add the following code:

```
unitCommand = new SqlCommand(
    "DELETE FROM UnitOfMeasure WHERE ID = @ID", linkToDB);
param = unitCommand.Parameters.Add("@ID", SqlDbType.BigInt, 0, "ID");
param.SourceVersion = DataRowVersion.Original;
UnitAdapter.DeleteCommand = unitCommand;
```

These statements define the *DELETE* query used to remove database records.

7. Just after the "Load the data from the database into the local editor" comment, within the *try* block, add the following two lines:

```
UnitAdapter.Fill(UnitTable);
UnitGrid.DataSource = UnitTable;
```

These statements perform the actual movement of data from the external database to the local *DataTable* copy. The *Fill* method also builds the basic schema within the *UnitTable* instance so that the incoming records have a place to reside.

8. Locate the *ActUpdate_Click* event handler. Within the *try* block, add the following statement:

```
UnitAdapter.Update(UnitTable);
```

This single line completes the round trip, moving changed data in the *UnitTable* instance back to the external data source.

9. Run the program. The form that appears displays all existing records from the *UnitOfMeasure* table in the sample database. Add a new sample record by entering **ml** in the *ShortName* column of the last (empty) row and **milliliter** in the *FullName* column of the same row. Click Update to move these changes to the database. When you perform that update, the data adapter retrieves the ID for the new record and displays it in the editor to the left of the values you entered.

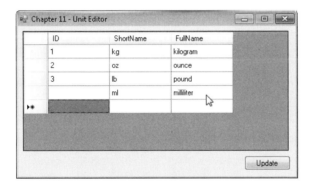

Syncing Data with a *SqlDataAdapter*: Visual Basic

1. Open the "Chapter 11 VB" project from the installed samples folder. The project includes a *Windows.Forms* class named *UnitEditor*, a simple database table editor.

2. Open the source code view for the *UnitEditor* form. Locate the *GetConnectionString* function, a routine that uses a *SqlConnectionStringBuilder* to create a valid connection string to the sample database. It currently includes the following statements:

```
builder.DataSource = "(local)\SQLExpress"
builder.InitialCatalog = "StepSample"
builder.IntegratedSecurity = True
```

Adjust these statements as needed to provide access to your own test database.

3. Locate the *UnitEditor_Load* event handler. This routine configures the main *SqlDataAdapter* used by the program to edit the *UnitOfMeasure* table from the sample database. Just after the "Build the selection query" comment, add the following statements:

```
unitCommand = New SqlCommand(
    "SELECT * FROM UnitOfMeasure ORDER BY ID", linkToDB)
UnitAdapter.SelectCommand = unitCommand
```

This code adds the required *SELECT* command to the adapter, extracting records (and indirectly, the schema) from the *UnitOfMeasure* table.

4. Just after the "Build the insertion query" comment, add the following code:

```
unitCommand = New SqlCommand(
    "INSERT INTO UnitOfMeasure (ShortName, FullName) " &
    "VALUES (@ShortName, @FullName); SET @ID = @@IDENTITY;", linkToDB)
unitCommand.Parameters.Add(
    "@ShortName", SqlDbType.VarChar, 15, "ShortName")
unitCommand.Parameters.Add(
    "@FullName", SqlDbType.VarChar, 50, "FullName")
With unitCommand.Parameters.Add("@ID", SqlDbType.BigInt, 0, "ID")
    .Direction = ParameterDirection.Output
End With
UnitAdapter.InsertCommand = unitCommand
```

This block adds the *INSERT* portion of the query set. The three parameters transfer the table content, with two parameters (*@ShortName* and *@FullName*) included for data returning to the database, and the third parameter (*@ID*) coming back.

5. Just after the "Build the revision query" comment, add the following lines:

```
unitCommand = New SqlCommand(
    "UPDATE UnitOfMeasure SET ShortName = @ShortName, " &
    "FullName = @FullName WHERE ID = @ID", linkToDB)
unitCommand.Parameters.Add(
    "@ShortName", SqlDbType.VarChar, 15, "ShortName")
unitCommand.Parameters.Add(
    "@FullName", SqlDbType.VarChar, 50, "FullName")
With unitCommand.Parameters.Add("@ID", SqlDbType.BigInt, 0, "ID")
    .SourceVersion = DataRowVersion.Original
End With
UnitAdapter.UpdateCommand = unitCommand
```

This *UPDATE* query is much like the *INSERT* query added in the previous step, but it also uses data from the original version of the edited *DataSet* row to help locate the matching record in the database.

6. Just after the "Build the deletion query" comment, add the following code:

```
unitCommand = New SqlCommand(
    "DELETE FROM UnitOfMeasure WHERE ID = @ID", linkToDB)
With unitCommand.Parameters.Add("@ID", SqlDbType.BigInt, 0, "ID")
    .SourceVersion = DataRowVersion.Original
End With
UnitAdapter.DeleteCommand = unitCommand
```

These statements define the *DELETE* query used to remove database records.

7. Just after the "Load the data from the database into the local editor" comment, within the *Try* block, add the following two lines:

```
UnitAdapter.Fill(UnitTable)
UnitGrid.DataSource = UnitTable
```

These statements perform the actual movement of data from the external database to the local *DataTable* copy. The *Fill* method also builds the basic schema within the *UnitTable* instance so that the incoming records have a place to reside.

8. Locate the *ActUpdate_Click* event handler. Within the *Try* block, add the following statement:

```
UnitAdapter.Update(UnitTable)
```

This single line completes the round trip, moving changed data in the *UnitTable* instance back to the external data source.

9. Run the program. The form that appears displays all existing records from the *UnitOfMeasure* table in the sample database. Add a new sample record by entering **ml** in the *ShortName* column of the last (empty) row and **milliliter** in the *FullName* column of the same row. Click Update to move these changes to the database. When you perform that update, the data adapter retrieves the ID for the new record and displays it in the editor to the left of the values you entered.

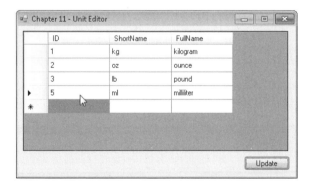

Table and Column Mapping

Sometimes it isn't convenient or even possible to use the same table and column names between your local *DataTable* and the external database table, view, or generated results it represents. In such situations, use the *SqlDataAdapter.TableMappings* collection to define the naming changes between the external and internal versions of your table structures.

This system is especially useful when importing data into a *DataSet* in which named tables already exist. Remember that when *SqlDataAdapter* retrieves result sets from the database, it names the first set "Table," the second set "Table1," and so on. For example, suppose you use the *DataSet / String* syntax in the *Fill* method:

```
workAdapter.Fill(targetSet, "Grid")   ' Visual Basic version
```

The first table in *targetSet* is "Grid," the second is "Grid1," and so on. If the *DataSet* includes names that vary from these defaults, *Fill* will add new tables with the default names and schemas.

To coerce the data adapter into moving the incoming records into the correct table, add new *System.Data.Common.DataTableMapping* objects to the table mapping collection before calling the *Fill* method.

C#
```csharp
// ----- Using the basic external-internal syntax is quick.
workAdapter.TableMappings.Add("Table", "Employee");


// ----- Adding a DataTableMapping instance works also.
DataTableMapping nameChange = new DataTableMapping();
nameChange.SourceTable = "Table1";
nameChange.DataSetTable = "Customer";
workAdapter.TableMappings.Add(nameChange);
```

Visual Basic
```vb
' ----- Using the basic external-internal syntax is quick.
workAdapter.TableMappings.Add("Table", "Employee")


' ----- Adding a DataTableMapping instance works also.
Dim nameChange As New DataTableMapping
nameChange.SourceTable = "Table1"
nameChange.DataSetTable = "Customer"
workAdapter.TableMappings.Add(nameChange)
```

It's not just table names that can be mapped; the data adapter supports column name mappings as well.

```csharp
C#
// ----- Start with the table name.
DataTableMapping employeeMap =
    workAdapter.TableMappings.Add("Table", "Employee");

// ----- Then add the columns. Columns not mentioned here
//       import using the source column names.
employeeMap.ColumnMappings.Add("Employee ID", "ID");
employeeMap.ColumnMappings.Add("Current Department", "DeptID");
```

```vbnet
Visual Basic
' ----- Start with the table name.
Dim employeeMap As DataTableMapping =
    workAdapter.TableMappings.Add("Table", "Employee")

' ----- Then add the columns. Columns not mentioned here
'       import using the source column names.
employeeMap.ColumnMappings.Add("Employee ID", "ID")
employeeMap.ColumnMappings.Add("Current Department", "DeptID")
```

You are not required to set up a mapping for every incoming table or column. The data adapter includes two properties that establish the rules for handling missing targets. The *SqlDataAdapter.MissingMappingAction* property determines what should be done when the table and column mapping rules do not include one of the incoming tables or columns (or any of them). It is set to one of the *MissingMappingAction* enumerated values.

- ■ ***MissingMappingAction.Passthrough***   Even though there is no mapping, the table or column is added to the target schema using the default incoming name. This is the default setting.

- ■ ***MissingMappingAction.Ignore***   The missing table or column is ignored, and its incoming data for that table or column is discarded.

- ■ ***MissingMappingAction.Error***   The mapping process generates an exception when it finds an unmapped table or column.

The second property for managing mapping exceptions is the *SqlDataAdapter.Missing SchemaAction*. This property indicates what should be done when the target *DataSet* or *DataTable* does not already include the incoming mapped or unmapped table or column name. Its options somewhat parallel those used for the missing mapping action.

- **MissingSchemaAction.Add**   Any table or column names missing from the target schema are added automatically. This is the default setting.

- **MissingSchemaAction.AddWithKey**   The same as the *MissingSchemaAction.Add* option, but primary key and other constraint settings are imported along with the basic schema.

- **MissingSchemaAction.Ignore**   Any incoming table or column names not already found in the target schema are discarded, and the data values associated with those elements are excluded from import.

- **MissingSchemaAction.Error**   The import process generates an exception on any missing table or column in the schema. The target schema is not modified at all.

Summary

This chapter was a culmination of all that you gained through the earlier chapters. In the *SqlDataAdapter* (and its siblings for other providers), the data sets, tables, connections, commands, and parameters come together to provide a flexible and consistent method for importing data easily from an external data source and migrating modifications to that data back out to the database.

The *SqlDataAdapter* class enables this data communication through a set of four platform-specific statements: *SELECT, INSERT, UPDATE,* and *DELETE,* or their stored procedure equivalents. ADO.NET includes the *SqlCommandBuilder* tool to assist you in developing at least some of these statements. For more advanced implementations, the data adapter's table mappings feature lets you control how data comes into memory-resident storage.

Chapter 11 Quick Reference

To	Do This
Import a database table into a *DataTable* through an adapter	Create the *DataTable* instance.
	Create a *SqlDataAdapter*, supplying both a record selection query and a valid connection.
	Call the adapter's *Fill* method, passing it the *DataTable* instance.
Return modified records to a database through an adapter	Create a *SqlDataAdapter*, supplying both a record selection query and valid connection.
	Provide the adapter's *InsertCommand*, *UpdateCommand*, and *DeleteCommand*, either directly or by using a *SqlCommandBuilder*.
	Call the adapter's *Fill* method, passing it the *DataTable* or *DataSet* instance as needed.
	Make changes to the data.
	Call the adapter's *Update* method, passing it the *DataTable* or *DataSet* instance.
Prevent incoming data from modifying the existing *DataSet* schema	Set the *SqlDataAdapter* instance's *MissingSchemaAction* property to *MissingSchemaAction.Ignore*.

Chapter 12
Guaranteeing Data Integrity

After completing this chapter, you will be able to:

- Understand ADO.NET's use of optimistic concurrency

- Perform transactions that include multiple record updates

- Spread transactions across multiple databases

Database programming would be a meaningless task if there were no way to guarantee the integrity of the data. Having a single user update a single record with no one else to interrupt the process is one thing. But what happens when you have dozens—or hundreds—of users all trying to update records in the same tables, or even the same records, at the same time?

Welcome to the world of *transactions*—database operations that enable multiple record updates to be treated as a single unit. This chapter introduces ADO.NET's take on the transaction and how your code can work with the database to ensure safe and sound data.

Note The exercises in this chapter all use the same sample project: a program that simulates the transfer of funds between bank accounts. Although you will be able to run the application after each exercise, the expected results for the full application might not appear until you complete all exercises in the chapter.

Transactions and Concurrency

In today's Web-based, highly-scalable 24/7/365 world, it's a given that multiple users will attempt to simultaneously modify the content in your database. As long as each user is updating different records, concerns about data conflicts occurring between those users are minimal. But when two users start competing for the same records, the safety of the data itself becomes a serious issue.

Consider two users, Alice and Bob, who are using the same event reservations system to purchase tickets for an upcoming concert. Because the seats for the concert are numbered, only a single user can purchase a numbered ticket for a specific seat. The sales system sells tickets in two steps: (1) it reads the reservations table to locate the next empty seat, and (2) it updates the record to assign a user to the previously looked-up seat.

Figure 12-1 shows three possible scenarios when Alice and Bob use the system at approximately the same time.

Scenario #1	Scenario #2	Scenario #3
Alice: Read	Alice: Read	Alice: Read
Alice: Write	Bob: Read	Bob: Read
Bob: Read	Alice: Write	Bob: Write
Bob: Write	Bob: Write	Alice: Write

FIGURE 12-1   The risks of multiuser access to data.

Assume that seats 100 and 101 are available and will be reserved in that order. In Scenario #1, Alice completes her transaction for seat 100 before Bob even begins requesting an open seat, so there aren't any data conflicts. But Scenarios #2 and #3 show potential problems. Depending on how the system is designed, it's possible that either Bob or Alice will be without a reservation. In Scenario #3, if the system tells both Alice and Bob that 100 is the next seat available, Alice will get the reservation even through Bob updated the system first. This "last one wins" situation is a common difficulty to be overcome in database development.

Another potential problem occurs when a database update takes place in multiple parts. When you transfer money from your savings account to your checking account, the database records (at least) two distinct updates: (1) the debit of funds from the savings account, and (2) the credit of those same funds into the checking account. As long as both operations occur, the record of the transfer is sound. But what happens if the database crashes after the withdrawal of funds from the savings account, but before those funds make it into the checking account?

Databases attempt to resolve all these conflicts and more by employing transactions. A *transaction* is a single unit of database work that is guaranteed to maintain the integrity and reliability of the data. It does this by adhering to *ACID*, the four rules that define the transaction, which are as follows:

- **Atomicity**   The transaction is all or nothing. If any part of the transaction cannot complete, whether due to invalid data, constraint limitations, or even a hardware failure, the entire transaction is cancelled and undone. After this reversal completes, the state of the involved records is the same as if the transaction never occurred.

- **Consistency**   The transaction, when complete, will leave the database in a valid state. This aspect of transactions often details with constraints. For example, when deleting a parent record, child records bound by a foreign key constraint must be modified to remove the parent reference, deleted from the database, or if they remain, the transaction must be canceled.

- **Isolation**   This property has to do with multiuser scenarios. When a transaction is active, other users or processes that attempt to access the involved records are not allowed to see those records in a semicomplete state. The database must either provide those other processes with the pretransaction content of the records, or force those processes to *block*, or wait, until the transaction is complete.

- **Durability**   Durable transactions are robust enough to overcome any type of database failure, and if they are damaged so that they cannot be recovered, they are ultimately reversed. Modern databases achieve this using *transaction logs*, a secondary repository of all database modifications that can be "played back" to recover damaged data if needed.

Robust databases such as SQL Server ensure that updates made to individual records meet all these ACID requirements. For updates made to multiple records, especially those that involve different tables, ACID applies only if you specifically wrap the updates within the database's platform-specific implementation of a transaction.

A transaction begins when you specifically tell the database that you need one, and it ends when you either *commit* the transaction—making all changes that took place within the transaction permanent—or issue a *rollback*—a cancelling or reversal of the entire transaction.

Database systems also employ *record locking*: the temporary protection of records, record blocks, or entire tables from use by other processes during the lifetime of a transaction or other data operation. The isolation property of ACID is a typical record-locking function, although there are other manual and automated actions in which a database will lock records. Record locking allows programmers to resolve the seat reservation issues previously posed by Alice and Bob. If Alice locks seat 100 pending completion of the reservation process, Bob will not have access to that record. Instead, he must either wait until the reservation system makes a seat number available or reserve a seat that is not currently locked.

> **Note**   Although record locking is a traditional method of protecting records, it is often not efficient, and sometimes not even possible, when dealing with disconnected, highly-scalable systems such as busy web sites. Such systems must use other methods of protecting records that must be restricted to a single user or session. Some of these alternatives are described in this chapter, on page 194.

Concurrency is the art of when to apply a record lock. There are two main flavors of concurrency:

- **Pessimistic concurrency**   Records destined to be updated are locked when they are first accessed and read. Only the user holding the lock has full access to the record, including the ability to modify it. At some point, the record must be released, either through a formal release of the lock or through an update-and-commit process that completes the update. Pessimistic concurrency is useful when allowing two users update access to the same record could prove problematic.

- **Optimistic concurrency**   Records are left unlocked during the read-write interval and are locked by the database only at the moment of update. This type of record locking is good for those times when records are rarely or never accessed by two users at once, or when the risks associated with having two users update those records in parallel are small. Limited locks allow for high scalability, although with the increased potential for data conflicts.

ADO.NET, with its focus on disconnected data processing, uses optimistic concurrency. Unfortunately, this method leaves some applications open to data conflicts of the type experienced by Alice and Bob. There are data-specific methods that help avoid, or even eliminate, these problems, even when pessimistic concurrency is not available. The *SqlCommandBuilder* class uses one such method when it builds data modification statements for the target database table. Consider an update statement that modifies several fields in a customer table:

```
UPDATE Customer SET FullName = @NewName,
    Address = @NewAddress, Phone = @NewPhone
    WHERE ID = @OriginalID
```

If User A and User B are both updating the record at the same time, with User A modifying *Address* and User B correcting *Phone*, the "last one wins" rule will apply in the absence of pessimistic concurrency. *SqlCommandBuilder* attempts to reduce such issues by including all the original data values in the update query's *WHERE* clause.

```
UPDATE Customer SET FullName = @NewName,
    Address = @NewAddress, Phone = @NewPhone
    WHERE ID = @OriginalID
    AND FullName = @OriginalName
    AND Address = @OriginalAddress
    AND Phone = @OriginalPhone
```

This changes the update system to "first one wins" because any changes made to the record will fail to match some of the "original" values submitted by the second user—one that still has the original premodified image of the record—and thus prevent the update request from making additional changes without first obtaining the "new original" version of the record. In SQL Server table updates, a *rowversion* column can be used in the same way because interim updates to the record change that column's value automatically.

```
/* ----- versiontrack column is of type rowversion. */
UPDATE Customer SET FullName = @NewName,
    Address = @NewAddress, Phone = @NewPhone
    WHERE ID = @OriginalID
    AND versiontrack = @OriginalRowVersion
```

Note Some database platforms support statements that let you sidestep ADO.NET's preference for optimistic concurrency. The Oracle *SELECT* statement, for example, includes a *FOR UPDATE* clause that applies a persistent lock to the record until it is modified in a subsequent statement or is otherwise released.

Depending on how you manage your ADO.NET database connections and connection-pooling options, such SQL statements might provide access to true pessimistic concurrency. If you choose to use such features, be sure to fully test your implementation, and be aware of changes to ADO.NET in future releases that might affect your use of such statements.

Using Local Transactions

ADO.NET includes support for transactions with a single database through the *System. Data.Common.DbTransaction* class. In the SQL Server provider, this base class is overridden by the *System.Data.SqlClient.SqlTransaction* class. The OLE DB and ODBC providers implement transactions through the *System.Data.OleDb.OleDbTransaction* and *System.Data. Odbc.OdbcTransaction* classes, respectively.

Note The remaining discussion of transactions focuses on the SQL Server provider's implementation. The OLE DB and ODBC implementations are identical, although some of the internal aspects vary by target database. Some OLE DB or ODBC-accessible databases might not support transactions.

Using a transaction to enclose multiple update statements is simple:

1. Open a connection to the database with a *SqlConnection* object.

2. Create a *SqlTransaction* instance on that connection.

3. Issue SQL statements within the context of the transaction.

4. Either commit or roll back the transaction.

5. Close the database connection.

Instead of creating instances of *SqlTransaction* directly, you generate connection-specific transactions using the *SqlConnection* object's *BeginTransaction* method. Transactions work only on open database connections, so you must call the connection object's *Open* method first.

```csharp
C#
using (SqlConnection linkToDB = new SqlConnection(connectionString))
{
    linkToDB.Open();
    SqlTransaction envelope = linkToDB.BeginTransaction();
```

```vb
Visual Basic
Using linkToDB As SqlConnection = New SqlConnection(connectionString)
    linkToDB.Open()
    Dim envelope As SqlTransaction = linkToDB.BeginTransaction()
```

After obtaining a transaction object, add it to any *SqlCommand* objects that should be part of the transaction.

```csharp
C#
// ----- Include the transaction in the SqlCommand constructor.
SqlCommand updateCommand = new SqlCommand(sqlText, linkToDB, envelope);

// ----- Or add it to an existing SqlCommand object.
SqlCommand updateCommand = new SqlCommand(sqlText, linkToDB);
updateCommand.Transaction = envelope;
```

```vb
Visual Basic
' ----- Include the transaction in the SqlCommand constructor.
Dim updateCommand As New SqlCommand(sqlText, linkToDB, envelope)

' ----- Or add it to an existing SqlCommand object.
Dim updateCommand As New SqlCommand(sqlText, linkToDB)
updateCommand.Transaction = envelope
```

After you've issued all the transaction-specific commands, you can commit or roll back the entire transaction by calling the *SqlTransaction* object's *Commit* or *Rollback* method.

C#

```
// ----- Commit the transaction.
envelope.Commit();

// ----- Rollback the transaction.
envelope.Rollback();
```

Visual Basic

```
' ----- Commit the transaction.
envelope.Commit()

' ----- Rollback the transaction.
envelope.Rollback()
```

You should always call *Commit* or *Rollback* explicitly. If you dispose of the object or allow it to go out of scope without calling one of these two methods, the transaction will be rolled back, but at a time determined by the .NET garbage collection system.

Both *Commit* and *Rollback*—and the initial *BeginTransaction* call as well—generate exceptions if there is a database or local failure in the transaction. Always surround these calls with exception handling statements.

C#

```
try
{
    envelope.Commit();
}
catch (Exception ex)
{
    MessageBox.Show("Error saving data: " + ex.Message);
    try
    {
        envelope.Rollback();
    }
    catch (Exception ex2)
    {
        // ----- Although the rollback generated an error, the
        //       transaction will still be rolled back by the
        //       database because it did not get a commit order.
        MessageBox.Show("Error undoing the changes: " + ex2.Message);
    }
}
```

```vb
Visual Basic
Try
    envelope.Commit()
Catch ex As Exception
    MessageBox.Show("Error saving data: " & ex.Message)
    Try
        envelope.Rollback()
    Catch ex2 As Exception
        ' ----- Although the rollback generated an error, the
        '       transaction will still be rolled back by the
        '       database because it did not get a commit order.
        MessageBox.Show("Error undoing the changes: " & ex2.Message)
    End Try
End Try
```

If you include *SELECT* statements in your transactions, especially on records that will not be modified as part of the transaction, there is a chance that these selected records might become locked during the transaction, preventing other users from making modifications to them, or even reading them. Depending on the configuration of your SQL Server instance, *SELECT* statements might apply "read locks" on the returned records by default. To avoid such locks, exclude *SELECT* statements from your transactions or use the *WITH (NOLOCK)* hint in your SQL Server *SELECT* statements.

```sql
SELECT * FROM OrderEntry WITH (NOLOCK)
WHERE OrderDate >= DATEADD(day, -3, GETDATE())
```

Processing with a Local Transaction: C#

1. Open the "Chapter 12 CSharp" project from the installed samples folder. The project includes a *Windows.Forms* class named *AccountTransfer*, which simulates the transfer of funds between two bank accounts.

2. Open the code for the *AccountTransfer* class. Locate the *GetConnectionString* function, which is a routine that uses a *SqlConnectionStringBuilder* to create a valid connection string to the sample database. It currently includes the following statements:

```csharp
builder.DataSource = @"(local)\SQLExpress";
builder.InitialCatalog = "StepSample";
builder.IntegratedSecurity = true;
```

Adjust these statements as needed to provide access to your own test database.

3. Locate the *TransferLocal* routine. This code performs a transfer between two bank accounts records using a local *SqlTransaction* instance. A *using* block fills most of the procedure's body. Just inside this *using* statement, immediately after the comment "The database must be opened to create the transaction," add the following code:

```
linkToDB.Open();

// ----- Prepare a transaction to surround the transfer.
envelope = linkToDB.BeginTransaction();
```

These statements open the database connection (a requirement for using transactions) and start the transfer's transaction.

4. Just after the "Prepare and perform the withdrawal" comment, add the following statements:

```
sqlText = @"UPDATE BankAccount SET Balance = Balance - @ToTransfer
    WHERE AccountNumber = @FromAccount";
withdrawal = new SqlCommand(sqlText, linkToDB, envelope);
withdrawal.Parameters.AddWithValue("@ToTransfer", toTransfer);
if (OptFromChecking.Checked)
    withdrawal.Parameters.AddWithValue("@FromAccount", CheckingAccountID);
else
    withdrawal.Parameters.AddWithValue("@FromAccount", SavingsAccountID);
```

These lines create a parameterized *UPDATE* query within the context of the *envelope* transaction. The presence of *envelope* as the final argument to the *SqlCommand* constructor provides this context.

5. Just after the "Prepare and perform the deposit" comment, add the following lines:

```
sqlText = @"UPDATE BankAccount SET Balance = Balance + @ToTransfer
    WHERE AccountNumber = @ToAccount";
deposit = new SqlCommand(sqlText, linkToDB, envelope);
deposit.Parameters.AddWithValue("@ToTransfer", toTransfer);
if (OptFromChecking.Checked)
    deposit.Parameters.AddWithValue("@ToAccount", SavingsAccountID);
else
    deposit.Parameters.AddWithValue("@ToAccount", CheckingAccountID);
```

This block is the same as in the previous step, but it performs the second half of the two-statement transaction.

6. Just after the "Perform the transfer" comment within the *try* block, add these three statements:

```
withdrawal.ExecuteNonQuery();
deposit.ExecuteNonQuery();
envelope.Commit();
```

This set of lines performs the actual transaction, issuing distinct *UPDATE* queries for the withdrawal and deposit halves of the atomic transaction. The third method call, *Commit*, makes the transaction permanent. Any failure on any of these three lines raises an exception in the subsequent *catch* block.

7. Just after the "Do a rollback instead" comment, within the inner *try* block, add the following line:

```
envelope.Rollback();
```

This line undoes the transaction in case of failure in the previous step.

8. Run the program. The form that appears lets you transfer funds between a checking and a savings account. If you try to transfer an amount greater than the amount in the source account, the transaction fails due to "check constraints" defined on the SQL Server table that prevent negative values. Select From Checking To Savings as the transfer type and enter **1000** in the Transfer Amount field (or any value that exceeds the balance in the checking account). Click Transfer. The error that occurs triggers a rollback of the transaction. In contrast, operations that transfer funds within the limits of the source account's balance result in a successful, committed transfer.

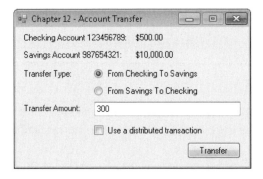

Processing with a Local Transaction: Visual Basic

1. Open the "Chapter 12 VB" project from the installed samples folder. The project includes a *Windows.Forms* class named *AccountTransfer*, which simulates the transfer of funds between two bank accounts.

2. Open the code for the *AccountTransfer* class. Locate the *GetConnectionString* function, which is a routine that uses a *SqlConnectionStringBuilder* to create a valid connection string to the sample database. It currently includes the following statements:

```
builder.DataSource = "(local)\SQLExpress"
builder.InitialCatalog = "StepSample"
builder.IntegratedSecurity = True
```

Adjust these statements as needed to provide access to your own test database.

3. Locate the *TransferLocal* routine. This code performs a transfer between two bank account records using a local *SqlTransaction* instance. A *Using* block fills most of the procedure's body. Just inside this *Using* statement, immediately after the comment "The database must be opened to create the transaction," add the following code:

```
linkToDB.Open()

' ----- Prepare a transaction to surround the transfer.
envelope = linkToDB.BeginTransaction()
```

These statements open the database connection (a requirement for using transactions) and start the transfer's transaction.

4. Just after the "Prepare and perform the withdrawal" comment, add the following statements:

```
sqlText = "UPDATE BankAccount SET Balance = Balance   @ToTransfer " &
    "WHERE AccountNumber = @FromAccount"
withdrawal = New SqlCommand(sqlText, linkToDB, envelope)
withdrawal.Parameters.AddWithValue("@ToTransfer", toTransfer)
If (OptFromChecking.Checked = True) Then
    withdrawal.Parameters.AddWithValue("@FromAccount", CheckingAccountID)
Else
    withdrawal.Parameters.AddWithValue("@FromAccount", SavingsAccountID)
End If
```

These lines create a parameterized *UPDATE* query within the context of the *envelope* transaction. The presence of *envelope* as the final argument to the *SqlCommand* constructor provides this context.

5. Just after the "Prepare and perform the deposit" comment, add the following lines:

```
sqlText = "UPDATE BankAccount SET Balance = Balance + @ToTransfer " &
    "WHERE AccountNumber = @ToAccount"
deposit = New SqlCommand(sqlText, linkToDB, envelope)
deposit.Parameters.AddWithValue("@ToTransfer", toTransfer)
If (OptFromChecking.Checked = True) Then
    deposit.Parameters.AddWithValue("@ToAccount", SavingsAccountID)
Else
    deposit.Parameters.AddWithValue("@ToAccount", CheckingAccountID)
End If
```

This block is the same as in the previous step, but it performs the second half of the two-statement transaction.

6. Just after the "Perform the transfer" comment within the *Try* block, add these three statements:

```
withdrawal.ExecuteNonQuery()
deposit.ExecuteNonQuery()
envelope.Commit()
```

This set of lines performs the actual transaction, issuing distinct *UPDATE* queries for the withdrawal and deposit halves of the atomic transaction. The third method call, *Commit*, makes the transaction permanent. Any failure on any of these three lines raises an exception in the subsequent *Catch* block.

7. Just after the "Do a rollback instead" comment, within the inner *Try* block, add the following line:

```
envelope.Rollback()
```

This line undoes the transaction in case of failure in the previous step.

8. Run the program. The form that appears lets you transfer funds between a checking and a savings account. If you try to transfer an amount greater than the amount in the source account, the transaction fails due to "check constraints" defined on the SQL Server table that prevent negative values. Select From Checking To Savings as the transfer type and enter **1000** in the Transfer Amount field (or any value that exceeds the balance in the checking account). Click Transfer. The error that occurs triggers a rollback of the transaction. In contrast, operations that transfer funds within the limits of the source account's balance result in a successful, committed transfer.

Employing Savepoints

Normally a transaction is an all-or-nothing operation. However, the SQL Server provider also includes support for *savepoints*, which are named partial transactions that can be independently rolled back.

 Note Savepoints are available only with the SQL Server provider. The OLE DB and ODBC providers do not support this feature.

To add a savepoint to a transaction, call the *SqlTransaction* object's *Save* method, passing it the name of the new savepoint.

C#

```csharp
// ----- Run the pre-savepoint transaction statements.
SqlCommand firstCommand = new SqlCommand(sqlText1, linkToDB, envelope);
firstCommand.ExecuteNonQuery();

// ----- Mark this place for possible partial rollback.
envelope.Save("HalfwayPoint");

// ----- Run the post-savepoint transaction statements.
SqlCommand secondCommand = new SqlCommand(sqlText2, linkToDB, envelope);
secondCommand.ExecuteNonQuery();
```

Visual Basic

```vbnet
' ----- Run the pre-savepoint transaction statements.
Dim firstCommand As New SqlCommand(sqlText1, linkToDB, envelope)
firstCommand.ExecuteNonQuery()

' ----- Mark this place for possible partial rollback.
envelope.Save("HalfwayPoint")

' ----- Run the pre-savepoint transaction statements.
Dim secondCommand As New SqlCommand(sqlText2, linkToDB, envelope)
secondCommand.ExecuteNonQuery()
```

Calling the *Rollback* method will roll the transaction back to the very beginning, undoing all statements issued in the context of the transaction. Calling *Rollback* and passing it a savepoint name argument also rolls back the transaction, but only to the state at which the indicated savepoint occurred. In the previous code block, the following statement will roll back the transaction to just after the processing of *firstCommand*, undoing the effects of *secondCommand*:

C#

```csharp
envelope.Rollback("HalfwayPoint");
```

Visual Basic

```vbnet
envelope.Rollback("HalfwayPoint")
```

You can issue as many savepoints as you need within a transaction. You must still issue a final *Commit* or *Rollback* on the transaction to save or cancel the transaction's overall changes.

Using Distributed Transactions

The .NET Framework includes support for *distributed transactions* through the Microsoft Distributed Transaction Coordinator (MSDTC). This system allows an ACID-enabled transaction to span multiple databases on different servers. Platforms beyond standard relational databases can also participate in MSDTC-distributed transactions as long as they provide full *commit/rollback* support for included operations.

Distributed transactions occur through the *System.Transactions.TransactionScope* class. This class is not part of ADO.NET, but ADO.NET does include automatic support for it when you use it in your application. To access this class, you must add a reference to the *System.Transactions.dll* library in your application through the Project | Add Reference menu command in Visual Studio.

To begin a distributed transaction, create an instance of *TransactionScope*.

```
C#
using System.Transactions;

// ----- Later...
using (TransactionScope envelope = new TransactionScope())
{
    // ----- Include all relevant ADO.NET commands here.
```
```
Visual Basic
Imports System.Transactions

' ----- Later...
Using envelope As TransactionScope = New TransactionScope()
    ' ----- Include all relevant ADO.NET commands here.
```

That's it. As long as the *TransactionScope* object is valid (not disposed), all new ADO.NET database connections become part of the distributed transaction. You don't need to use *SqlTransaction* objects or provide support for distributed transactions; it's automatic.

The *TransactionScope* instance monitors all relevant activity until it is disposed (by calling *Dispose* or letting the object go out of scope), at which time the entire transaction is either committed or rolled back. By default, the transaction is rolled back. To ensure that the transaction is committed, call the *TransactionScope* object's *Complete* method.

C#

```csharp
using (TransactionScope envelope = new TransactionScope())
{
    // ----- Include all relevant ADO.NET commands here, then...
    envelope.Complete();
}
```

Visual Basic

```vb
Using envelope As TransactionScope = New TransactionScope()
    ' ----- Include all relevant ADO.NET commands here, then...
    envelope.Complete()
End Using
```

For those times when you want to specifically exclude a connection (and its associated commands) from the active *TransactionScope*, add *"Enlist=False"* to the connection string.

```
Data Source=MyServer;Integrated Security=True;
    Initial Catalog=MyDatabase;Enlist=False
```

If you have a connection that is not enlisted in the overall transaction, you can move it into the transaction scope using the connection's *EnlistTransaction* method. After a connection is part of a transaction scope, it cannot be delisted.

Note When running an application that creates a distributed transaction, you might receive the following error: "MSDTC on server '*servername*' is unavailable". This typically indicates that the Distributed Transaction Controller service is not running. Start the service through either the Services applet or the Component Services applet, both of which can be found in the Administrative Tools section of the Windows Control Panel.

Processing with a Distributed Transaction: C#

> **Note** This exercise uses the "Chapter 12 CSharp" sample project and continues from where the previous exercise in this chapter left off.

1. Open the code for the *AccountTransfer* class. Locate the *TransferDistributed* function. This code performs a transfer between two bank account records using a distributed transaction. The body of the routine hosts two nested *using* blocks.

```
// ----- Create the withdrawal and deposit connections.
using (SqlConnection sourceLink =
    new SqlConnection(GetConnectionString()))
{
    using (SqlConnection destLink =
        new SqlConnection(GetConnectionString()))
    {
        // ----- Lots of database-related code here...
    }
}
```

2. Surround the two nested *using* blocks with a third outer *using* block.

```
using (TransactionScope envelope = new TransactionScope())
{
    // ----- The two original nested using blocks appear here...
}
```

This statement block creates the *TransactionScope*, which is the object responsible for managing the distributed transaction.

3. Just after the "Transfer complete. Commit the transaction" comment, add the following line:

```
envelope.Complete();
```

This method call commits the entire transaction.

4. Run the program. In the local-transaction sample earlier in this chapter, attempting to overdraw funds caused the transaction to fail in the first half of the two-part update: the withdrawal portion. You can force a failure in the second half of the transaction by selecting a transfer in the opposite direction and entering a negative value (with an absolute value that exceeds the target account) in the Transfer Amount field.

   Select From Savings To Checking as the transfer type and enter **-1000** (negative 1000) in the Transfer Amount field—or any value that, if positive, would exceed the balance in the checking account. Select the Use A Distributed Transaction field and then click Transfer. The error that occurs triggers a rollback of the distributed transaction due to a check constraint failure in the deposit portion (the second half) of the transaction.

Processing with a Distributed Transaction: Visual Basic

> **Note** This exercise uses the "Chapter 12 VB" sample project and continues from where the previous exercise in this chapter left off.

1. Open the code for the *AccountTransfer* class. Locate the *TransferDistributed* function. This code performs a transfer between two bank account records using a distributed transaction. The body of the routine hosts two nested *Using* blocks.

```vb
' ----- Create the withdrawal and deposit connections.
Using sourceLink As SqlConnection =
        New SqlConnection(GetConnectionString())
    Using destLink As SqlConnection =
            New SqlConnection(GetConnectionString())
        ' ----- Lots of database-related code here...
    End Using
End Using
```

2. Surround the two nested *Using* blocks with a third outer *Using* block.

```vb
Using envelope As TransactionScope = New TransactionScope()
    ' ----- The two original nested using blocks appear here...
End Using
```

This statement block creates the *TransactionScope*, which is the object responsible for managing the distributed transaction.

3. Just after the "Transfer complete. Commit the transaction" comment, add the following line:

```vb
envelope.Complete()
```

This method call commits the entire transaction.

4. Run the program. In the local-transaction sample earlier in this chapter, attempting to overdraw funds caused the transaction to fail in the first half of the two-part update: the withdrawal portion. You can force a failure in the second half of the transaction by selecting a transfer in the opposite direction and entering a negative value (with an absolute value that exceeds the target account) in the Transfer Amount field.

Select From Savings To Checking as the transfer type and enter **-1000** (negative 1000) in the Transfer Amount field—or any value that, if positive, would exceed the balance in the checking account. Select the Use A Distributed Transaction field, and then click Transfer. The error that occurs triggers a rollback of the distributed transaction due to a check constraint failure in the deposit portion (the second half) of the transaction.

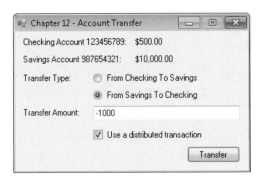

Summary

This chapter introduced the *SqlTransaction* class and its distributed counterpart, *TransactionScope*. Both tools allow you to treat multiple discrete database updates as a single, undivided whole. This provides a greater level of data reliability when the risks associated with a partial data update are high.

ADO.NET's disconnected model lends itself well to the optimistic concurrency data locking model. It's a common scenario for systems where the chance of simultaneous updates to a single record is very low. For situations where pessimistic concurrency and a more preemptive record locking strategy have been the norm, ADO.NET might require you to try different ways of accomplishing the same tasks.

Chapter 12 Quick Reference

To	Do This
Process statements using a local transaction	Open a connection to a database using *SqlConnection*.
	Call the connection object's *BeginTransaction* method to obtain the transaction object.
	Call the necessary SQL statements for data modification, including the transaction object in each *SqlCommand*.
	Call the transaction object's *Commit* method to save the changes.
Roll back a local transaction	Create a valid *SqlConnection* and process data modification statements as needed.
	Call the transaction object's *Rollback* method.
Process statements using a distributed transaction	Start the MSDTC if not already running.
	Create an instance of *TransactionScope*.
	Process your SQL statements as needed, excluding the use of *SqlTransaction*.
	If the transaction is successful, call the *TransactionScope* object's *Complete* method.
	Call the *TransactionScope* object's *Dispose* method.

Part III
Entity Framework

Chapter 13: Introducing the Entity Framework

Chapter 14: Visualizing Data Models

Chapter 15: Querying Data in the Framework

Chapter 16: Understanding Entities Through Objects

Chapter 13
Introducing the Entity Framework

After completing this chapter, you will be able to:

- Understand the high-level concepts of the ADO.NET Entity Framework

- Distinguish between the three main Entity Framework modeling layers

- Identify the general relationships between database elements and parallel elements in the Entity Framework

ADO.NET has been included with the .NET Framework since its initial release in 2002. As the primary data layer of the Framework, it provides great general-purpose access to external data sources. Starting with Service Pack 1 of Visual Studio 2008 (and the associated .NET Framework version 3.5), Microsoft enhanced ADO.NET with a library of additional function-ality known as the *Entity Framework* (EF). The question is this: Why? Why would Microsoft augment a system that already provided sufficient features to work with both internal and external data in a generic, convenient format?

This chapter answers that question by introducing the Entity Framework and its major con-ceptual components. It focuses on the two primary benefits of using the Framework on top of ADO.NET's core data functionality: (1) the ability to focus on the conceptual view of how data fits together instead of on the physical view of how it is stored in the database; and (2) the move away from the database-centric reality of independent tables joined in relation-ship toward a true object-oriented model in which related data values are treated as integral members of each other's data worldviews.

 Note The four EF-related chapters in this book offer only a brief introduction to the flexible and extensive Entity Framework. For expanded coverage of the Framework and how to use it in your projects, review the Visual Studio online help. The Microsoft Press book *Programming the Microsoft® ADO.NET Entity Framework* provides a more detailed exploration of EF and its components.

Understanding the Entity Framework

ADO.NET provides convenient programmer access to content located in an external data source or crafted within the application. One of the data layer's core strengths is its capabil-ity to simulate the *logical implementation* of the underlying data source. Database tables stored in a relational database such as SQL Server can be brought into an application, complete with constructs that emulate the join relationships and columnar data types of each imported table. Foreign keys play an important role in bringing data together, both in the database and in the *DataSet* representation.

By processing the data that comes into your program through a *DataReader* or by adjusting the *TableMapping* rules associated with a *DataAdapter*, you can modify the presentation of the incoming data structures from the way they appear in the underlying database. Yet even with such modifications, many *DataSet* and *DataTable* representations of external data tend to resemble the logical view of the source data.

When working with tables of customers and orders, an associated *DataSet* will often contain *Customer* and *Order DataTable* objects that are little more than local copies of the true tables. Although this benefit is very useful for developers focused on a specific database schema, it is also a disadvantage, especially when changes to the external schema must be constantly reflected in code. The table-specific focus of the *DataSet* also forces applications to work with data according to the dictates and limitations of the database, instead of on the enhanced features that languages such as C# and Visual Basic bring to the data processing table. Additionally, ADO.NET's use of generic object collections for row values removes the strongly typed benefits of programming in .NET.

Note Visual Studio 2005 and version 2.0 of the .NET Framework introduced *strongly typed DataSets*. These wizard-generated classes, derived from *DataSet* and ADO.NET's other disconnected table classes, added imported table and column definitions as true class members. Strongly typed data sets are still available in Visual Studio 2010. However, the Entity Framework provides enhanced database interaction capabilities and additional features that often make it a better option for defining strongly typed views of external data. Strongly typed data sets are not discussed further in this book.

The Entity Framework helps resolve such issues by putting the focus on the *conceptual implementation* of the data; a class-based view of how all the data works together. Instead of working with distinct table records that refer to each other's records indirectly through foreign key values, EF objects expose these relationships as true object-oriented class memberships. Where a *DataSet* may contain separate *Customer* and *Order* tables that need to have their records joined manually in code, a *Customer* entity class generated by the Entity Framework includes an *OrderEntries* member, with each customer instance already aware of its associated orders. Foreign keys are still important, but the Framework figures out how to use them, leaving code free to access the results in a true instance-based environment.

Defining the Entity Framework's Terms

The Entity Framework works with different types of flat, relational, and hierarchical data sources—not just traditional databases such as SQL Server—so the names used for the different components of the Framework were selected to reflect those different usage options. Still, in light of its standard ADO.NET underpinnings and its excellent support for SQL Server and similar databases, it is helpful to understand its features as they relate to relational database concepts.

- **Model**   The Entity Framework is, above all, a system for designing conceptual models of your data. These models are saved in an XML format from which the Framework generates the specific source code classes. All terms defined here (entity, association, and so on) are primarily model-based, although the Framework generates classes and code that makes them more than just items in a model diagram.

- **Entity**   The core of the Entity Framework is, naturally, the *Entity*. With its ADO.NET core, you might think, incorrectly, that an entity finds its parallel in the *DataSet* or *DataTable*. Instead, the parallel for an entity is a single table row, a record, a *DataRow*. A customer entity is a single customer, with a distinct name, address, set of orders, and so on. The Framework generates the custom classes (known as *Entity Types*) from which specific entity objects are instantiated.

- **Entities**   The plural form of an entity has a separate existence in the Entity Framework, implemented as a generic collection of a specific entity. Similar in concept to a table or a *DataTable*, entities are created by the Framework to expose enumerable instances of a specific custom entity. This parent-child relationship smoothes the transition from table-row-style database content to inheritable class-based data management.

- **Property**   The field or column members of an entity (similar to *DataColumn* instances in a *DataTable*) are known as *properties*. This makes sense because they are implemented as standard class properties, complete with configurable getters and setters. One or more properties in an entity are designated as the *entity key*, which uniquely defines each entity. All entities require an entity key. Multiple properties can be defined together as a *complex type*, sort of a user-defined data type for entities.

- **Association**   A relationship established between two entities is known as an *association*, and is defined through an *association type*. Similar to a database-level table join or a *DataRelation* in standard ADO.NET, associations define the single or multicolumn connections between different entities. The properties on either end of the relationship are known as *association ends*. The cardinality of an association (or in EF parlance, the multiplicity of its association endpoints; whether the association is one-to-one, one-to-many, and so on) helps determine how the association exposes data. Unlike the *DataRelation* implementation, associations are true bidirectional access points between entity instances. An entity can exist even if the tables that provide the content for associated entities lack a database-level join specification.

- **Association set**   All association instances for a defined association type appear as a distinct collection called an *association set*. On the model side of the Framework, an association set contains the field definitions that describe a single association between two tables.

- **Navigation property**   A *navigation property* exposes the available data at the other end of an association. For instance, in a customer-order association, the *Orders* navigation property on a *Customer* entity object provides access to the zero or more *Order* entity instances associated with the specific customer. When viewed from the order side of that same relationship, a customer-targeted navigation property on an *Order* entity instance links to the *Customer* object to which that order belongs. An entity can also contain foreign keys to an associated entity, but these keys provide less direct access to related data.

- **Entity set**   An *entity set* is the logical container for an entity *and any other entities derived from that first entity*. For example, a *PastDueOrder* entity definition and the *Order* definition from which it derives would appear together in a single entity set. The closest parallel in a relational database might be a table and any views created that use only content from that base table.

- **Entity container**   One or more entity sets appear within the context of an *entity container*, the outermost conceptual construct within the Entity Framework. When writing code that interacts with entities, you will always start by creating an instance of an entity container, known as a *context*. The entity container is a lot like a database or *DataSet*, each with its collection of tables (entities).

Entity Framework models define an entity container, which in turn includes entity sets and association sets. An entity set contains one or more (derived) entity types. Entities are defined by their properties, both simple and complex. The definition of an association always includes the two endpoints that join related entities. Classes generated by the Framework implement in code the entities, properties, and associations defined in the model.

Understanding the Entity Framework's Layers

In the Entity Framework, you define all the entities, associations, entity sets, and so on through XML schema dialects. The Framework uses the XML-defined model to generate classes in Visual Basic or C#. These classes implement the data environment described by the model. Each model includes three main layers that help isolate the programmatic access to the data from the database-managed storage of the raw data. The three layers are the conceptual model (or conceptual layer), the storage model (storage layer), and the mappings (mapping layer).

Understanding the Conceptual Model

For developers, the *conceptual model* is frequently the primary focus in setting up an Entity Framework experience. This layer defines the *Entity Data Model* (EDM), the data organization concepts that will find their way into generated application-side instantiated classes. The conceptual model is defined with the *Conceptual Schema Definition Language* (CSDL), which is an XML schema definition. In your project, CSDL files have a .csdl extension.

 Note As discussed in the following text and in the next chapter, models generated using Visual Studio design tools store the resulting XML content in a file with an .edmx file extension. The XML specifications for the three model layers all appear in this single file instead of in separate files with their own file extensions.

Whenever the model changes, the Framework can generate a new set of implementation classes, simplifying the process of propagating database-level changes into your application's source code.

Each model defines a *namespace* in which its entities, associations, and other key components appear. Like standard .NET namespaces, EF namespaces help group related entities under a common name and allow for differentiation between otherwise identically named entities.

 Note Visual Studio includes a *Generate Database Wizard* that can use a valid CSDL model to generate a SQL Server database with all needed tables and supporting elements. Use of the wizard is beyond the scope of this book. For information on this tool, search for "Generate Database Wizard" in the Visual Studio 2010 online help.

Understanding the Storage Model

The *storage model* identifies the underlying database-level elements that support the conceptual model. Sometimes called the *logical model*, the storage model layer defines the application-side experience of a database-side logical (and ultimately, physical) implementation.

Like the conceptual model, the storage model includes entity and association definitions in a model-language syntax, independent of any specific database. But it also contains database-specific commands (queries and stored procedures) that will eventually find their way to ADO.NET connection and command objects.

Your code defines the storage model using the *Store Schema Definition Language* (SSDL), another XML schema definition. SSDL files use the extension .ssdl.

Understanding the Model Mappings

The *model mapping* layer provides the glue between the conceptual model and the storage model. Using the *Mapping Specification Language* (MSL), the mapping indicates how entities, properties, and associations in the conceptual model tie to specific items in the storage model, which in turn defines the path to the database home for each piece of data. Mapping files use an .msl file extension.

Using the Entity Framework

Using a model in the Entity Framework requires four essential steps:

1. Build the model.

2. Generate the objects.

3. Instantiate a context.

4. Run queries within the context.

Building the Model

As mentioned previously, an Entity Framework model appears as XML content using three distinct XML schemas. The Visual Studio online help includes full documentation for these schema languages, so it is possible to handcraft your schema design. However, most developers will likely appreciate a more visual approach to crafting conceptual and logical models, and the map that links them. For this reason, Microsoft included in Visual Studio the *ADO.NET Entity Data Model Designer*, a drag-and-drop entity design experience that manages an EF model's conceptual, storage, and mapping layer options.

The Designer's generated XML content (stored with an .edmx file extension in your project) encapsulates all three portions of the schema definition using CSDL, SSDL, and MSL. When designing an entity model based on an existing database, the Designer's *Entity Data Model Wizard* imports tables, views, and stored procedure definitions from any supported database format. Chapter 14, "Visualizing Data Models," shows the *Entity Data Model Designer* and its associated wizard in action.

The following CSDL content presents an Entity Framework conceptual model of two related tables: *Customer* (with *ID* and *FullName* fields) and *Order* (with *ID*, *OrderDate*, and *Total*, plus a *Customer* foreign key):

```xml
<EntityContainer Name="StepSampleConnection" LazyLoadingEnabled="true">
  <EntitySet Name="Customers" EntityType="StepByStep.Customer" />
  <EntitySet Name="OrderEntries" EntityType="StepByStep.OrderEntry" />
  <AssociationSet Name="CustOrderLinkSet" Association="CustOrderLink">
    <End Role="Customer" EntitySet="Customers" />
    <End Role="OrderEntry" EntitySet="OrderEntries" />
  </AssociationSet>
</EntityContainer>
<EntityType Name="Customer">
  <Key>
    <PropertyRef Name="ID" />
  </Key>
  <Property Name="ID" Type="Int64" Nullable="false" />
  <Property Name="FullName" Type="String" Nullable="false"
      MaxLength="50" FixedLength="false" />
  <Property Name="PhoneNumber" Type="String" MaxLength="15"
      FixedLength="false" />
  <NavigationProperty Name="OrderEntries" Relationship="CustOrderLink"
      FromRole="Customer" ToRole="OrderEntry" />
</EntityType>
<EntityType Name="OrderEntry">
  <Key>
    <PropertyRef Name="ID" />
  </Key>
  <Property Name="ID" Type="Int64" Nullable="false" />
  Property Name="Customer" Type="Int64" Nullable="false" />
  <Property Name="OrderDate" Type="DateTime" Nullable="false" />
  <Property Name="Total" Type="Decimal" Nullable="false"
    Precision="19" Scale="4" />
  <NavigationProperty Name="OrderCustomer" Relationship="CustOrderLink"
      FromRole="OrderEntry" ToRole="Customer" />
</EntityType>
<Association Name="CustOrderLink">
  <End Role="Customer" Type="StepByStep.Customer" Multiplicity="1" />
  <End Role="OrderEntry" Type="StepByStep.OrderEntry" Multiplicity="*" />
  <ReferentialConstraint>
    <Principal Role="Customer">
      <PropertyRef Name="ID" />
    </Principal>
    <Dependent Role="OrderEntry">
      <PropertyRef Name="Customer" />
    </Dependent>
  </ReferentialConstraint>
</Association>
```

The *<EntityContainer>* entry defines the core of the model, with its listing of *<EntitySet>* and *<AssociationSet>* tags. Entity sets are fully defined down to the column level in separate *<EntityType>* blocks. Likewise, *<AssociationSet>* entries depend on *<Association>* definitions found elsewhere in the XML.

The storage model and mapping XML sections provide equivalent definition experiences using their respective SSDL and MSL design languages.

Generating the Objects

The XML content for an Entity Framework model is not immediately usable in your code to manage data. Instead, a set of data objects must be generated from the conceptual and storage models and from the mapping layer.

When you add models to a project using the *ADO.NET Entity Data Model Designer*, this data object generation happens automatically. Saved changes to the model trigger a generation of Visual Basic or C# code-behind in a separate .vb (Visual Basic) or .cs (C#) source code "designer" file.

When designing entity models manually, after creating the distinct conceptual model, storage model, and mapping layer files in your project, you must generate the object layer using *edmgen.exe*, which is a command-line tool included with Visual Studio.

> **Note** Use of the *edmgen.exe* tool is beyond the scope of this chapter. See the Visual Studio online help for details on using this tool.

The generated object layer builds classes for each entity; classes that derive from the *EntityObject* base class found in the *System.Data.Objects* namespace (along with many EF-related class definitions). Much of this class' content defines ordinary public properties that are based on the property definitions in the conceptual model. As an example, here is the definition for the *Customer.FullName* property, as generated by Visual Studio:

```
C#
[EdmScalarPropertyAttribute(EntityKeyProperty=false, IsNullable=false)]
[DataMemberAttribute()]
public global::System.String FullName
{
    get
    {
        Return _FullName;
    }
    set
    {
        OnFullNameChanging(value);
        ReportPropertyChanging("FullName");
        _FullName = StructuralObject.SetValidValue(value, false);
        ReportPropertyChanged("FullName");
        OnFullNameChanged();
    }
}
Private global::System.String _FullName;
```

Visual Basic

```vb
<EdmScalarPropertyAttribute(EntityKeyProperty:=false, IsNullable:=false)>
<DataMemberAttribute()>
Public Property FullName() As Global.System.String
    Get
        Return _FullName
    End Get
    Set
        OnFullNameChanging(value)
        ReportPropertyChanging("FullName")
        _FullName = StructuralObject.SetValidValue(value, False)
        ReportPropertyChanged("FullName")
        OnFullNameChanged()
    End Set
End Property
Private _FullName As Global.System.String
```

Other class elements allow the Entity Framework to manage the entire lifetime of an entity, from its initial retrieval from the database to its concurrency-aware update of that same database with modified entity content.

Instantiating the Context

All access to live content as represented by the model is through a *context*, an instance of *System.Data.Objects.ObjectContext*. A context is an instantiated version of the *<EntityContainer>* that exposes all entities and associations defined in the model.

To create a context, instantiate a new *ObjectContext* object, passing it a connection string, which typically contains the name given to the entity container (stored in the *<EntityContainer>* tag's *name* attribute).

C#

```csharp
// ----- The default name of an entity container in visually designed
//       models always ends in "Entities."
ObjectContext context = new ObjectContext("name=SalesOrderEntities");
```

Visual Basic

```vb
' ----- The default name of an entity container in visually designed
'       models always ends in "Entities."
Dim context As New ObjectContext("name=SalesOrderEntities")
```

The context object provides access to all available data in the entities, plus general information about the model-made-real.

Running Framework Queries

The Entity Framework provides four key methods for querying data exposed by the entity model.

- Write SQL-like queries using the *Entity SQL* language. Chapter 15, "Querying Data in the Framework," discusses these queries and their syntax.

- Use query builder methods, a system that employs query-like class methods, such as *Where* and *OrderBy*, on entity collections to obtain the desired results. (Internally, the Entity SQL language converts its queries to query builder format for processing.) Chapter 16, "Understanding Entities Through Objects," introduces the core concepts and methods involved in these queries.

- Use the C# and Visual Basic LINQ sublanguages to query the entity objects directly. Chapters 17 through 20 focus on the LINQ aspects of querying ADO.NET data. Chapter 19, "Using LINQ to Entities," demonstrates using LINQ to query model-generated entities.

- Allow queries via HTTP requests using WCF Data Services. Chapter 22, "Providing RESTful Services with WCF Data Services," provides a brief description of this somewhat indirect way of accessing EF content.

The simplest possible query involves asking the context for all instances of a particular entity. The following statements use the context object's *CreateObjectSet* method to generate a collection of *Customer* (entity) instances:

```
C#
ObjectSet<Customer> query =
    context.CreateObjectSet<Customer>();
foreach (Customer oneCustomer in query)
{
    // ----- Take action on each Customer instance, such as...
    AddCustomerToReport(oneCustomer.FullName);
}
```

```
Visual Basic
Dim query As ObjectSet(Of Customer) =
    context.CreateObjectSet(Of Customer)()
For Each oneCustomer As Customer In query
    ' ----- Take action on each Customer instance, such as...
    AddCustomerToReport(oneCustomer.FullName)
Next oneCustomer
```

Summary

This chapter provided an overview of the major concepts in ADO.NET's new Entity Framework functionality. Although much more complex than the ADO.NET class library that enables it, EF is also much more flexible in its ability to provide an object-oriented development experience when interacting with externally stored data. With its supporting visual designer, its XML definition layers, and its query capabilities, the Entity Framework provides a formalized method of interacting with raw data in a way that best matches the conceptual model that the data was designed to represent.

The next three chapters delve even deeper into the usability features of the Entity Framework. Chapter 14 focuses on the visual design environment that most programmers will use to create EF-centric applications. Chapters 15 and 16 introduce specifics on working with data through the objects of a generated conceptual model.

Chapter 13 Quick Reference

To	Do This
Define a model for business objects or similar programmatic elements	Design a conceptual model using the *Conceptual Schema Definition Language* (CSDL), either manually or through Visual Studio's entity design features.
Access EF-modeled data at runtime	Create an instance of *ObjectContext*, passing it the name of the entity container.
	Use the methods and properties of the context to retrieve the data.
	Optionally, use one of EF's query tools to access and modify data.
Generate an object layer manually	Use the *edmgen.exe* command-line tool.

Chapter 14
Visualizing Data Models

After completing this chapter, you will be able to:

- Design an entity model using drag-and-drop techniques
- Describe how Visual Studio converts Entity Framework models to source code
- Import objects from an existing database into the Entity Framework

ADO.NET's Entity Framework (EF) rests on a foundation of XML schema files. From the conceptual model used in your applications to the mapping links between your code and an external database, EF stores its core modeling data using three different XML schema languages. If you already understand XML, using these schema variants is not overwhelming. But trying to handcraft three layers of modeling data for the dozens or even hundreds of database objects that support a complex enterprise application is a considerable undertaking.

Fortunately, Visual Studio includes the *ADO.NET Entity Data Model Designer*, a visual design tool that makes model design as simple as adding controls to a Windows Forms application. This chapter shows you how to use the Designer and its various design elements. Whether you are importing an existing database schema into an application or creating custom entities for an application's internal use, the Entity Data Model Designer will help you move from the model design phase to actual software development quickly and easily.

Designing an Entity Framework Model

Given the complexity of the Entity Framework, the Entity Data Model Designer included with Visual Studio is surprisingly simple. All you need to use it is an existing Visual Studio project.

Using the Entity Data Model Wizard

You can build a model using the Entity Data Model Designer starting from a blank slate, letting you model new entities as needed within your application. For many projects, though, you'll create the base model from the logical objects stored in an existing database. When you add a new Entity Data Model (EDM) to your project, Visual Studio prompts you to import tables, stored procedures, and other objects from an existing database using the *ADO.NET Entity Data Model Wizard*.

> **Note** The wizard's capability to build a model from an existing database can be limited by security rights and restrictions imposed on your database account. Make sure you have sufficient rights to the database tables and elements that you will model in your application.

Similar to the Data Source Configuration Wizard demonstrated in Chapter 1, "Introducing ADO.NET 4," the Entity Data Model Wizard guides you through the database selection and connection process, which serves four main purposes:

- **To build the connection string for both the model and the target database.** Built upon standard ADO.NET connection strings, this wizard adds EF-specific metadata key-value pairs that help the Framework access the three XML-based modeling layers.

```
metadata=res://*/Model1.csdl|res://*/Model1.ssdl|res://*/Model1.msl;
provider=System.Data.SqlClient;
provider connection string='Data Source=(local)\SQLExpress;
Initial Catalog=StepSample;Integrated Security=True;
Connect Timeout=30;User Instance=True'
```

  In this sample, the expected SQL Server connection string comes after three resource references that identify the Conceptual Schema Definition Language (CSDL), Store Schema Definition Language (SSDL), and Mapping Specification Language (MSL) modeling documents.

- **To build an application-side storage layer that parallels the database-side tables, views, and stored procedures specified in the wizard.** This layer appears within your application using the SSDL schema language, a layer that is only indirectly accessible through the model designer.

- **To create a conceptual model of the imported storage items.** At first, this model will be nearly identical to the logical organization of the storage layer. You will have the opportunity to adjust this model to meet the needs of your application. This layer is created using the CSDL schema and is presented in the visual designer as a series of database modeling objects on a design surface.

- **To link the storage and conceptual models with mappings using the MSL schema language.** An additional Visual Studio panel called the Mapping Details panel lets you modify the mapping relationships for all entities and associations included in the conceptual model.

That's a lot of activity. Fortunately, the wizard performs most of it through a few point-and-click actions.

Importing Database Tables as Entities

1. Create a new Windows Forms application (or almost any standard Visual Studio application) using either C# or Visual Basic.

2. In the Visual Studio development environment, select the Project | Add New Item menu command. When the Add New Item dialog box appears, select ADO.NET Entity Data Model from the list of template items. Change the default item name to **SalesOrder.edmx**. Click Add.

3. The Entity Data Model Wizard appears. On the Choose Model Contents panel, select Generate From Database; then click Next.

4. On the Choose Your Data Connection panel, either select an existing connection to the book's sample database from the drop-down list of connections or click New Connection to locate the sample database.

 Note The Visual Studio 2010 Entity Framework tools do not support SQL Server 2000 or earlier. When importing objects from a SQL Server database, you must use SQL Server 2005 or higher.

The EF-modified connection string appears in the middle of the panel. If you use SQL Server security with a plain-text password, the wizard will ask you to indicate whether to store this unsecured connection string. For this example, select Yes if prompted. The Save Entity Connection Settings In App.Config As option near the bottom of the panel should already be selected. Under this field, enter **SalesOrderEntities** as the configuration name. Click Next.

5. The Choose Your Database Objects panel appears.

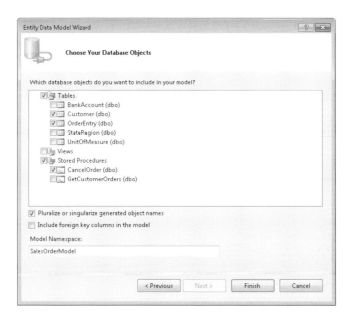

In this hierarchical list of objects, select the Customer and OrderEntry tables, plus the CancelOrder stored procedure. The Include Foreign Key Columns In The Model field is already selected, which in this case will add the *OrderEntry.Customer* database field as a distinct conceptual property. Maintaining this setting also limits your ability to modify the mapping details between the two tables. Clear this field. Enter **SalesOrderModel** as the Model Namespace. Click Finish to close the wizard and generate the model.

Note Imported views and table-valued stored procedures are read-only in the model. You can modify the model to add support for updates if you provide the relevant SQL commands or stored procedures yourself.

6. The model appears in the main Visual Studio window as *SalesOrder.edmx*. The design surface includes distinct *Customer* and *OrderEntry* entities that are connected by a line.

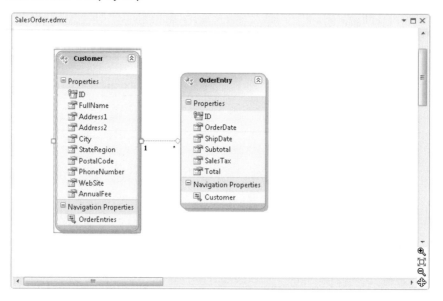

Entity Data Model Designer

The design surface of the Entity Data Model Designer hosts visual representations of entities and associations. If you have worked with other third-party entity-relationship modeling tools, the presentation should be familiar. Each entity appears as a collapsible rectangle with the name of the entity in bold at the top. Below the name is a list of defined entity properties, followed by any navigation properties.

Associations appear as lines connecting related entities. Although the line does not indicate which properties are joined by the association, the cardinality (that is, the multiplicity of the association endpoints) does appear as indicators on either end of the line.

The bottom-right corner of the Designer includes four display controls that let you adjust the view of the model. From top to bottom, the four controls are: Zoom In, Zoom To 100%,

Zoom Out, and Move Via A Thumbnail View. Right-click on the design surface to see additional view management options through a shortcut menu.

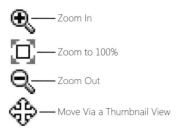

Zoom In

Zoom to 100%

Zoom Out

Move Via a Thumbnail View

The Designer's main purpose is to simplify the creation and editing of entities and their associations. You perform most of these editing activities by clicking entities, entity properties, or associations. You then use the Visual Studio Properties panel to modify the various settings of the selected entity, property, or association. Right-clicking entities, properties, associations, or even on the design surface provides access to additional editing and model management features.

A full listing of editing activities is available in the Visual Studio online help. The following list shows some the main tasks you can accomplish using the Model Designer:

- **Edit entities**   To add a new entity, right-click the design surface and select Add | Entity from the shortcut menu. The Add Entity dialog box that appears lets you specify the new entity name, its primary key (if any), and any inheritance relationship it has to an existing entity.

On the design surface, select an existing entity and use the Visual Studio Properties panel to manage its basic settings. To remove an entity, click that entity in the Designer and press Delete.

- **Edit properties**   To create a new property within an entity, right-click the entity and select one of the Add | Property choices from the shortcut menu. The Designer supports three types of properties: scalar properties, which are simple types such as strings and numbers; navigation properties, which enable natural links between different entities; and complex properties, a grouping of other simple types based on some conceptual relationship. Complex types—such as an *Address* type that contains distinct street, city, and postal code properties—can be defined independently by right-clicking the design surface and selecting the Add | Complex Type shortcut command.

- **Edit associations**   Add a new association by right-clicking an entity and choosing Add | Association from the shortcut menu. The Add Association dialog box that appears lets you define the endpoints of the association, including the multiplicity of each end.

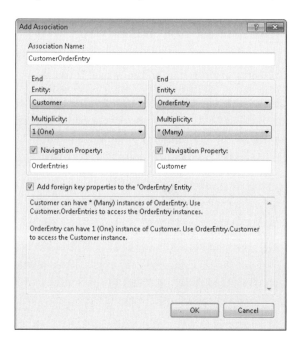

Select an association and use the Visual Studio Properties panel to manage its settings. (Most of the settings are unavailable if the association is based on a storage layer foreign key relationship.) To remove an association, click its line in the Designer and press Delete.

- **Refactor complex types**   The Designer can craft a new complex property (and its underlying complex type) from an entity's existing properties. To create such a complex property, select all involved properties within the visual entity. Right-click the selected group and choose Refactor Into New Complex Type from the shortcut menu.

- **Edit function imports**   Function imports are database-level stored procedures as expressed through an entity container. Once defined, calling a stored procedure is as simple as making a normal class-based method call. The Add Function Import dialog box, available through the Designer's Add | Function Import shortcut command, lets you locate and define these new function calls.

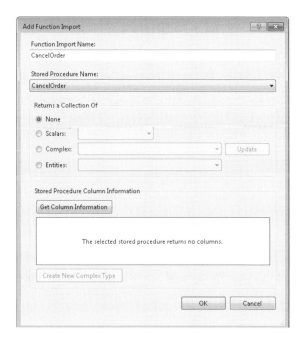

The dialog box can auto-detect the procedure's return type, although you might need to make slight adjustments. Having an accurate return type allows you to use a defined function with the different editing operations of an entity or entity component.

- **Auto-update the model**   If the underlying database objects change in a way that affects the model, you can refresh the model by using the Update Model From Database shortcut command through a right-click on the design surface.

Each time you save changes to your model (or allow it to be auto-saved as configured through your Visual Studio preferences), Visual Studio regenerates the Visual Basic or C# source code object layer representation of the model. To view this code, open the *<model-name>.Designer.cs* or *<modelname>.Designer.vb* file from the Solution Explorer panel.

> **Note** Visual Basic hides this file by default. To access the file, click the Show All Files toolbar button within the Solution Explorer panel.

Any changes you make within this designer file will be lost the next time Visual Studio generates the model's object layer. *You should not make changes directly to this file!* However, because the generated code consists of standard .NET classes, you can add a partial class file to your project or use other language-specific or Entity Framework–specific features to enhance the generated content.

> **Note** Visual Studio uses the "default code generator" when building a model's object layer. You can override this default, and even write your own object layer generation rules, by adjusting some of the default model settings. See the "Managing the Object Layer" section on page 241 of this chapter for information on controlling the code generation process.

Changes made to the model do not propagate back to the underlying database. The purpose of the model is to provide a meaningful conceptual view of the data to your application, a view that does not need to exactly match the logical structure of the database.

Creating a Complex Property from Scalar Properties

> **Note** This exercise continues the previous exercise in this chapter.

1. In the *Customer* entity on the Entity Data Model Designer's design surface, use the mouse along with the Shift or Control keys to select all the following properties at the same time: *Address1, Address2, City, StateRegion,* and *PostalCode*.

2. Right-click the group and then select Refactor Into New Complex Type from the short cut menu.

The Designer will replace the previously selected properties with a single property named *ComplexProperty*.

3. Right-click the *ComplexProperty* property and then choose Rename from the shortcut menu. Change the name of the property to **Address**.

4. Save changes to the model or the project to regenerate the object layer.

Working with the Mapping Details Panel

The focus of the Designer's visual design surface is on the conceptual model, the CSDL content as expressed through a convenient Visual Studio editor. The Entity Framework design tools also include a *Mapping Details* panel that lets you modify the mapping layer (the MSL content) as it relates to the conceptual model.

Note Although you can build a storage layer manually using the SSDL schema language, and although the Entity Data Model Wizard generates SSDL content based on an external data source, the Entity Data Model Designer does not include features that let you directly modify the storage layer.

If not already available in your Visual Studio Integrated Development Environment (IDE), access the Mapping Details panel by right-clicking the model's visual design surface and selecting Mapping Details from the shortcut menu.

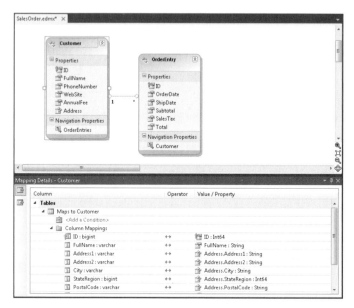

To use the Mapping Details panel, select an entity from the visual design surface. The panel displays all column mappings already defined for the entity, with storage model properties on the left half and conceptual model properties to their right. To modify the conceptual property for a storage model property, click in the *Value / Property* column to the right of the storage model property name and use its drop-down list to select a different conceptual model property.

The Mapping Details panel lets you link properties from multiple storage layer entities (that is, from multiple tables, views, or table-emitting stored procedures from the target database) to a single conceptual model entity. With an entity still selected on the visual design surface, click the ghosted <Add A Table Or View> row in the Mapping Details panel.

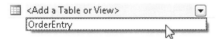

Select one of the available entities from the drop-down list. After the new storage layer properties appear in the panel, modify each property as needed to define the proper data relationships.

By selecting an association within the visual designer surface, the Mapping Details panel will also let you modify the mapped settings for that association.

> **Note** This ability to edit the association mapping does not apply to associations tied to imported foreign key relationships.

Another useful feature of the Mapping Details panel is the ability to define conditions for mapped entities. For example, you might want to limit the loaded orders for a customer to just those that have not yet been shipped. By adding a condition to the OrderEntry entity that looks for non-NULL values in the *ShipDate* property, the Entity Framework will automatically limit the orders managed by the model's application.

> **Note** If a storage layer property is used as a condition, it cannot be used as a standard mapped property within the conceptual model.

Adding a Mapping Condition to an Entity

> **Note** This exercise continues the previous exercise in this chapter.

1. If you haven't yet displayed the Mapping Details panel, open it by right-clicking the Entity Data Model Designer's design surface and choosing Mapping Details from the shortcut menu.

2. Select the *OrderEntry* entity on the visual design surface. The mapping details for that entity should appear in the Mapping Details panel.

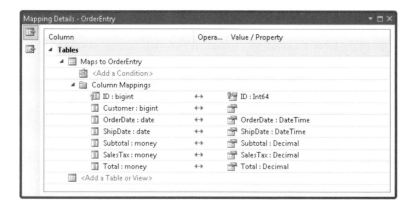

3. On the column mapping for the *ShipDate : date* storage layer property, click the *ShipDate : DateTime* value in the *Value / Property* column. You'll see a drop-down list of options. Select <Delete> from this list to clear the mapping.

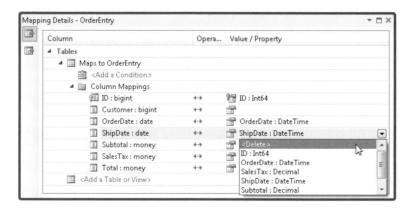

4. Near the top of the Mapping Details panel, just below the Maps To OrderEntry row, click the ghosted <Add A Condition> item and select ShipDate from the drop-down list.

5. In the *Operator* column of the new When ShipDate row, select Is.

6. In the *Value / Property* column of the When ShipDate row, select Not Null.

7. On the visual design surface, click the *ShipDate* property in the *OrderEntry* entity. Press Delete to remove the *ShipDate* property.

8. Save changes to the model to generate the new object layer content.

The upper-left corner of the Mapping Details panel includes two toolbar buttons.

—— Map Entity to Tables / Views

—— Map Entity to Functions

The top button lets you update the mappings for an entity using the storage layer tables and other similar storage items. The bottom button lets you specify database-level stored procedures, exposed as entity functions, that manage the insert, update, or deletion of individual entities within its entity set.

Use a Stored Procedure to Manage Entity Data

> **Note** This exercise continues the previous exercise in this chapter.

1. Select the *OrderEntry* entity on the visual design surface.

2. Click the Map Entity To Functions toolbar button (the lower button) on the Mapping Details panel.

3. Select the <Select Delete Function> row and then select CancelOrder from the drop-down list.

4. The Mapping Details panel detects the properties required for the selected function. In this case, a single *orderID* integer must be mapped to an entity value. In the *Property* column of the *CancelOrder* row, choose ID : Int64 for the parameter property. *ID* is the primary key for the *OrderEntry* entity.

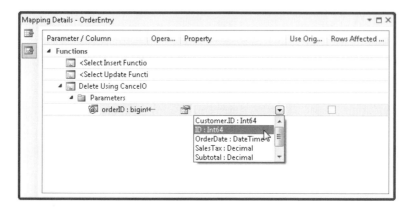

5. Save changes to the model to generate the new object layer content.

Using the Model Browser

Visual Studio's *Model Browser* panel is a hierarchical item selection panel similar to the Solution Explorer panel. When an Entity Framework visual model is active, the Model Browser displays the various components of both the conceptual and storage layers. By browsing and selecting the entities, properties, and other features of a model through this panel, you can view and modify the settings of each selected item through the standard Visual Studio Properties panel.

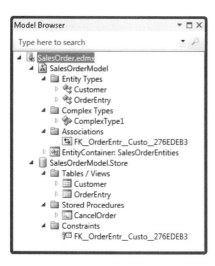

The Model Browser is an essential part of the visual model designer, because some features can be created and managed only through the browser. For example, you can add, edit, and delete individual properties from an existing complex type only by accessing that complex type through the Model Browser panel.

Managing the Object Layer

Visual Studio generates the source code for an entity model in your project each time you save changes to that model. The generated object layer is a set of Entity Framework-aware classes that exist as standard C# or Visual Basic source code.

By default, Visual Studio generates the model source code using its "default code genera-tor." You can view this setting within the Entity Data Model Designer by selecting the design surface of the visual model and then viewing the *Code Generation Strategy* property in the Properties panel. For wizard-generated models, this is set to **Default**.

For advanced needs, Visual Studio allows you to fully manage the code generation process by adding a *code generation item* to your project. These standard Visual Basic or C# language files are also known as *text templates* and include a .tt file extension. Visual Studio provides two types of code-generation items for use with Entity Framework models:

- **ADO.NET EntityObject Generator**   This is the default type, and the same type Visual Studio uses internally by default to generate the object layer for a model.

- **ADO.NET Self-Tracking EntityObject Generator**   This advanced generator is useful for n-tier projects in which the code that modifies EF-managed data exists in a differ-ent layer from the code that manages the structural interactions between entities and model layers.

To add a custom code generator to your project, use Visual Studio's Project | Add New Item menu command, and choose either ADO.NET EntityObject Generator or ADO.NET Self-Tracking EntityObject Generator as the new item type. You can also add these items by right-clicking the visual modeler design surface and selecting Add Code Generation Item from the shortcut menu.

When you add a new code generation item to your project, Visual Studio makes two Entity Framework-related changes:

1. The *Code Generation Strategy* property for your model changes from Default to None.

2. Within the new .tt file, a reference to the CSDL portion of your model appears near the top of the code generation source code.

The modification of text templates is beyond the scope of this book. For details on the content of code generation items and how to modify them, search for "Generated Code Overview" within the Visual Studio online help.

Summary

This chapter continued the overview of the Entity Framework by introducing the ADO.NET Entity Data Model Designer and its associated database import wizard. These tools simplify one of the most common tasks performed when developing applications that use the Entity Framework: importing existing database logical objects into a new Framework model.

Now that you have an accessible model, you can write code that queries the data managed by that model. The next two chapters introduce two common methods of querying EF data: retrieving entity data using Entity SQL and accessing objects directly through the Entity Framework's Object Services layer.

Chapter 14 Quick Reference

To	Do This
Add a new Entity Framework model to a project	Open or create a Visual Studio project.
	Select Project	Add New Item.
	Select ADO.NET Entity Data Model as the new item type then click Add.
	When the wizard appears, select either Generate From Database or Empty Model.
	Complete the wizard steps and modify the model as needed.
Use a stored procedure to update database-side content from entity changes	Include the stored procedure in the model, either through the initial wizard import or by using the Designer's Add	Function Import shortcut command.
	Select the entity in the visual designer.
	Open the Mapping Details panel.
	Click the Map Entities To Functions toolbar button (the lower button) within the panel.
	In the panel's list of functions, click the <Select Update Function> row then select the stored procedure.
	If needed, assign entity properties to the stored procedure's parameters.
Create a new complex type for later use in an entity	Open the Model Browser panel.
	Expand the conceptual model portion of the browser tree.
	Right-click the Complex Types branch then select Create Complex Type from the shortcut menu.
	Rename the new complex type.
	Right-click the complex type to add new properties using the various Add	Property shortcut menus.
Refresh the model after making database-level structural changes	Right-click the model's design surface then select Update Model From Database from the shortcut menu.

Chapter 15
Querying Data in the Framework

After completing this chapter, you will be able to:

- Describe the Entity SQL language and its purpose

- Create basic queries using Entity SQL

- Use the Entity Provider to access data based in an entity model

The Entity Framework (EF) is a markedly different way of interacting with data traditionally found in relational databases and similar external data stores. With its focus on coercing everything into .NET objects, it brings a familiarity to the data management process. But for those who are used to retrieving data through databases such as SQL Server and their SQL-based data query languages, moving to an object-centric paradigm doesn't necessarily feel like an improvement.

Fortunately, the Entity Framework includes a tool that helps bridge the data query gap between SQL-based systems and Framework model-based objects: *Entity SQL*. This query language has all the flavor and feeling of SQL, but it runs its queries against the entities and properties of an Entity Data Model (EDM).

This chapter provides a brief overview of Entity SQL, including examples of how to use it in your code. Visual Studio's online help includes full documentation on the language. If you are already comfortable with SQL, it should take you no time at all to retrieve model data using this new yet familiar language.

Note This chapter assumes you have some familiarity with the SQL language, especially as expressed in SQL Server's Transact-SQL (T-SQL) language.

The exercises in this chapter all use the same sample project, a tool that queries Entity Framework data using Entity SQL. Although you will be able to run the application after each exercise, the expected results for the full application might not appear until you complete all exercises in the chapter.

Getting to Know Entity SQL

Entity SQL is based in part on the T-SQL imperative query language found in Microsoft's SQL Server product. Despite this lineage, there are some significant differences between T-SQL and Entity SQL:

- **Entity SQL is a selection-only language.**   Whereas T-SQL includes support for data manipulation language (DML) and data definition language (DDL), Entity SQL supports only data retrieval. The focus is on the *SELECT* statement; *INSERT, UPDATE,* and *DELETE* are not available. When updates are needed, the standard Entity Framework tools take over.

- **None of the batch query or stored procedure functionality found in T-SQL is available in Entity SQL.**   Entity SQL does include support for custom functions, but they exist only to augment a related *SELECT* statement.

- **T-SQL focuses on the logical tables and rows in the database.**   Even when an Entity Framework model targets a SQL Server database, Entity SQL queries focus on the data as expressed through the conceptual model.

Writing Basic Queries

Entity SQL selection queries follow the same general syntax as those of standard SQL: with *SELECT, FROM, WHERE, GROUP BY,* and *ORDER BY* clauses.

```
SELECT list-of-fields
FROM one-or-more-tables
WHERE Boolean-expression
GROUP BY aggregate-grouping-fields
ORDER BY sort-by-fields
```

As with standard SQL, all fields included anywhere within the query must tie back to a table or entity that is specified in the *FROM* clause or in a subquery. The *FROM* clause usually lists its sources from the available entities in the model—that is, to the entity collections that themselves contain individual entities. These entity collections commonly use pluralized names.

```
-- This is probably not correct
SELECT ... FROM Customer

-- But this is valid with its pluralized name
SELECT ... FROM Customers
```

The *SELECT* clause is a comma-delimited list of the values to be returned in each result row. In Entity SQL, every reference to a field value or property must include its associated entity name or an alias to that name. In T-SQL, you can create a simple query without such references.

```
SELECT ID, FullName FROM Customers
```

In Entity SQL, table references are required.

```
SELECT Customers.ID, Customers.FullName FROM Customers
```

It is more common to use table aliases.

```
SELECT c.ID, c.FullName FROM Customers AS c
```

Entity SQL does not support the * symbol used in SQL to specify all columns in a table. To return the entire content of each matching row, use the table alias by itself in the *SELECT* clause, or list the columns and properties individually.

```
SELECT c FROM Customers AS c
```

In this statement, the values returned are instances of *Customer*, which is the entity from the application's data model. Each data value returned from an Entity SQL query is, naturally, expressed through a .NET object instance of some primitive or custom type. When relevant, a query will return instances of an entity type or custom type from the model. If your *SELECT* clause doesn't correlate to a modeled data type, the query engine will return the data as a collection of an *anonymous type*, a sort of impromptu nameless class that contains properties that match the fields in the *SELECT* list.

To include more than a single entity in the *FROM* clause, use the *JOIN* keyword.

```
SELECT c.FullName, o.OrderDate, o.Total
FROM Customers AS c
JOIN OrderEntry AS o ON c.ID = o.Customer
```

JOIN is a shortcut for *INNER JOIN*, which is the default type of inter-entity join. Entity SQL also supports outer joins (*LEFT OUTER JOIN, RIGHT OUTER JOIN,* and *FULL OUTER JOIN*) and cross joins (*CROSS JOIN*). The *FROM* clause also supports "applies," which was introduced in SQL Server 2005 (*CROSS APPLY* and *OUTER APPLY*) and can be used with dependent or correlated entities. In all cases, the *ON* keyword specifies the fields on which to establish the join.

The *ORDER BY* clause allows for a comma-delimited list of the fields by which the results should be sorted, from left to right. The *ASC* and *DESC* modifiers from SQL are available in Entity SQL.

```
SELECT c.ID, c.FullName
FROM Customers AS c
ORDER BY c.FullName DESC
```

By default, the data returned from an Entity SQL query is in the form of a table of rows—actually, a collection of object instances that all use the same named or anonymous type. This is true even when the *SELECT* clause includes only a single value and the query returns only a single row.

```
-- This single-row, single-column query still returns a row.
SELECT c.FullName FROM Customers AS c WHERE c.ID = 1
```

You can force the query to return the result (in each returned record) as a distinct value instead of as a row containing one distinct value. To accomplish this, use the *VALUE* keyword before the field specification.

```
-- This query returns a value, not a row of values.
SELECT VALUE c.FullName FROM Customers AS c WHERE c.ID = 1
```

Using Literals, Operators, and Expressions

Entity SQL includes a wide variety of literal types that can be included in your queries. Table 15-1 lists these literal types.

TABLE 15-1 Literals Available in Entity SQL

Literal Type	Triggering Action
Integer	By default, integer literals are 32-bit signed integers (*Int32*). You can change the sign or size of the integer by appending literal codes to the value: *U* for 32-bit unsigned literals (*UInt32*), *L* for 64-bit signed values (*Int64*), and *UL* for 64-bit unsigned numbers (*UInt64*). For instance, the literal *123UL* is a 64-bit unsigned value.
	If you need to include other integer types in your results, the *CAST* function lets you coerce a value into another data type:
	`SELECT CAST(123 AS System.Int16) AS ServiceCode, ...`
Floating-point Value	Any numeric literal that includes a decimal point is considered a double-precision floating-point value (*Double*). To create a single-precision floating-point value (*Single*), append the letter *f* to the literal, as in *123.45f*. Literals of type *Decimal* appear with a trailing *M*, as in *123.45M*.
String	Strings can appear between either single or double quotes and are non-Unicode by default. To treat a literal as a Unicode string, attach an *N* to the start of the literal, as in *N'abc'*.
Boolean	Entity SQL supports the *true* and *false* keywords for use as Boolean values.
Date and Time	All date values must include the time component; time values can be used without an associated date portion. Dates (or dates with times) use the *DATETIME* keyword followed by a specially formatted date and time in single quotes:
	`DATETIME 'YYYY-MM-DD hh:mm[:ss[.fffffff]]'`
	That is, a full year-month-day date followed by military-format time with optional seconds, with or without a fractional seconds portion.
	Time values use the *TIME* keyword and omit the date portion:
	`TIME 'hh:mm[:ss[.fffffff]]'`
	The date-time-offset literal, a variation of *DATETIME*, includes an offset of hours and minutes, plus or minus, from the specified base date and time. This is useful for time zone offsets and other purposes that require times and dates managed from a reference clock:
	`DATETIMEOFFSET 'YYYY-MM-DD hh:mm[:ss[.fffffff]] {+|-}hh:mm'`

Literal Type	Triggering Action
GUID	To include a literal GUID, use the *GUID* keyword followed by the dash-embedded GUID within single quotes. `GUID '28CA0BAE-27C9-446E-8DEB-C32E071C4B1A'`

Binary Content	Create binary content (for graphics and similar non-text data) using the *BINARY* keyword, followed by the hex-formatted binary content in single quotes (attaching *X* to the start of the quoted binary content also works):
	
	`BINARY 'A2AAE82303FF...'`
	`-- or...`
	`X'A2AAE82303FF...'`

Null Value	The keyword *null* represents a NULL value in any data type. Using NULL values in some types of calculations always produces a NULL result.

Entity SQL supports most of the common operators available in other SQL variants. The math operators (+, -, *, /, and %, which represent addition, subtraction or negation, multiplication, division, and modulo operations, respectively) work on either integer or floating point values. The + operator also doubles as a string concatenation tool.

The comparison operators (=, <> or !=, <, >, <=, >=) can be used with numeric, string, date, or other relevant data types, typically within the *WHERE* clause of a statement. The *IN* operator matches one from a parenthesized set of options or subquery results. Similarly, the *EXISTS* keyword returns *true* if a subquery includes any valid results.

The logical operators *AND, OR,* and *NOT* combine different logical expressions, and can be replaced with the C-like synonyms &&, ||, and !, respectively. The special *IS* and *IS NOT* operators enable comparisons with the *null* literal.

As in SQL, simple field references can be replaced with expressions that include or exclude any specific field. Parentheses can be included for grouping within complex expressions. The following statement includes an expression in the *SELECT* clause, as well as both logical and comparison operators in the *WHERE* clause:

```
-- Get the post-tax total for each unshipped, chargeable order.
SELECT o.OrderID, o.SubTotal * o.TaxRate AS OrderTotal
FROM AllOrders AS o
WHERE o.ShipDate IS NULL AND o.SubTotal > 0
```

As shown in the preceding code block, comment lines begin with two hyphens.

In addition to operator-induced data manipulation, Entity SQL includes several canonical functions that accept expressions and properties as arguments and return a calculated result.

- **Math functions**   *Abs* returns the absolute value of its integer or decimal argument. The *Power* function raises a base to an exponent. The three functions *Ceiling, Floor,* and *Round* truncate and round decimal values.

- **String functions**   The available string functions are closely tied with those used for .NET strings. *Concat* joins two strings together just like the + operator. *LTrim, RTrim,* and *Trim* remove excess whitespace. *Left, Right,* and *Substring* return a portion of a string with an identified location and length. *ToLower* and *ToUpper* return a new case-altered string. *StartsWith, EndsWith,* and *Contains* are Boolean functions that return *true* if a partial string match is found. *IndexOf* is similar to those three functions, but returns a numeric position for the match. *Length* returns the character length of a string. *Replace* and *Reverse* both return new strings after applying the relevant changes to the content.

- **Date and time functions**   Entity SQL includes several *Add...* functions (such as *AddMinutes*) that add (or subtract when negative) time value to a date/time base. Similarly named *Diff...* functions (such as *DiffYears*) report the differences between two source date/time arguments. Distinct *Year, Month, Day, Hour, Minute, Second, Millisecond,* and *DayOfYear* functions return the specific component of a source date or time. *Truncate* returns a date without its time portion. Other functions let you retrieve the current date and time or build a new date and time from integer components.

- **Bitwise functions**   Instead of overloading the logical operators with bitwise functionality, Entity SQL includes distinct bitwise functions: *BitWiseAnd, BitWiseNot, BitWiseOr,* and *BitWiseXor.*

- **Other functions**   The *NewGuid* function returns a newly generated and unique GUID value. The *CAST* function lets you force a data value into another (allowed) type using the syntax *CAST(original-value AS new-data-type).*

In addition to these built-in functions, Entity SQL includes a series of SQL Server-specific functions. They are equivalent in functionality to their T-SQL counterparts, and they all begin with the prefix "SqlServer."

```
SELECT SqlServer.DATEPART("day", o.OrderDate) AS OrderDay
FROM OrderEntries AS o WHERE o.ID = 2932
```

The "SqlServer" component of this statement is actually a reference to a namespace named "SqlServer." Instead of attaching this prefix each time you need it in a query, you can also apply the *USING* keyword to reference a namespace that you can then access throughout the query.

```
USING SqlServer;
SELECT DATEPART("day", o.OrderDate) AS OrderDay
FROM OrderEntries AS o WHERE o.ID = 2932
```

T-SQL's *CASE* keyword, the inline conditional switch statement, is available in Entity SQL as well. The *CASE* block can include any number of *WHEN* clauses and a single optional *ELSE* clause to return conditional results.

```
SELECT CASE
    WHEN o.OrderTotal > 0 THEN 'Standard Order'
    WHEN o.OrderTotal < 0 THEN 'Refund'
    ELSE 'No Charge'
END AS OrderType, ...
```

The *UNION, INTERSECT, EXCEPT,* and *OVERLAPS* keywords, as well as the *SET* function enable set operations on query results. *UNION* merges two result sets, whereas *INTERSECT* returns only those rows that appear in both sets. *EXCEPT* returns the first set with any rows in the second set removed. *OVERLAPS* returns *true* if any row appears in both sets being compared. *SET* returns a subset that includes only unique rows.

Grouping and Aggregating Entity Data

Entity SQL includes several *aggregate functions* that allow your query to generate summarized data across a range of included records. The following statement adds up all order totals in the *OrderEntry* table:

```
SELECT SUM(o.Total) AS TotalOfAllOrders
FROM OrderEntry AS o
```

In addition to *SUM*, which totals up a column of numeric values, the language includes the following aggregate functions:

- **COUNT and BIGCOUNT**   Counts the total number of records included in the query; or when passed a column name or calculated expression, returns the number of non-NULL results. Entity SQL does not support the *COUNT(*)* syntax typically used in other SQL variants. Instead, use *COUNT(0)*. *BIGCOUNT* is identical to *COUNT*, but returns a 64-bit integer instead of a 32-bit integer.

- **MAX and MIN**   These functions return the maximum or minimum value within the result set for the supplied column name or expression. Numbers, strings, dates, and other data types that support ordering of items can be used as arguments.

- **AVG**   Returns the average for the supplied column or expression across all included records. *AVG* supports numeric values only.

- **STDEV and STDEVP**   These functions calculate the standard deviation and the population-specific standard deviation across all rows for the specific column or expression.

- **VAR and VARP**   Related to the standard deviation, these two functions generate the statistical variance and the population-specific variance across all rows for the specific column or expression.

Entity SQL supports group-based aggregation with the *GROUP BY* clause.

```
-- Calculate last year's small monthly order totals.
SELECT WhichMonth, SUM(o.Total) AS TotalOfAllOrders
FROM OrderEntries AS o
WHERE Year(o.OrderDate) = Year(CurrentDateTime()) - 1
GROUP BY Month(o.OrderDate) AS WhichMonth
HAVING SUM(o.Total) < 1000
ORDER BY WhichMonth
```

As shown in the code, *HAVING* is also available, which acts like a *WHERE* clause on the post-aggregated content. One formatting difference from T-SQL is the placement of the aliased grouping field in the *GROUP BY* clause. In this sample code, *Month(o.OrderDate) AS WhichMonth* defines the group and appears in *GROUP BY* instead of in the more traditional *SELECT* location. Both the *SELECT* and *ORDER BY* clauses can reference this group by the alias.

Paging support appears in Entity SQL via the *SKIP* and *LIMIT* keywords. This enables paged results, commonly seen on web sites that split search results among multiple web pages. *SKIP* indicates the number of results to skip from the start of the result set. *LIMIT* tells how many rows to return from the top or from just after the skipped items.

```
-- Return page 2 from a list of matching products, 50 per page.
SELECT p.ID, p.ProductName, p.Description, p.Price
FROM Products AS p
ORDER BY ProductName SKIP 50 LIMIT 50
```

Similar to the *LIMIT* keyword, the *TOP* clause returns the first specified number of rows from the query. You cannot use *TOP* and *SKIP* in the same query; use *LIMIT* when *SKIP* is specified.

```
-- Don't return more than 200 matching products.
SELECT TOP 200 p.ID, p.ProductName, p.Description, p.Price
FROM Products AS p
WHERE p.ProductName LIKE @UserSearchValue
ORDER BY p.ProductName
```

The *DISTINCT* keyword removes any duplicate rows from a result set. This keyword is sometimes needed when too few columns exist to guarantee unique results, or when performing certain types of joins.

```
SELECT DISTINCT p.ProductName
FROM Products AS p
```

Although not specifically a grouping feature, Entity SQL does include the ability to use subqueries. These nested *SELECT* statements can appear in the *SELECT, FROM,* or *WHERE* clauses in the parent query. References to aliased entity names between the parent query and the subquery are permitted.

```
-- List the past-due customers.
SELECT c.FullName
FROM Customers AS c
WHERE c.ID IN (
  SELECT o.Customer FROM OrderEntries AS o
  WHERE o.PastDue = true)
```

Using Features Unique to Entity SQL

Entity SQL includes a few tremendously useful features that don't directly correspond to T-SQL language elements. Most of these features stem from the object-based nature of the data being queried: SQL Server doesn't have true navigation properties and its records don't exist as collections of table-row instances. The custom Entity SQL features directly address these and other Entity Framework enhancements.

In Entity SQL, the entities being queried and the results those queries produce are actually collections—generic collections hosting instances of a specific named or anonymous class type. Although you normally use the entity-based collections in your queries, you can also build your own collections within the query by using either a set of curly braces or the *MULTISET* function. A collection of integers, for example, appears as a comma-delimited list within curly braces.

```
{ 1, 2, 3 }
```

As interesting as this collection-building feature is, it becomes quite useful when combined with the *ROW* function, which lets you generate ad hoc entity-like records within the query text. The following query builds a pseudo-table of credit card types and joins it with the main *Payments* entity:

```
-- NOTE: This code is not fully valid according to credit
--       card issuer standards.
SELECT p.AccountNumber, x.CardType
FROM Payments AS p
INNER JOIN { ROW("3" AS FirstDigit, "American Express" AS CardType),
             ROW("4" AS FirstDigit, "Visa" AS CardType),
             ROW("5" AS FirstDigit, "MasterCard" AS CardType),
             ROW("6" AS FirstDigit, "Discover" AS CardType) } AS x
ON Left(p.AccountNumber, 1) = x.FirstDigit
```

Although Entity SQL does not support true stored procedures, it does provide a limited user-defined function capability. Using the *FUNCTION* keyword, you create user-defined functions within the same statement as the *SELECT* query and then use the function in the clauses of the query.

```
FUNCTION MonthHalf(whichDate System.DateTime) AS
(
  CASE WHEN Day(whichDate) < 16 THEN 'First Half'
  ELSE 'Second Half' END
)
SELECT o.OrderDate, MonthHalf(o.OrderDate)
FROM OrderEntries AS o
```

Entity SQL also includes native support for EF-modeled complex types and their relationships. The project examples in Chapter 14, "Visualizing Data Models," created a complex type called *Address* that contained the address-related properties of the *Customer* entity. Instead of accessing the city name of a customer as *Customer.City*, it became *Customer.Address.City*. Entity SQL supports this "multiple-dot" notation for complex types.

Sometimes it is useful to get a reference (similar to pointers in C-like languages or a *ByRef* parameter in Visual Basic) to persisted content. Entity SQL includes four functions that manage references. The *REF* function creates a reference for any entity or value; for example, *REF(Customer.FullName)* creates a reference to a customer's name. *DEREF* returns the original content for previously *REF*'d objects. The *CREATEREF* function generates a reference to an entity by supplying its entity type and its primary key value.

```
CREATEREF(SalesOrderEntities.Customer, 3)
```

The *KEY* function returns the primary key value used to create a reference with *CREATEREF*.

Running Entity SQL Queries

The Entity Framework includes two key ways of using Entity SQL queries to access entity managed data: using an *ObjectQuery* instance to query the entities within the context directly or using a more traditional ADO.NET provider-like interface.

Running Queries Using an *ObjectQuery*

The *System.Data.Objects.ObjectQuery(Of T)* class-processes an Entity SQL statement against an open EF context and returns the results as a collection of either named or anonymous instances.

```csharp
C#
// ----- SalesOrderEntities is an Entity Container.
using (SalesOrderEntities context =
        new SalesOrderEntities(GetConnectionString()))
{
    ObjectQuery<Customer> query =
        New ObjectQuery<Customer>(sqlText, context);
    // ... Other code as needed ...
}
```

```vbnet
Visual Basic
' ----- SalesOrderEntities is an Entity Container.
Using context As New SalesOrderEntities(GetConnectionString())
    Dim query As New ObjectQuery(Of Customer)(sqlText, context)
    ' ... Other code as needed ...
End Using
```

You must keep the context around as long as you need to access the *ObjectQuery* object's data, especially if the retrieved data includes content accessed through a navigation property. The generic *ObjectQuery* type works like a typical generic collection object, but it's not a true collection. When you create the *ObjectQuery* instance, the Entity Framework delays processing of the query until you specifically request data. Even then, it might decide to retrieve only the requested portion of the data. Keeping the context around during the entire data-retrieval process enables the *ObjectQuery* to fulfill any data requests you give it over time.

Note The object context and its related entity container in the conceptual model expose a *LazyLoadingEnabled* property. Changing this Boolean value alters the way that the Entity Framework loads data at the other end of a navigation property. Models built with the visual designer set this property to *True* by default, keeping unused navigation property data unloaded. Setting this value to *False* (the default for manually created models) provides more proactive loading of related data and might allow you to access such data even when the context is no longer available. You can adjust this property's value in the visual designer or within the context instance.

The preceding code creates an instance of *ObjectQuery* with a generic focus of *Customer,* presumably one of the entities in the Entity Data Model. The Entity SQL statement used to retrieve the results must generate entities of that type. Your code can also generate data values not tied to any predefined entity or custom type. These anonymous-type queries use the *System.Data.Common.DbDataRecord* class as the target generic type.

C#
```
ObjectQuery<Customer> query =
    New ObjectQuery<DbDataRecord>(sqlText, context);
```

Visual Basic
```
Dim query As New ObjectQuery(Of DbDataRecord)(sqlText, context)
```

Retrieving Entity Data Through an *ObjectQuery*: C#

1. Open the "Chapter 15 CSharp" project from the installed samples folder. The project includes a *Windows.Forms* class named *EntityQuery,* which is a tool for trying out EF queries.

2. Open the source code view for the *EntityQuery* form. Locate the *GetConnectionString* function; this is a routine that uses a *SqlConnectionStringBuilder* to create a valid connection string to the sample database. It currently includes the following statements:

    ```
    sqlPortion.DataSource = @"(local)\SQLExpress";
    sqlPortion.InitialCatalog = "StepSample";
    sqlPortion.IntegratedSecurity = true;
    ```

    Adjust these statements as needed to provide access to your own test database.

3. Locate the *ActSingleEntity_Click* event handler. This routine creates an *ObjectQuery* to retrieve *Customer* entities. Just after the "Retrieve the customer entities via a query" comment, within the *try* block, add the following statements:

```
ActiveContext = new SalesOrderEntities(GetConnectionString());
sqlText = @"SELECT VALUE Customer FROM Customers
    AS Customer ORDER BY Customer.FullName DESC";
query = new ObjectQuery<Customer>(sqlText, ActiveContext);
```

This code creates a context (*ActiveContext*) and then creates an *ObjectQuery* pseudo-collection for *Customer* entities. To guard against errors related to lazy loading of data, the context remains open after this code completes.

4. Run the program. Click the Single Entity button to view the results of this example's query.

Retrieving Entity Data Through an *ObjectQuery*: Visual Basic

1. Open the "Chapter 15 VB" project from the installed samples folder. The project includes a *Windows.Forms* class named *EntityQuery*, which is a tool for trying out EF queries.

2. Open the source code view for the *EntityQuery* form. Locate the *GetConnectionString* function; this is a routine that uses a *SqlConnectionStringBuilder* to create a valid connection string to the sample database. It currently includes the following statements:

```
sqlPortion.DataSource = "(local)\SQLExpress"
sqlPortion.InitialCatalog = "StepSample"
sqlPortion.IntegratedSecurity = True
```

Adjust these statements as needed to provide access to your own test database.

3. Locate the *ActSingleEntity_Click* event handler. This routine creates an *ObjectQuery* to retrieve *Customer* entities. Just after the "Retrieve the customer entities via a query" comment, within the *Try* block, add the following statements:

```
ActiveContext = New SalesOrderEntities(GetConnectionString())
sqlText = "SELECT VALUE Customer FROM Customers " &
    "AS Customer ORDER BY Customer.FullName DESC"
query = New ObjectQuery(Of Customer)(sqlText, ActiveContext)
```

This code creates a context (*ActiveContext*) and then creates an *ObjectQuery* pseudo-collection for *Customer* entities. To guard against errors related to lazy loading of data, the context remains open after this code completes.

4. Run the program. Click the Single Entity button to view the results of this example's query.

Running Queries Using a Provider

In standard ADO.NET data processing, SQL-based queries make their way to the target data through command and connection objects, and then ultimately through a provider such as the SQL Server ADO.NET provider.

The Entity Framework hosts its own data provider: the *EntityClient provider*. This provider exposes much of the same connection and command functionality available with the SQL Server and other native providers, but with the ability to query against entities in an Entity Data Model. The key classes for the EntityClient provider appear in the *System.Data. EntityClient* namespace.

Using the EntityClient provider to query data covers the same general steps as are performed with other providers:

1. Create and open a connection using the *EntityConnection* class and a connection string.

2. Create an *EntityCommand* instance and then add the connection and the Entity SQL statement to it.

3. If the query contains @-prefixed parameters, add parameters objects as needed.

4. Call one of the command object's *Execute* methods to process the query and return data results.

The command object includes the *ExecuteNonQuery* method for running queries with no return results; the *ExecuteScalar* method, which returns a single result; and *ExecuteReader*, which returns a single-pass data reader, *EntityDataReader*. What is missing is the data adapter with its capability to move incoming data into a *DataTable* or *DataSet* instance. Considering all the other data-manipulation tools included with the Entity Framework, this is a small omission. But if you need to push entity data into a standard ADO.NET structure, you will have to do so manually.

When using the *EntityCommand.ExecuteReader* method to generate a data reader, you must pass *CommandBehavior.SequentialAccess* as a behavior argument.

C#
```
results = query.ExecuteReader(CommandBehavior.SequentialAccess);
```

Visual Basic
```
results = query.ExecuteReader(CommandBehavior.SequentialAccess)
```

This option is normally used when retrieving binary large objects (BLOBs) and other large content blocks from the database, but its use is required with the EntityClient provider, even when returning minimal content. The side effect of using the sequential access option is that each returned row's data values must be retrieved in the same order in which they appear in the SQL statement and can be accessed only once each. After you read a field, it's time to move on to the next one.

The following exercise shows the EntityClient provider in action, using a parameterized query and a data reader to shuttle results into a *DataTable* instance.

Retrieving Entity Data Through a Provider: C#

 Note This exercise continues the previous exercise in this chapter.

1. Locate the *ActDataTable_Click* event handler; this is a routine that copies entity-based data into a standard ADO.NET *DataTable* instance. Because the data will be shuttled manually into an existing data table, the routine includes code to build the receiving table.

   ```
   resultsAsTable = new DataTable;
   resultsAsTable.Columns.Add("CustomerID", typeof(long));
   resultsAsTable.Columns.Add("CustomerName", typeof(string));
   resultsAsTable.Columns.Add("AnnualFee", typeof(decimal));
   ```

   Most of the routine is contained within a *using* block that manages the provider connection.

   ```
   using (EntityConnection linkToDB =
       new EntityConnection(GetConnectionString()))
   {
       // ----- Most of the code appears here.
   }
   ```

2. Just after the "Retrieve the data via a parameterized query" comment, add the following statement:

   ```
   sqlText = @"SELECT CU.ID, CU.FullName, CU.AnnualFee
       FROM SalesOrderEntities.Customers AS CU
       WHERE CU.AnnualFee >= @MinFee ORDER BY CU.FullName";
   ```

   The EntityClient provider supports parameterized queries, as shown in these lines.

3. In the same section of code, within the *try* block that follows the newly added SQL statement, add these lines:

   ```
   query = new EntityCommand(sqlText, linkToDB);
   query.Parameters.AddWithValue("MinFee", 200);
   results = query.ExecuteReader(CommandBehavior.SequentialAccess);
   ```

   As mentioned previously, the *CommandBehavior.SequentialAccess* option is required.

4. Just after the "Move each row into the DataTable" comment, within one of the later *try* blocks, add the following code:

```
while (results.Read())
{
    oneRow = resultsAsTable.NewRow();
    oneRow["CustomerID"] = (long)results["ID"];
    oneRow["CustomerName"] = (string)results["FullName"];
    oneRow["AnnualFee"] = (decimal)results["AnnualFee"];
    resultsAsTable.Rows.Add(oneRow);
}
```

These lines move the data from the reader into the preconfigured *DataTable* instance. As is required by the sequential access flag used when creating the reader, the incoming fields are accessed in the order in which they appeared in the SQL query, and each field is accessed only once.

5. Run the program. Click the Data Table button to view the results of this example's query.

Retrieving Entity Data Through a Provider: Visual Basic

> **Note** This exercise continues the previous exercise in this chapter.

1. Locate the *ActDataTable_Click* event handler; this is a routine that copies entity-based data into a standard ADO.NET *DataTable* instance. Because the data will be shuttled manually into an existing data table, the routine includes code to build the receiving table.

```
resultsAsTable = New DataTable
resultsAsTable.Columns.Add("CustomerID", GetType(Long))
resultsAsTable.Columns.Add("CustomerName", GetType(String))
resultsAsTable.Columns.Add("AnnualFee", GetType(Decimal))
```

Most of the routine is contained within a *Using* block that manages the provider connection.

```
Using linkToDB As New EntityConnection(GetConnectionString())
    ' ----- Most of the code appears here.
End Using
```

2. Just after the "Retrieve the data via a parameterized query" comment, add the following statement:

```
sqlText = "SELECT CU.ID, CU.FullName, CU.AnnualFee " &
    "FROM SalesOrderEntities.Customers AS CU " &
    "WHERE CU.AnnualFee >= @MinFee ORDER BY CU.FullName"
```

The EntityClient provider supports parameterized queries, as shown in these lines.

3. In the same section of code, within the *Try* block that follows the newly added SQL statement, add these lines:

```
query = New EntityCommand(sqlText, linkToDB)
query.Parameters.AddWithValue("MinFee", 200)
results = query.ExecuteReader(CommandBehavior.SequentialAccess)
```

As mentioned previously, the *CommandBehavior.SequentialAccess* option is required.

4. Just after the "Move each row into the DataTable" comment, within one of the later *Try* blocks, add the following code:

```
Do While (results.Read() = True)
    oneRow = resultsAsTable.NewRow()
    oneRow!CustomerID = CLng(results!ID)
    oneRow!CustomerName = CStr(results!FullName)
    oneRow!AnnualFee = CDec(results!AnnualFee)
    resultsAsTable.Rows.Add(oneRow)
Loop
```

These lines move the data from the reader into the preconfigured *DataTable* instance. As is required by the sequential access flag used when creating the reader, the incoming fields are accessed in the order in which they appeared in the SQL query, and each field is accessed only once.

5. Run the program. Click the Data Table button to view the results of this example's query.

Summary

This chapter reviewed the Entity SQL language and its usage within .NET applications. Entity SQL is built with the same basic query language syntax found in SQL Server's Transact-SQL and in other variations of SQL. Although there are some differences when dealing with the object nature of the Entity Framework, teams already working with SQL will have little trouble integrating Entity SQL into their applications.

Although Entity SQL is great for organizations that have a large investment in SQL technologies, it might not be the most straightforward EF-query tool for your needs. The upcoming chapters introduce additional ways that Entity Framework data can be accessed within your software and your business logic.

Chapter 15 Quick Reference

To	Do This
Select entity records using Entity SQL	Write your query using the Entity SQL language. Create an instance of the entity context. Create an instance of *ObjectQuery*<class>, where *class* is an entity type, EF custom type, or *DbDataRecord*. Access the members of the *ObjectQuery* instance.
Select the ID of all *Product* entity instances	Use a query similar to the following: `SELECT p.ID FROM Products AS p` If the collection of entities was designed with a plural name, use that plural name in the query.
Select a single value as a data-type value instead of as a row containing that value	Use the *SELECT VALUE* syntax.

Chapter 16

Understanding Entities Through Objects

After completing this chapter, you will be able to:

- Access the properties of an entity through a standard object instance

- Add, update, and delete database content by modifying object properties

- Carry out query-like actions using standard method calls

One of the main advantages of the Entity Framework (EF) is that you can manage database content using standard .NET objects that reflect the conceptual nature of the data. Behind the scenes, various XML models, generated language code blocks, and provider interactions make this possible. But the complexity exists solely to fulfill the promise of providing simplicity in handling the main business logic of your application. Imagine being able to modify the *Name* property of a *Customer* object in code and have that change propagate to the database— all without having to write any of the code to make that happen.

This chapter introduces *Object Services*, the part of the Entity Framework that makes that promise a reality. This Framework layer makes the transition from database to model to objects—or vice versa—possible. In a way, the Entity Framework *is* the Object Services layer because that layer is responsible for the core functionality of the Framework. Visual Studio makes working with the Framework easy because access to its functionality is enhanced by visual designers and Entity SQL scripts. This chapter focuses on the objects themselves; you'll see how to add, modify, and remove them in a way that directly affects the external data store.

 Note The exercises in this chapter all use the same sample project, which is a tool that provides editing features for a table of customers. While you will be able to run the application after each exercise, the expected results for the full application might not appear until you complete all exercises in the chapter.

Managing Entity Data Through Objects

Object Services manages the entire lifetime of data through the Entity Framework, from determining how to translate the storage-layer model into the appropriate provider-level actions, to shuttling data through the model and into usable .NET objects. Earlier chapters in this book introduced some of these modeling concepts. This time, the focus is on the last part: exposing data through objects.

Accessing Entity Data Through Objects

The object layer source code that Object Services generates from the Conceptual Schema Definition Language (CSDL)-based conceptual model consists of classes that derive from a set of generic base classes. Each conceptual model element has some object-level counterpart that appears as C# or Visual Basic source code in the ModelName.*Designer.cs* or ModelName.*Designer.vb* file. The following base classes play key support roles in implementing the conceptual model in code:

- *System.Data.Objects.DataClasses.EntityObject* This is the base class for all entities. If your entity model includes a *Customer* entity, the generated code includes a *Customer* class that derives from this *EntityObject* class. Individual entity properties appear as standard .NET properties within the derived class.

- *System.Data.Objects.DataClasses.ComplexObject* When an entity includes a complex type (such as the *Address* complex type crafted in the "Entity Data Model Designer" section on page 230 of Chapter 14, "Visualizing Data Models"), that type derives from the *ComplexObject* base class.

- *System.Data.Objects.ObjectSet(Of TEntity)* Entities—the table-style collection of individual entity instances—derive from this generic base class. *ObjectSet* implements the *IEnumerable* interface for a collection-like experience.

- *System.Data.Objects.ObjectQuery(Of T)* Although generated entity objects are not based on this class, it still plays a key role in Entity Framework data activities. Any time you query entity data—whether through an Entity SQL query, the LINQ tools discussed later in this book, or the query builder methods introduced in the second half of this chapter—the returned results exist as some form of *ObjectQuery*. It also serves as the base class for *ObjectSet(Of TEntity)*.

- *System.Data.Objects.ObjectContext* This is the class-based embodiment of an entire conceptual model, also called the *entity container*. The generated entity container provides access to all entity and association instances within your application. You must create an instance of a derived *ObjectContext* to interact with Entity Framework data.

Additional classes implement associations, association endpoints, and other class-based expressions of conceptual model elements. The derived classes also draw on the storage and mapping layers to carry out the various data activities requested by your code.

The following code, already introduced in an earlier chapter, shows some typical statements used to access external data through model-generated objects:

C#

```csharp
// ----- Always start by creating an object context. Create an instance of
//       either ObjectContext, or of the derived entity container class.
using (SalesOrderEntities context =
        new SalesOrderEntities(GetConnectionString()))
{
    // ----- Option 1: Derived entity collections expose contained
    //       entity sets directly.
    results = context.Customers;


    // ----- Option 2: The CreateObjectSet method returns all entity
    //       instances for the named entity type.
    results = context.CreateObjectSet<Customer>();


    // ----- Option 3: Run an Entity SQL query to retrieve some
    //       or all entity instances.
    results = new ObjectQuery<Customer>(sqlText, context);


    // ----- Option 4: Use query builder methods, shown later.


    // ----- Option 5: Use LINQ, shown later.
}
```

Visual Basic

```vbnet
' ----- Always start by creating an object context. Create an instance of
'       either ObjectContext, or of the derived entity container class.
Using context As New SalesOrderEntities(GetConnectionString())
    ' ----- Option 1: Derived entity collections expose contained
    '       entity sets directly.
    results = context.Customers


    ' ----- Option 2: The CreateObjectSet method returns all entity
    '       instances for the named entity type.
    results = context.CreateObjectSet(Of Customer)()


    ' ----- Option 3: Run an Entity SQL query to retrieve some
    '       or all entity instances.
    results = New ObjectQuery(Of Customer)(sqlText, context)


    ' ----- Option 4: Use query builder methods, shown later.


    ' ----- Option 5: Use LINQ, shown later.
End Using
```

Depending on how you configured your conceptual model, this code might not actually retrieve any data from the database because by default the Entity Framework defers data access until the data is needed. Therefore, in many cases, you must access individual entities or their properties to initiate a true database query.

After you have a set of entity instances, you can scan through them as you do with any other collection. The entity properties of each instance method appear as standard .NET class properties, so you can access them from code just like any other strongly typed property.

C#
```csharp
foreach (Customer oneCustomer in results)
{
    SendInvoicesToCustomer(oneCustomer.ID, oneCustomer.FullName);
}
```

Visual Basic
```vbnet
For Each oneCustomer As Customer In results
    SendInvoicesToCustomer(oneCustomer.ID, oneCustomer.FullName)
Next oneCustomer
```

Complex types use a multidotted property notation.

C#
```csharp
VerifyPostalCode(oneCustomer.Address.PostalCode);
```

Visual Basic
```vbnet
VerifyPostalCode(oneCustomer.Address.PostalCode)
```

This same syntax also works for content at the other end of a navigation property.

C#
```csharp
// ----- Assume that State is a navigation property.
location = oneCustomer.Address.City + ", " +
    oneCustomer.Address.State.Abbreviation;
```

Visual Basic
```vbnet
' ----- Assume that State is a navigation property.
location = oneCustomer.Address.City & ", " &
    oneCustomer.Address.State.Abbreviation
```

Modifying Entity Data Through Objects

Accessing data through properties is great, but if that is all the Entity Framework could do, it wouldn't be a tremendous improvement over standard ADO.NET. Fortunately, the Entity Framework also supports data updates. Entities and properties you retrieve through the context are fully editable—assuming that the underlying database elements are editable.

The entity container supports updates to existing entity properties, the addition of new entity instances, and the removal of existing entity instances. All changes propagate back to the database, and all take into account the constraints and business logic rules you impose on the conceptual layer, the storage layer, the mapping layer, and the external data store.

Modifying existing properties is the easiest action to take. After retrieving an entity, you modify it by simply setting one of its properties to the new value.

C#
```
oneCustomer.AnnualFee += 50;
```

Visual Basic
```
oneCustomer.AnnualFee += 50
```

Just as with ADO.NET, you must take one additional step that is needed to accept all pending changes. To accept changes in the Entity Framework, call the *SaveChanges* method of the active context object. This completes the update process and persists all changes to the underlying data source.

C#
```
context.SaveChanges();
```

Visual Basic
```
context.SaveChanges()
```

Adding new entities is a little more involved, but it parallels what you would normally do with a collection of objects in .NET. To add a new *Customer* entity to the model, and ultimately to the database table or tables that manage customer data, follow four simple steps:

1. Create a new instance of the *Customer* entity.

2. Fill in its properties.

3. Add the new entity instance to the context or the context's exposed set of customers.

4. Call the context object's *SaveChanges* method.

Here's an example that adds a new customer:

```csharp
C#
using (SalesOrderEntities context =
        new SalesOrderEntities(connectionString))
{
    // ----- Step 1: Create a new Customer instance.
    Customer oneCustomer = new Customer();

    // ----- Step 2: Fill in the properties.
    oneCustomer.FullName = "Fourth Coffee";
    // ...and so on...

    // ----- Step 3: Add the Customer to the context.
    context.AddObject("Customers", oneCustomer);
    // ...or...
    context.Customers.AddObject(oneCustomer);

    // ----- Step 4: Confirm the change.
    context.SaveChanges();
}
```

```vbnet
Visual Basic
Using context As New SalesOrderEntities(connectionString)
    ' ----- Step 1: Create a new Customer instance.
    Dim oneCustomer As New Customer

    ' ----- Step 2: Fill in the properties.
    oneCustomer.FullName = "Fourth Coffee"
    ' ...and so on...

    ' ----- Step 3: Add the Customer to the context.
    context.AddObject("Customers", oneCustomer)
    ' ...or...
    context.Customers.AddObject(oneCustomer)

    ' ----- Step 4: Confirm the change.
    context.SaveChanges()
End Using
```

The *ObjectContext.AddObject* method accepts the name of the entity set (normally the plural name of the entity) and the new entity instance. Alternatively, you can call *AddObject* from the existing collection (as in *context.Customers.AddObject*), passing only the new entity instance as an argument.

Note Each generated entity exposes two events for each core property: *OnPropertyChanging* and *OnPropertyChanged*, where the "Property" portion matches the associated property name. Use these events to add appropriate business logic to any entity modifications.

Your code is responsible for supplying all required property values (those that don't accept NULL values and that don't have defaults). If neither the conceptual model nor the underlying database provides primary key values, your code must supply them as well.

 Note If you neglect to call *SaveChanges*, not only will the changes not be persisted to the database but you will also not receive any warning about the unsaved content.

To remove an existing entity from the model, call the *DeleteObject* method—the counterpart of *AddObject*—passing it the instance to be deleted.

C#
```
// ----- Delete a Customer from the context.
context.DeleteObject(oneCustomer);
// ...or...
context.Customers.DeleteObject(oneCustomer);
```

Visual Basic
```
' ----- Delete a Customer from the context.
context.DeleteObject(oneCustomer)
' ...or...
context.Customers.DeleteObject(oneCustomer)
```

If an entity or one or more of its underlying database tables are configured to cascade deletes, other related entities or data values can be removed in response to a *DeleteObject* call.

Be sure to call *SaveChanges* after completing one or more entity adds, updates, or deletes. If saving your data modifications causes other data side effects (perhaps due to triggers at the database level), you can call the context object's *Refresh* method to force an eventual reload of any new or modified values.

C#
```
context.Refresh(RefreshMode.StoreWins);
```

Visual Basic
```
context.Refresh(RefreshMode.StoreWins)
```

The *Refresh* method includes a *RefreshMode* parameter that tells the method how to deal with data conflicts between the data source and the local EF model's content. Passing a value of *RefreshMode.StoreWins* will bring any modifications found in the data source into the local entity sets, overwriting any out-of-date information stored within the EF context. *RefreshMode.ClientWins*, the other available option, updates data in the data source to bring it in line with the model's view of those associated data records.

By default, the Entity Framework will build the appropriate *INSERT, UPDATE,* and *DELETE* statements needed by each entity as found in the storage layer, taking into account the data fields, the primary keys, and the relationships for each entity. You can override this behavior and supply your own table-specific modification functions in the mapping layer. These functions ultimately tie to stored procedures within the linked database. In the *Entity Data Model Designer*, use the Map Entity To Functions button on the Mapping Details panel to specify each stored procedure. The "Adding a Mapping Condition to an Entity" exercise on page 237 in Chapter 14 demonstrated this process.

Modifying a Database Through Entity Objects: C#

1. Open the "Chapter 16 CSharp" project from the installed samples folder. The project includes *Windows.Forms* classes named *CustomerEditor* and *CustomerDetail*, which let a user modify records in the sample database's *Customer* table.

2. Open the source code view for the *CustomerEditor* form. Locate the *GetConnectionString* function; this is a routine that uses a *SqlConnectionStringBuilder* to create a valid connection string to the sample database. It currently includes the following statements:

```
sqlPortion.DataSource = @"(local)\SQLExpress";
sqlPortion.InitialCatalog = "StepSample";
sqlPortion.IntegratedSecurity = true;
```

Adjust these statements as needed to provide access to your own test database.

3. Open the source code view for the *CustomerDetail* form. Locate the *SaveFormData* function. This routine updates an entity's properties with data supplied by the user. Just after the "Update the individual fields" comment, add the following statements:

```
toUpdate.FullName = CustomerName.Text.Trim();
if (Address1.Text.Trim().Length > 0)
    toUpdate.Address1 = Address1.Text.Trim();
else
    toUpdate.Address1 = null;
if (Address2.Text.Trim().Length > 0)
    toUpdate.Address2 = Address2.Text.Trim();
else
    toUpdate.Address2 = null;
```

```
if (CityName.Text.Trim().Length > 0)
    toUpdate.City = CityName.Text.Trim();
else
    toUpdate.City = null;
if (ItemData.GetItemData(StateName.SelectedItem) != -1L)
    toUpdate.StateRegion = ItemData.GetItemData(StateName.SelectedItem);
else
    toUpdate.StateRegion = null;
if (PostalCode.Text.Trim().Length > 0)
    toUpdate.PostalCode = PostalCode.Text.Trim();
else
    toUpdate.PostalCode = null;
if (PhoneNumber.Text.Trim().Length > 0)
    toUpdate.PhoneNumber = PhoneNumber.Text.Trim();
else
    toUpdate.PhoneNumber = null;
if (WebSite.Text.Trim().Length > 0)
    toUpdate.WebSite = WebSite.Text.Trim();
else
    toUpdate.WebSite = null;
toUpdate.AnnualFee = AnnualFee.Value;
```

Most of the properties in the *Customer* entity are nullable, allowing even numeric properties to be assigned a value of *null*.

4. Just after the "Update the database" comment, inside the *try* block, add the following
   statements:

```
if (this.ActiveCustomer == null)
{
    this.ActiveContext.Customers.AddObject(toUpdate);
    this.ActiveCustomer = toUpdate;
}
this.ActiveContext.SaveChanges();
return true;
```

These lines perform the actual add or update of the *Customer* entity. The call to
SaveChanges flushes all changes out to the database.

5. Run the program. When the list of customers appears, click Add or select a customer
   and click Edit. When the *CustomerDetail* form appears, add or update the individual field
   values. When you're finished, click OK. If you added or modified a customer name, that
   change will be reflected in the list of customer names back on the *CustomerEditor* form.

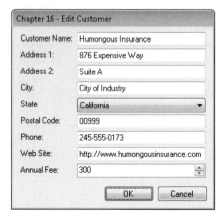

Note At this point, the Delete button on the *CustomerEditor* form does not work. The example that appears later in this chapter on page 283 adds the necessary code to enable the customer removal feature.

Modifying a Database Through Entity Objects: Visual Basic

1. Open the "Chapter 16 VB" project from the installed samples folder. The project includes *Windows.Forms* classes named *CustomerEditor* and *CustomerDetail*, which let a user modify records in the sample database's *Customer* table.

2. Open the source code view for the *CustomerEditor* form. Locate the *GetConnectionString* function; this is a routine that uses a *SqlConnectionStringBuilder* to create a valid connection string to the sample database. It currently includes the following statements:

```
sqlPortion.DataSource = "(local)\SQLExpress"
sqlPortion.InitialCatalog = "StepSample"
sqlPortion.IntegratedSecurity = True
```

Adjust these statements as needed to provide access to your own test database.

3. Open the source code view for the *CustomerDetail* form. Locate the *SaveFormData* function. This routine updates an entity's properties with data supplied by the user. Just after the "Update the individual fields" comment, add the following statements:

```
toUpdate.FullName = CustomerName.Text.Trim
If (Address1.Text.Trim.Length > 0) Then _
    toUpdate.Address1 = Address1.Text.Trim Else _
    toUpdate.Address1 = Nothing
If (Address2.Text.Trim.Length > 0) Then _
    toUpdate.Address2 = Address2.Text.Trim Else _
    toUpdate.Address2 = Nothing
If (CityName.Text.Trim.Length > 0) Then _
    toUpdate.City = CityName.Text.Trim Else _
```

```
        toUpdate.City = Nothing
If (ItemData.GetItemData(StateName.SelectedItem) <>  1&) Then _
        toUpdate.StateRegion = ItemData.GetItemData(
        StateName.SelectedItem) Else toUpdate.StateRegion = Nothing
If (PostalCode.Text.Trim.Length > 0) Then _
        toUpdate.PostalCode = PostalCode.Text.Trim Else _
        toUpdate.PostalCode = Nothing
If (PhoneNumber.Text.Trim.Length > 0) Then _
        toUpdate.PhoneNumber = PhoneNumber.Text.Trim Else _
        toUpdate.PhoneNumber = Nothing
If (WebSite.Text.Trim.Length > 0) Then _
        toUpdate.WebSite = WebSite.Text.Trim Else _
        toUpdate.WebSite = Nothing
toUpdate.AnnualFee = AnnualFee.Value
```

Most of the properties in the *Customer* entity are nullable, allowing even numeric properties to be assigned a value of *Nothing*.

4. Just after the "Update the database" comment, inside the *Try* block, add the following
statements:

```
If (Me.ActiveCustomer Is Nothing) Then
    Me.ActiveContext.Customers.AddObject(toUpdate)
    Me.ActiveCustomer = toUpdate
End If
Me.ActiveContext.SaveChanges()
Return True
```

These lines perform the actual add or update of the *Customer* entity. The call to
SaveChanges flushes all changes out to the database.

5. Run the program. When the list of customers appears, click Add or select a customer
and click Edit. When the *CustomerDetail* form appears, add or update the individual field
values. When you're finished, click OK. If you added or modified a customer name, that
change will be reflected in the list of customer names back on the *CustomerEditor* form.

Note At this point, the Delete button on the *CustomerEditor* form does not work. The example that appears later in this chapter on page 284 adds the necessary code to enable the customer removal feature.

Using Query Builder Methods

Entity SQL and entity-specific LINQ queries (discussed in upcoming chapters) are useful tools for accessing Entity Framework-managed data because they both provide a SQL-like experience, which is based, in part, on the desire to provide an English-like experience. As programmer-friendly as these methods are, they aren't in a form that is easily processed by languages such as C# and Visual Basic. The *SELECT* statements and the pseudo-language content of a LINQ query must first be molded into a form that the relevant language compiler can process. Enter query builder methods.

Query builder methods are ordinary .NET extension methods that apply the subtasks of a SQL-query to an entity or to the larger entity collection. An *extension method* is a feature of .NET that lets developers add method-like functionality to a class without having access to the source code for that class. For example, the following code adds a *DelimSubstring* method to the *System.String* data type that returns a delimited substring:

```csharp
C#
public static class StringExtensions
{
    // ----- The "this" keyword defines the extension target.
    public static String DelimSubstring(this String origString,
            String delim, int position)
    {
        // ----- Return a base-1 delimited substring from a larger string.
        String pieces[];

        // ----- Don't bother if there is no string to split.
        if (origString == null) return null;
        if (origString.Length == 0) return "";
        if (position <= 0) return "";

        // ----- Break the string into delimited parts.
        pieces = origString.Split(new String[] {delim},
            StringSplitOptions.None);

        // ----- Locate and return the requested portion.
        if (pieces.Count < position) return "";
        return pieces(position - 1);
    }
}
```

Visual Basic
```vb
' ----- Namespace for the <Extension()> attribute.
Imports System.Runtime.CompilerServices

Module StringExtensions
    <Extension()>
    Public Function DelimSubstring(ByVal origString As String,
            ByVal delim As String, ByVal position As Integer) As String
        ' ----- Return a base-1 delimited substring from a larger string.
        Dim pieces() As String

        ' ----- Don't bother if there is no string to split.
        If (origString Is Nothing) Then Return Nothing
        If (origString.Length = 0) Then Return ""
        If (position <= 0) Then Return ""

        ' ----- Break the string into delimited parts.
        pieces = origString.Split(New String() {delim},
            StringSplitOptions.None)

        ' ----- Locate and return the requested portion.
        If (pieces.Count < position) Then Return ""
        Return pieces(position - 1)
    End Function
End Module
```

To use an extension method, call it as a method on the target data type or class.

C#
```csharp
String phoneNumber = "206-555-1234";
String areaCode = phoneNumber.DelimSubstring("-", 1);
```

Visual Basic
```vb
Dim phoneNumber As String = "206-555-1234"
Dim areaCode As String = phoneNumber.DelimSubstring("-", 1)
```

The Entity Framework includes extension methods for common Entity SQL clauses, including *Select, GroupBy,* and *Union.* These methods can be used on instances of *ObjectSet* and *ObjectQuery,* which are two Framework base classes (introduced earlier in this chapter) that act as collections for named or anonymous entity types.

Consider this simple Entity SQL statement that selects a few fields from *Customer* entities:

```
SELECT c.FullName, c.WebSite
FROM Customers AS c
ORDER BY c.FullName
```

You can apply query builder methods to a set of customer entities to generate the same results.

C#
```
ObjectQuery<DbDataRecord> query =
    context.Customers.Select("it.FullName, it.WebSite").OrderBy("it.FullName");
```

Visual Basic
```
Dim query As ObjectQuery(Of DbDataRecord) =
    context.Customers.Select("it.FullName, it.WebSite").OrderBy("it.FullName")
```

This code uses the *Select* and *OrderBy* query builder methods to replicate the *SELECT* and *ORDER BY* Entity SQL clauses. In fact, internally the Entity Framework does something similar, breaking the clauses and components of a complex query into distinct method calls. (Both Entity SQL and LINQ convert their queries into a "command tree" that executes in much the same way as the query builder example shown here.)

The "it" keyword used within the content of each query builder method provides a way of referring to the current named or anonymous type as viewed from each builder method. It's somewhat similar to the *this* keyword in C#, or the *Me* keyword in Visual Basic, both of which allow classes to reference their own members. You can change the "it" term to something else by setting the *Name* property of the *ObjectSet* or *ObjectQuery* instance being enhanced by the extension method.

All query builder methods return a generic *ObjectQuery* instance, either an entity type, a modeled complex type, or the ad hoc *ObjectQuery(Of DbDataRecord)* type. Table 16-1 lists the standard query builder methods provided by the Entity Framework.

TABLE 16-1 Query Builder Methods

Query Builder Method	Entity SQL Equivalent	Description
Select	SELECT	Returns all original instances in the base class, but with only those properties specified in the string argument. The argument is a comma-delimited list of fields, properties, or expressions, as is normally used in a SELECT statement.
SelectValue	SELECT VALUE	Similar to Select, but returns only a single property or value. The returned value must be a simple type, an EF-defined complex type, or a modeled entity type.
Distinct	SELECT DISTRICT	Removes duplicates from the collection of data instances. Distinct doesn't work on instances that contain BLOBs or other database-level large-data fields.
Where	WHERE	Applies a conditional rule to the instances in the base query, returning only those that match. The string argument is the same as you would normally use in a WHERE clause.
GroupBy	GROUP BY	Groups results by one or more fields. The method accepts two string arguments: (1) a comma-delimited list of the grouping fields, or what would normally appear in a SQL GROUP BY clause; and (2) a comma-delimited list of projected fields, or what would normally appear in the SELECT clause.
OrderBy	ORDER BY	Uses a comma-delimited list of property or field names to order a collection of instances. When used, the OrderBy method should always appear at the end of a statement that includes multiple query builder methods.
Top	TOP, LIMIT	Returns just the top number of instances from the base collection, which is indicated by the passed-in argument. When used after (to the right of) the Skip method, Top acts like the LIMIT clause in an Entity SQL query.
Skip	SKIP	Skips over the number of instances indicated by the passed-in count, returning all instances after the skipped portion.
OfType	OFTYPE	For conceptual models that include inherited types, this method returns only those instances that are truly instances of the specified base or derived type.
Union	UNION	Combines a base query with another passed-in query, returning the full set with duplicates removed.
UnionAll	UNION ALL	Same as the Union method, but with duplicates retained.
Intersect	INTERSECT	Merges the base query with the contents of another query argument and returns only those instances that are found in both.

Query Builder Method	Entity SQL Equivalent	Description
Except	*EXCEPT*	Returns all records in the original collection except those found in the collection passed as an argument to this method. `query1.Except(query2)` Returns *query1* records not found in *query2*.

Those query builder methods that accept property names or expressions can use @-prefixed parameters. The parameter values appear as additional arguments to the query method. The following statement uses a parameter in a *Where* method call:

```
C#
query = context.Customers.Where("it.ID = @lookupID",
    new ObjectParameter("lookupID", 3422));
```

```
Visual Basic
query = context.Customers.Where("it.ID = @lookupID",
    New ObjectParameter("lookupID", 3422))
```

When using the *Union, UnionAll, Intersect,* or *Except* methods, the parameters applied to the two source query collections are merged. Thus the same parameter name cannot appear in both source queries.

This restriction on duplicate parameter names exists because of the way query builder methods process the core data. As with Entity SQL processing, the query builder methods delay processing of data until your code attempts to access actual data from the query, such as trying to access the value of an individual entity property.

Instead of applying changes to the entity sets and instance collections as the query builder methods are encountered, each method instead helps craft one or more database-level queries that perform the actual data retrieval. You can view this composed SQL statement by accessing the *CommandText* property of the final query builder method in your set. As an example, here's the SQL command text produced by the previous query (the one that includes the *@lookupID* parameter):

```
SELECT VALUE it
FROM ([SalesOrderEntities].[Customers]) AS it
WHERE it.ID = @lookupID
```

Queryable Extension Methods

The collection of results returned by each of the query builder methods is *ObjectQuery(Of T),* a generic type that implements the *IQueryable* interface. This interface supports its own set of extension methods (from the *System.Linq.Queryable* type) that can be used to augment the results returned by query builder methods.

One of the simplest of these methods is *First*, which returns the topmost instance in the query collection. It is the same as using the *Top* query builder method, but it returns results of type *IQueryable.*

Other *Queryable* methods, such as *Count* and *Max*, provide results that parallel the Entity SQL aggregate functions. For a full list of these methods, look up the "Queryable Class (System.Linq)" entry in the Visual Studio online help.

Note Many of the *Queryable* extension methods accept lambda functions as arguments. Lambdas act as a type of inline function that the extension method calls for each instance in the collection being processed. Visual Basic and C# have specific syntax rules for crafting lambda expressions. See the Visual Studio online help for information on using lambda expressions.

Using Query Builder Methods: C#

Note This exercise continues the previous exercise in this chapter.

1. Open the source code view for the *CustomerEditor* form. Locate the *ActDelete_Click* event handler; this is a routine that manages the removal of *Customer* records. Just after the "Locate the customer record" comment (but before the *if* statement that follows it), add the following code:

```
whichCustomer = ActiveContext.Customers.Where("it.ID = @lookupID",
    new ObjectParameter("lookupID", ItemData.GetItemData(
    AllCustomers.SelectedItem))).First();
```

This statement uses a parameterized *Where* query builder method to select one of the customer entities by *ID*. It also calls the *First* extension method, one of the *Queryable* methods.

2. Run the program. To test the code, select a customer from the list and then click Delete. If the program prompts you to delete the customer, it successfully located the entity by *ID*.

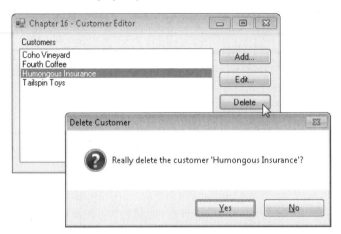

Using Query Builder Methods: Visual Basic

Note This exercise continues the previous exercise in this chapter.

1. Open the source code view for the *CustomerEditor* form. Locate the *ActDelete_Click* event handler; this is a routine that manages the removal of *Customer* records. Just after the "Locate the customer record" comment (but before the *If* statement that follows it), add the following code:

```
whichCustomer = Me.ActiveContext.Customers.Where("it.ID = @lookupID",
    New ObjectParameter("lookupID", ItemData.GetItemData(
    AllCustomers.SelectedItem))).First()
```

This statement uses a parameterized *Where* query builder method to select one of the customer entities by *ID*. It also calls the *First* extension method, one of the *Queryable* methods.

2. Run the program. To test the code, select a customer from the list and then click Delete. If the program prompts you to delete the customer, it successfully located the entity by *ID*.

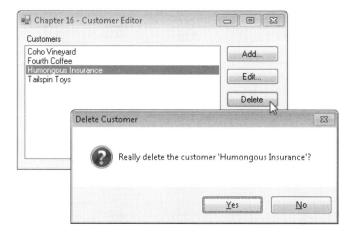

Summary

This chapter introduced Object Services—the core of the Entity Framework—and its conceptual model-centric way of dealing with data. The ability to modify database-level content through seemingly simple object properties is what EF is all about. There is some work involved in getting to that point; work that is thankfully supported by wizards and other tools supplied with Visual Studio.

Microsoft added extension methods to both Visual Basic and C# initially to support the then-new LINQ functionality. But beyond this core technology, Microsoft also added ready-to-use methods that bring SQL-query functionality to ordinary object method calls. By stringing a few or even a few dozen of these calls together, you can generate results that match even the most complex hand-crafted SQL database queries.

Chapter 16 Quick Reference

To	Do This
Modify a database field through an entity property	Create a context instance for the conceptual model.
	Access an entity from the context.
	Modify the desired property value by assigning a new value to it.
	Call the context object's *SaveChanges* method.
Use a query builder method to sort *Customer* entities by the *FullName* field	Create a context instance for the conceptual model.
	Access the collection of entities to be sorted.
	Call the collection object's *OrderBy* extension method, passing it *"it.FullName"* as the order-by clause.

Part IV
LINQ

Chapter 17: Introducing LINQ

Chapter 18: Using LINQ to DataSet

Chapter 19: Using LINQ to Entities

Chapter 20: Using LINQ to SQL

Chapter 17
Introducing LINQ

After completing this chapter, you will be able to:

- Understand the purpose of LINQ in your applications

- Identify the different LINQ providers

- Craft typical LINQ queries using ordinary .NET objects

SQL has proved to be a popular language for retrieving and manipulating data. It is found in most major database systems, and even data libraries that aren't necessarily tied to a database—including the Entity Framework (EF)—use variants of SQL to access tabular or similarly shaped data.

Given its consistency in the programming industry, it comes as no surprise that Microsoft would endow both Visual Basic and C# with a SQL-like syntax for data retrieval purposes. LINQ, introduced into Visual Studio with its 2008 release (and the accompanying .NET Framework version 3.5), enables SQL-style queries that can analyze and retrieve data stored in databases, XML, and even ordinary .NET objects and collections.

This chapter introduces LINQ in both its C# and Visual Basic forms. This is the first of four chapters that cover the querying technology. Chapters 18 through 20 discuss specific flavors of LINQ—flavors that tie directly to features of ADO.NET and the Entity Framework.

 Note The four LINQ-related chapters in this book offer only a brief introduction to the LINQ query language and its extensibility. For expanded coverage of LINQ and how to use it in your projects, review the Visual Studio online help. The upcoming Microsoft Press book, *Programming Microsoft® LINQ in .NET Framework 4*, provides a detailed overview of LINQ and its features.

Getting to Know LINQ

LINQ enables SQL-style language queries against a variety of data types. The queries are part of the language syntax in both C# and Visual Basic, meaning that you get full IntelliSense during query development. LINQ supports a wide range of queryable data types, including most types of collections, arrays, and anything else that supports the *IEnumerable(Of T)* or *IQueryable(Of T)* interfaces.

LINQ was a major enhancement to Microsoft's .NET language offerings; it brought several syntax additions to both Visual Basic and C#. To support these changes, it was necessary to add many new technologies, all of which are now available even when you're not using LINQ in your applications. Some of the more significant technologies you might encounter when using LINQ include the following:

- **Anonymous types**   Entity SQL used these nameless types to generate results that didn't tie to any predefined entity type or complex type. LINQ uses them for much the same purpose, allowing your code to project queries that include property sets not tied to any custom class defined in your source code.

- **Nullable types**   The .NET Framework has always supported nullable reference types, allowing your code to assign a value of *null* (C#) or *Nothing* (Visual Basic) to, say, a string instance variable. Nullable types extend this same support to value types, such as *System.Int32* and *System.Bool*. LINQ uses nullable types to represent fields that contain missing values in query results.

- **Lambda expressions**   Lambdas are function definitions that enable lightweight, callable logic in an in-line experience. LINQ uses lambda expressions to define the specifics of each query operation, among other tasks.

- **Extension methods**   These methods let you add functionality to an existing class definition, even if you don't have access to the class source code. Query builder methods, discussed in Chapter 16, "Understanding Entities Through Objects," are extension methods. In fact, those same query builder methods provide much of the core functionality for LINQ.

- **Object initializers**   Object initializers provide a convenient way of setting the properties of a new object instance, all in a single source code statement. More important, this action is considered "in line," meaning that the resulting populated instance can be used right away in the same statement. New instances of objects generated by a LINQ query have their fields populated using this tool. A related feature known as *collection initializers* provides similar functionality for arrays and collections of individual objects.

- **Local type inference**   This feature lets the language compiler identify the data type of a variable on your behalf, all based on the type of content being assigned to the variable. LINQ depends heavily on inference, but you'll see it most clearly when assigning the results of a query to an untyped variable.

- **Relaxed delegates**   The .NET Framework enforces strong typing, not only in primitive data types but also in function delegates and signatures. But there is still room for variety through the use of function overloads. Relaxed delegates provide a form of function overloading to event handlers and delegates, allowing code to trigger handlers that don't necessarily conform to the official definition. The individual operations that make up a LINQ query use somewhat ad hoc handlers that are implemented through relaxed delegates.

- **Partial methods**   Partial methods allow classes (typically generated classes) to define methods that might or might not be implemented at compile time. The inclusion of these optional methods is left up to the programmer filling out the remainder of the partial class definition. You can enhance your queries with partial methods to add interactive processing while the LINQ query builds the results.

- **XML literals, XML axis properties, and embedded XML expressions**   Version 3.5 of the .NET Framework added several new XML-related technologies, including the somewhat exciting XML literals functionality included with Visual Basic. LINQ can query XML content, and these technologies are used for such queries.

You can read about all these features in detail in the Visual Studio online help.

LINQ provides a common SQL-like experience to data retrieval within your source code. But the syntax and features used change slightly depending on the type of data being queried. LINQ includes several *providers* that tie to the type of data accessed by the system.

- **LINQ to Objects**   This is LINQ in its most basic form: the ability to query ordinary .NET objects and collections. LINQ to Objects is the main focus of this chapter.

- **LINQ to DataSet**   ADO.NET *DataSet* instances have their own LINQ provider, enabling specialized queries against the related tables and column values defined within each set. Chapter 18, "Using LINQ to DataSet," introduces this *DataSet*-centric form of LINQ.

- **LINQ to Entities**   This provider enables LINQ queries against an Entity Data Model, whether generated by the EF's Entity Data Model Designer or crafted by hand in XML. An introduction to LINQ to Entities appears in Chapter 19, "Using LINQ to Entities."

- **LINQ to SQL**   The LINQ to SQL provider specifically targets data stored in a Microsoft SQL Server database. Information on the specifics of using this provider appears in Chapter 20, "Using LINQ to SQL."

- **LINQ to XML**   LINQ lets you query XML tags and attributes as if they were typical database elements. The LINQ to XML provider is not discussed in this book.

LINQ is extensible, so third parties can develop their own providers. Several special-purpose providers already exist, enabling access to formats as diverse as comma-separated values (CSV) and Wikipedia.

Using LINQ with .NET Objects

The LINQ to Objects provider enables queries against standard .NET arrays, collections, generic collections, and anything else that implements the *IEnumerable(Of T)* or *IQueryable(Of T)* interface. As in standard SQL, you form LINQ queries from operational clauses, such as *Select*, *Where*, and *Order By*.

> **Note** The capitalization and syntax of the clause keywords differ slightly between C# and Visual Basic. For readability purposes, I will use the Visual Basic form of these keywords when referring to them in the prose text, but all examples appear in both languages.

For the sample queries in this section, assume that the following two simple object collections, *transport* and *speed* (code shown as follows), already exist and are available to the query code:

```csharp
C#
var transport = new[] { new { Name = "Car", Wheels = 4, SpeedClass = 3 },
    new { Name = "Motorcycle", Wheels = 2, SpeedClass = 3 },
    new { Name = "Bike", Wheels = 2, SpeedClass = 2 },
    new { Name = "Unicycle", Wheels = 1, SpeedClass = 1 },
    new { Name = "Tricycle", Wheels = 3, SpeedClass = 1 },
    new { Name = "Semi", Wheels = 18, SpeedClass = 3 }};

var speed = new[] { new { ClassID = 1, Name = "Low",
        LowMaxSpeed = 1, HighMaxSpeed = 10 },
    new { ClassID = 2, Name = "Medium",
        LowMaxSpeed = 11, HighMaxSpeed = 50 },
    new { ClassID = 3, Name = "High",
        LowMaxSpeed = 51, HighMaxSpeed = 150 }};
```

```vbnet
Visual Basic
Dim transport = {New With {.Name = "Car", .Wheels = 4, .SpeedClass = 3},
    New With {.Name = "Motorcycle", .Wheels = 2, .SpeedClass = 3},
    New With {.Name = "Bike", .Wheels = 2, .SpeedClass = 2},
    New With {.Name = "Unicycle", .Wheels = 1, .SpeedClass = 1},
    New With {.Name = "Tricycle", .Wheels = 3, .SpeedClass = 1},
    New With {.Name = "Semi", .Wheels = 18, .SpeedClass = 3}}

Dim speed = {New With {.ClassID = 1, .Name = "Low",
        .LowMaxSpeed = 1, .HighMaxSpeed = 10},
    New With {.ClassID = 2, .Name = "Medium",
        .LowMaxSpeed = 11, .HighMaxSpeed = 50},
    New With {.ClassID = 3, .Name = "High",
        .LowMaxSpeed = 51, .HighMaxSpeed = 150}}
```

These collections are anonymous in that a formal class was not defined to hold each instance. Instead, C# and Visual Basic defined ad hoc (anonymous) classes based on the *With* clause in each new object instance.

LINQ's core implementation appears in the *System.Linq* namespace.

Starting a Query with the *From* Clause

The starting point for most LINQ queries is the *From* keyword. It serves much the same purpose as the *FROM* keyword in SQL, but andunlike the SQL variant, the LINQ *From* keyword appears first in typical query statements.

```
C#
// ----- Standalone From clauses are not supported in C#.
//       This next line will not compile, but serves only
//       to demonstrate the general syntax.
var results = from tr in transport;
```

```
Visual Basic
Dim results = From tr In transport
```

The *From* clause identifies the enumerable source of the query (*transport* in this case) and its single-instance operator (*tr*), also known as a *range variable*. It's akin to working with a collection of entities in the Entity Framework, where an individual entity is something distinct from the collection that contains it.

Your query need not be limited to anonymous results, either. If you know the data type of the query output, you should take advantage of this knowledge by using a target variable of the expected type.

```
C#
// ----- Standalone From clauses are not supported in C#.
//       This next line will not compile, but serves only
//       to demonstrate the general syntax.
IEnumerable<Customer> results = from cu in Customers;
```

```
Visual Basic
Dim results As IEnumerable(Of Customer) = From cu In Customers
```

The single-line *From* query is the simplest LINQ query you can form in Visual Basic (it is not supported in C#), and it doesn't do much more than express the source collection as *IEnumerable(Of T)*.

Projecting Results with the *Select* Clause

The *Select* keyword lets you create a *projection*, a transformation of the original columns or properties into a new subset of columns or properties. The output properties can include any of the source properties and can also include static values or calculated values.

The following statement projects four new properties from the original *speed* collection: a calculated string value, two of the original numeric properties, and a new property that involves a complex multiproperty calculation. When including multiple output properties in your projection, C# requires that the properties be contained in a new anonymous type definition (*new {}*). Visual Basic lets you retain a more SQL-like presentation, allowing you to list the fields without the object-creation syntax.

```
C#
var results = from sp in speed
    select new { Name = sp.Name.ToUpper(), sp.LowMaxSpeed, sp.HighMaxSpeed,
    SpeedRange = (sp.HighMaxSpeed - sp.LowMaxSpeed + 1) };
```

```
Visual Basic
Dim results = From sp In speed
    Select Name = sp.Name.ToUpper, sp.LowMaxSpeed, sp.HighMaxSpeed,
    SpeedRange = (sp.HighMaxSpeed - sp.LowMaxSpeed + 1)
```

This query is a little more interesting than a plain *From* clause. And it's interesting-looking as well because it gives the impression of a SQL-like query within the very syntax of the C# or Visual Basic source code. Behind the scenes, the language is coercing these queries into a typical method-based format so that it can be turned into standard .NET compiled code. If desired, you can skip the SQL-style coding and craft the method-style statements yourself. The following statement replicates the functionality of the SQL-style statement appearing just above.

```
C#
var results = speed.Select(sp => new { Name = sp.Name.ToUpper(),
    sp.LowMaxSpeed, sp.HighMaxSpeed,
    SpeedRange = sp.HighMaxSpeed - sp.LowMaxSpeed + 1 });
```

```
Visual Basic
Dim results = speed.Select(Function(sp) New With {
    .Name = sp.Name.ToUpper, sp.LowMaxSpeed, sp.HighMaxSpeed,
    .SpeedRange = sp.HighMaxSpeed - sp.LowMaxSpeed + 1})
```

Instead of the database-style query format, this version works directly with the extension methods and lambda expressions that form the basis of LINQ query processing.

Unless you specify otherwise, the output of a projection will be a new anonymous type. To force output of a specific type, include the type name when building the projection fields.

```C#
C#
IEnumerable<SimpleClass> results = from tr in transport
    select new SimpleClass { Name = tr.Name, NumValue = tr.SpeedClass };
```

Visual Basic
```
Dim results As IEnumerable(Of SimpleClass) = From tr In transport
    Select New SimpleClass With {.Name = tr.Name, .NumValue = tr.SpeedClass}
```

You can assign the results of any query to an inferred or manually-typed variable or use the results immediately in other statements that accept collections, such as the *For Each* (Visual Basic) or *foreach* (C#) statement.

```C#
C#
foreach (var oneVehicle in (from tr in transport select tr))
{
}
```

Visual Basic
```
For Each oneVehicle In (From tr In transport Select tr)

Next oneVehicle
```

Note Although you do not need to surround the LINQ query in parentheses when using it in a *For Each* statement in Visual Basic, leaving out the parentheses can sometimes cause confusion, especially within the development environment. In Visual Basic, there is no formal terminator (beyond a blank line) that indicates the end of a LINQ query. Therefore, if you immediately follow the loop's LINQ query with loop content, forgoing a blank line at the top of the loop's body, Visual Studio's code editor and its IntelliSense system might incorrectly assume that the query continues onto the next line. Adding the parentheses removes this interpretation.

Filtering Results with the *Where* Clause

The *Where* clause applies a filtering operation to the original collection, using the supplied filter to limit the results to just those that match the filter.

```C#
C#
var results = from tr in transport
    where tr.SpeedClass == 1
    select tr;
```

Visual Basic
```
Dim results = From tr In transport
    Where tr.SpeedClass = 1
    Select tr
```

Internally, LINQ uses the *Where* extension method and a lambda expression that expresses the condition that filters the original collection.

```csharp
C#
var results = transport.Where(tr => tr.SpeedClass == 1);
```

```vb
Visual Basic
Dim results = transport.Where(Function(tr) tr.SpeedClass = 1)
```

The *Where* clause supports all the conditional filtering elements you would expect from SQL, including the comparison operators (>=, <, and so on), the logical operators (*And, Or,* and *Not* in Visual Basic, &&, ||, and ! in C#), and support for complex expressions. Add parentheses as needed to allow for conditional grouping of filters.

```csharp
C#
var results = from tr in transport
    where tr.SpeedClass == 1 && tr.Name.EndsWith("cycle")
    select tr;
```

```vb
Visual Basic
Dim results = From tr In transport
    Where tr.SpeedClass = 1 And tr.Name Like "*cycle"
    Select tr
```

Sorting Results with the *Order By* Clause

The *Order By* clause sorts the projected and filtered results by one or more properties or expressions. Each sort field in the comma-separated list that follows the *Order By* keywords is processed from left to right. Optional *Ascending* (the default) and *Descending* modifiers appear after any of the sort fields.

```csharp
C#
var results = from tr in transport
    orderby tr.SpeedClass descending, tr.Name
    select tr;
```

```vb
Visual Basic
Dim results = From tr In transport
    Order By tr.SpeedClass Descending, tr.Name
    Select tr
```

LINQ uses the *OrderBy* (or its *OrderByDescending* counterpart) extension method to sort a projection on a field. When sorting on a single field, that method does a great job, but it always assumes that the records to be sorted have not been previously sorted. If you opt to develop a query using extension methods and try to string together multiple *OrderBy* methods, the results will be sorted *only* by the last (rightmost) *OrderBy* call.

C#
```
// ----- This sorts by tr.Name (ascending) ONLY!
var results = transport.OrderByDescending(
    tr => tr.SpeedClass).OrderBy(tr => tr.Name);
```

Visual Basic
```
' ----- This sorts by tr.Name (ascending) ONLY!
Dim results = transport.OrderByDescending(
    Function(tr) tr.SpeedClass).OrderBy(Function(tr) tr.Name)
```

To preserve the ordering imposed by earlier calls to *OrderBy* or *OrderByDescending*, LINQ provides the *ThenBy* and *ThenByDescending* extension methods. This pair sorts results just like their *OrderBy* complements, but they do so in conjunction with and subordinate to prior sorting requests.

C#
```
// ----- This sorts by SpeedClass (descending), Name (ascending).
var results = transport.OrderByDescending(
    tr => tr.SpeedClass).ThenBy(tr => tr.Name);
```

Visual Basic
```
' ----- This sorts by SpeedClass (descending), Name (ascending).
Dim results = transport.OrderByDescending(
    Function(tr) tr.SpeedClass).ThenBy(Function(tr) tr.Name)
```

Selecting Linked Results with the *Join* Keyword

As in standard SQL, LINQ supports queries that combine results from two or more object collections. LINQ has direct support for inner joins and cross joins, and indirect support for left outer joins through the generation of hierarchical query results. Standard LINQ queries do not support right outer joins and full outer joins.

To build a cross join, which generates all possible combinations of two incoming collections, simply include both of the collections in *From* clauses. Visual Basic allows multiple comma-delimited sources in the *From* clause; in C#, you must provide distinct *From* clauses.

```C#
var results = from tr in transport
    from sp in speed
    select new { tr.Name, tr.SpeedClass, SpeedName = sp.Name };
```

Visual Basic
```
Dim results = From tr In transport, sp In speed
    Select tr.Name, tr.SpeedClass, SpeedName = sp.Name
```

To change this cross join into an inner join (which includes only those record combinations that match based on a condition), add a *Where* clause that indicates the relationship between the two collections in the *From* clause.

```C#
var results = from tr in transport
    from sp in speed
    where tr.SpeedClass == sp.ClassID
    select new { tr.Name, tr.SpeedClass, SpeedName = sp.Name };
```

Visual Basic
```
Dim results = From tr In transport, sp In speed
    Where tr.SpeedClass = sp.ClassID
    Select tr.Name, tr.SpeedClass, SpeedName = sp.Name
```

You can also create inner joins using the *Join* clause, which is a syntax closer to standard SQL *JOIN* syntax. Similar to *From*, *Join* identifies a collection and its range variable, but it also includes an *On* clause that documents the joined fields.

```C#
var results = from tr in transport
    join sp in speed on tr.SpeedClass equals sp.ClassID
    select new { tr.Name, tr.SpeedClass, SpeedName = sp.Name };
```

Visual Basic
```
Dim results = From tr In transport
    Join sp In speed On tr.SpeedClass Equals sp.ClassID
    Select tr.Name, tr.SpeedClass, SpeedName = sp.Name
```

Note that you use the *Equals* keyword rather than an equals sign to pair the joined fields. For multicolumn relationships, the *On* clause includes an *And* keyword that works much like the conditional *And* clause.

LINQ can create hierarchical results, known as *group joins*, which simulate a database-level left outer join. This type of joined query can include a subordinate set of results within one field of each parent record. For instance, a group join between customer and order collections can generate a set of customer objects, each of which includes an *Orders* field containing a full collection of orders for that customer.

The syntax to produce a group join parallels that of a standard inner join, but you add the *Group* keyword just before *Join* (Visual Basic only). An additional *Into* clause defines the columns or properties of the subordinate collection. Within this clause, the special *Group* keyword refers to the entire collection (again, Visual Basic only).

C#
```
// ----- Generates a set of speed records, with each record
//       containing the speed record name plus a "Members"
//       property that is itself a collection of transport
//       records associated with the parent speed record.
var results = from sp in speed
    join tr in transport on sp.ClassID equals tr.SpeedClass
    into Members
    select new { SpeedGroup = sp.Name, Members };
```

Visual Basic
```
' ----- Generates a set of speed records, with each record
'       containing the speed record name plus a "Members"
'       property that is itself a collection of transport
'       records associated with the parent speed record.
Dim results = From sp In speed
    Group Join tr In transport On sp.ClassID Equals tr.SpeedClass
    Into Members = Group
    Select SpeedGroup = sp.Name, Members
```

Limiting the Queried Content

In Visual Basic, LINQ includes several SQL-style keywords that limit the amount of data returned by its queries.

The *Distinct* clause removes duplicate rows from the results. It typically appears after the entire *Select* clause in Visual Basic. C# supports *Distinct* only in its extension method form.

```
C#
var results = (from tr in transport
    orderby tr.Wheels
    select tr.Wheels).Distinct();
```

Visual Basic
```
Dim results = From tr In transport
    Select tr.Wheels Distinct
    Order By Wheels
```

The *Skip* and *Take* clauses let you generate paged results, returning a limited number of objects in the output collection. Each keyword is followed by a numeric count that indicates the
number of records to skip (*Skip*) or include (*Take*). You can use either or both of these clauses
in your query. Using the *Take* clause alone parallels the functionality of the *TOP* keyword in
SQL Server.

```
C#
// ----- Use extension method form in C#.
var results = (from tr in transport
    select tr).Take(5);
```

Visual Basic
```
Dim results = From tr In transport
    Take 5
```

Because LINQ queries are processed in the order in which their clauses appear, you will probably want to use an *Order By* clause *before* applying either *Skip* or *Take*, not after.

The *Skip While* and *Take While* clauses work just like *Skip* and *Take*, but rather than a number,
each accepts a conditional expression applied to each successive instance in the generated
query results.

Some of the extension methods associated with the *IQueryable* interface can also be used
to limit the results. They are applied to the completed query when using the SQL-like syntax.
When using LINQ's extension method syntax, they appear as additional methods on the end
of the statement, as was done with the C# samples for *Distinct* and *Take*.

```
C#
// ----- Returns just the first result, not a collection.
var result = (from tr in transport select tr).First();

// ----- Counts the returned records.
int result = (from tr in transport select tr).Count();
```

Visual Basic
```
' ----- Returns just the first result, not a collection.
Dim result = (From tr In transport).First


' ----- Counts the returned records.
Dim result As Integer = (From tr In transport).Count
```

Summarizing Data Using Aggregates

LINQ includes several data aggregation functions that summarize data across the entire result set or within subgroups when used with the *Group By* clause.

In Visual Basic, if a query exists only to generate a single aggregate value, replace the *From* clause with an *Aggregate* clause. It starts out just like the *From* clause, with its source collection name and its range variable. This is followed by an *Into* clause that indicates the summary function.

Visual Basic
```
' ----- What is the maximum wheel count on any vehicle?
Dim result As Integer = Aggregate tr In transport
    Into Max(tr.Wheels)
```

You can also use the extension method form of *Max* (or other aggregates), which works in both Visual Basic and C#.

C#
```
// ----- What is the maximum wheel count on any vehicle?
int result = transport.Max(tr => tr.Wheels);
```
Visual Basic
```
' ----- What is the maximum wheel count on any vehicle?
Dim result As Integer = transport.Max(Function (tr) tr.Wheels)
```

LINQ includes the aggregate functions common to most database systems: *Count* (or *LongCount*, which is functionality identical to *Count*, but returns a *System.Int64 value*); *Sum*; *Min*; *Max*; and *Average*. Two additional functions, *Any* and *All*, return a Boolean value indicating whether any or all of the objects in the collection passed some conditional query.

C#
```
// ----- Do any vehicles have three wheels?
bool result = transport.Any(tr => tr.Wheels == 3);
```

Visual Basic
```
' ----- Do any vehicles have three wheels?
Dim result As Boolean = Aggregate tr In transport
    Into Any(tr.Wheels = 3)
```

The *Group By* clause collects aggregate summaries within unique and identifiable groups. Use it instead of the *Aggregate* clause to summarize data by category. Like *Aggregate*, it includes an *Into* clause that lists the summary functions (useful in Visual Basic) or indicates the target group identifier (C#). The comma-delimited list of fields used in categorizing the data appears between the *By* and *Into* keywords. A special member of the created aggregate, *Key*, presents the unique grouping value for each subsection.

C#
```
// ----- Vehicles by wheel count.
var results = from tr in transport
    group tr by tr.Wheels into g
    orderby g.Key
    select new { g.Key, HowMany = g.Count(tr => true) };
```

Visual Basic
```
' ----- Vehicles by wheel count.
Dim results = From tr In transport
    Group By tr.Wheels Into HowMany = Count(True)
    Order By Wheels
```

In Visual Basic, the *Group By* class performs an implicit *Select* of both the grouping columns and the aggregate results, so you don't need to include your own *Select* clause unless you want to further project the results.

Applying Set Operations

Table 16-1 in Chapter 16 includes some extension methods that perform set operations: *Union*, *UnionAll*, *Intersect*, and *Except*. SQL-style LINQ queries do not have specific keywords for these features, but you can still use the extension methods directly to combine multiple collections. The following query adds the *Union* extension method to one query, passing a second query as an argument:

C#

```csharp
var allTheNames = (from tr in transport
    select tr.Name).Union(
    from sp in speed
    select sp.Name);
```

Visual Basic

```vb
Dim allTheNames = (From tr In transport
    Select tr.Name).Union(
    From sp In speed
    Select sp.Name)
```

The queries to be combined can be as complex as you want, but the results must be merge-compatible.

Summary

This chapter provided a glimpse into LINQ and its capability to apply SQL-style queries to ordinary .NET object collections. The clauses that form the basis of each query including *From, Select,* and *Order By* parallel their SQL counterparts in both meaning and functionality. Although there are some differences that stem from LINQ's data-agnostic way of processing information, the ability to use the familiar SQL paradigm directly in the syntax of the C# and Visual Basic languages brings together two great data processing worlds to meet your data management needs.

For added power, you can use the *IEnumerable(Of T)* and *IQueryable(Of T)* extension methods, among others, to enhance the processed results. Although not covered in this chapter, it is possible to write your own extension methods that integrate into LINQ queries as first-class processing features.

The next three chapters delve deeper into the specific flavors of LINQ that pertain to the ADO.NET experience.

Chapter 17 Quick Reference

To	Do This
Join two collections together with an "inner join"	Include the *Join* keyword in the LINQ query, specifying the linked columns with the *On* keyword.
	Alternatively, include both collections in the *From* clause; use a *Where* condition to indicate the link.
Get a count of records in a query	Use the *Aggregate* clause followed by an *Into Count(x)*.
	The argument to *Count* is a Boolean expression; use *True* to include all records.
Return the results of a query minus any results found in a second query	Use the *Except* extension method: `(query1).Except(query2)`

Chapter 18
Using LINQ to DataSet

After completing this chapter, you will be able to:

- Prepare a *DataTable* instance so that it uses the *IEnumerable* interface

- Treat ADO.NET table values as first-class members of a LINQ query

- Cast type-neutral column values as strongly typed query values

LINQ processes data from a variety of sources, but those sources must first be expressed in a form that LINQ can use. For instance, LINQ expects that all incoming data be stored in a collection, one that conforms to either the *IEnumerable(Of T)* or the *IQueryable(Of T)* interface.

The LINQ to DataSet provider endows ordinary ADO.NET *DataTable* objects with the ability to participate fully in LINQ queries. It does this by adding the necessary LINQ requirements to relevant ADO.NET classes. This chapter introduces these enhancements and shows you how to employ them to extract data from data sets using the power of LINQ.

Understanding the LINQ to DataSet Provider

ADO.NET's *DataTable* class, as a logical collection of data-laden objects, is the perfect candidate for inclusion in LINQ queries. Unfortunately, it exhibits two aspects that make it less than useful with LINQ: (1) it implements neither *IEnumerable(Of T)* nor *IQueryable(Of T)*, and (2) the data values contained in each *DataRow* instance exist as *System.Object* instances and only indirectly express their true types through *DataColumn* definitions.

To overcome these deficiencies, the LINQ to DataSet provider adds new extension methods to both the *DataTable* and *DataRow* classes. These new features appear in the *System.Data.DataSetExtensions* assembly (found in the *System.Data.DataSetExtensions.dll* library file).

The assembly defines two classes, *DataTableExtensions* and *DataRowExtensions*, that include new extension methods for the *DataTable* and *DataRow* classes, respectively. For data tables, there is a new *AsQueryable* method that acts as the gateway for bringing ADO.NET data into a LINQ query.

On the *DataRow* side, a new *Field(Of T)* method moves each data column value from a ge-neric, semi-typeless existence to a strongly typed presence within your queries. It is still up to you, as the programmer, to correctly indicate the type of each field as you add them to the LINQ query syntax. But once defined, you can apply all the standard operators to those fields, including them in projections, filters, and other types of expressions.

> **Note** You can use *DataRow* values within LINQ queries without applying the *Field(Of T)* exten-sion method. However, these fields will still pose as *System.Object* instances. This might prevent you from carrying out certain types of query actions on specific fields. Also, you must still resolve the data type of each field before using it in post-query processing.
>
> LINQ to DataSet also lets you craft queries that use *ADO.NET Typed Data Sets*; however, the Entity Framework supercedes most of the advantages of typed data sets. Therefore, LINQ queries against typed data sets are not discussed in this book.

Writing Queries with LINQ to DataSet

With the exception of the new enumerated methods specific to LINQ to DataSet, using ADO.NET *DataTable* objects in LINQ queries is identical to using standard collection objects. The first step involves converting a data table to its enumerable equivalent using the *and*, which can be applied to any *DataTable* instance.

```
C#
// ----- Customer is an existing DataTable instance.
var results = from cu in Customer.AsEnumerable()
    select cu;
```
```
Visual Basic
' ----- Customer is an existing DataTable instance.
Dim results = From cu In Customer.AsEnumerable()
    Select cu
```

Although the LINQ to DataSet provider includes "DataSet" in its name, the focus in LINQ queries is on the *DataTable* class. LINQ to DataSet does not consider a *DataTable* instance's presence in an overall *DataSet* to be significant, nor does it examine any *DataRelationship* objects when processing queries that contain multiple *DataTable* instances. You must link tables together using LINQ's standard *Join* operator or use the *Where* clause to create an implicit join.

```
C#
// ----- Explicit join.
var results = from cu in Customer.AsEnumerable()
    join ord in Order.AsEnumerable() on cu.ID equals ord.CustomerID
    select...

// ----- Implicit join
var results = from cu in Customer.AsEnumerable()
    from ord in Order.AsEnumerable()
    where cu.ID == ord.CustomerID
    select...
```

Visual Basic
```
' ----- Explicit join.
Dim results = From cu In Customer.AsEnumerable()
    Join ord In Order.AsEnumerable() On cu.ID Equals ord.CustomerID
    Select...

' ----- Implicit join
Dim results = From cu In Customer.AsEnumerable(), ord In Order.AsEnumerable()
    Where cu.ID = ord.CustomerID
    Select...
```

After making the tables part of the query, you can access each row's individual column values as if they were typical LINQ query properties. As mentioned previously, LINQ will not automatically ascertain the data type of any given column; you must explicitly cast each field to its proper type.

To cast a field, add the *Field* extension method to the end of the range variable (the range variables in the previous code sample are *cu* and *ord*). Because the implementation of *Field* uses generics, you must also attach a type name using the language-appropriate syntax. Pass the name of the column as an argument to *Field*.

```
C#
var results = from cu in Customer.AsEnumerable()
    orderby cu.Field<string>("FullName")
    select new { CustomerName = cu.Field<string>("FullName") };
```

Visual Basic
```
Dim results = From cu In Customer.AsEnumerable()
    Select CustomerName = cu.Field(Of String)("FullName")
    Order By CustomerName
```

The *Field* method includes a few overloaded variations. In addition to field names, you can use a zero-based column position to locate field data, although this might reduce readability in your queries. An additional argument lets you specify the *DataRowVersion* to use. By default, queries use the *DataRowVersion.Current* version of the row.

Even when enumerated *DataTable* objects play a key role in a LINQ query, they need not be the only source of data involved. Part of LINQ's appeal is that it allows you to write queries that involve data from disparate sources. You can mix LINQ to Objects and LINQ to DataSet content in the same query simply by including each source in the *From* clause.

```csharp
C#
// ----- Build an ad hoc collection, although you could also
//       include a fully realized class.
var statusTable[] = { new { Code = "P", Description = "Active Order" },
    new { Code = "C", Description = "Completed / Shipped" },
    new { Code = "X", Description = "Canceled" }};

// ----- Link ADO.NET and Object collections in one query.
var results = from ord in Order.AsEnumerable()
    join sts in statusTable on
        ord.Field<string>("StatusCode") equals sts.Code
    orderby ord.Field<long>("ID")
    select new { OrderID = ord.Field<long>("ID"),
    CurrentStatus = sts.Description };
```

```vbnet
Visual Basic
' ----- Build an ad hoc collection, although you could also
'       include a fully realized class.
Dim statusTable = {New With {.Code = "P", .Description = "Active Order"},
    New With {.Code = "C", .Description = "Completed / Shipped"},
    New With {.Code = "X", .Description = "Canceled"}}

' ----- Link ADO.NET and Object collections in one query.
Dim results = From ord In Order.AsEnumerable()
    Join sts In statusTable On _
        ord.Field(Of String)("StatusCode") Equals sts.Code
    Select OrderID = ord.Field(Of Long)("ID"),
    CurrentStatus = sts.Description
    Order By OrderID
```

As in LINQ to Objects, the actual processing of a LINQ to DataSet query does not occur until your code references content from a constructed query. However, all the involved *DataTable* instances must already be filled with valid data before you make the query. When dealing with data from external sources, you must bring any data you plan to include in a LINQ query into the relevant *DataTable* instances before passing the objects through LINQ. If you use a *DataAdapter* to load data, call its *Fill* method before using LINQ to extract data.

> **Note** The *DataAdapter* object's *Fill* method loads all requested data into local *DataSet* memory. If the tables you need to query with LINQ are large and you aren't able to first reduce the number of ADO.NET-managed rows, you might wish to consider alternatives to LINQ to DataSet. LINQ to Entities, discussed in Chapter 19, "Using LINQ to Entities," can process external data without the need to load full tables into memory.

Querying with LINQ to DataSet: C#

1. Open the "Chapter 18 CSharp" project from the installed samples folder. The project includes a *Windows.Forms* class named *OrderViewer*, which is a simple order-list viewer.

2. Open the source code view for the *OrderViewer* form. Locate the *GetConnectionString* function; this is a routine that uses a *SqlConnectionStringBuilder* to create a valid connection string to the sample database. It currently includes the following statements:

```
sqlPortion.DataSource = @"(local)\SQLExpress";
sqlPortion.InitialCatalog = "StepSample";
sqlPortion.IntegratedSecurity = true;
```

   Adjust these statements as needed to provide access to your own test database.

3. Locate the *ActView_Click* event handler. This routine displays a list of orders for either all customers in the database or for a specific customer by ID number. Just after the "Retrieve all customer orders" comment, add the following statement:

```
var result = from cu in customerTable.AsEnumerable()
    from ord in orderTable.AsEnumerable()
    from sts in statusTable
    where cu.Field<long>("ID") == ord.Field<long>("Customer")
    && ord.Field<string>("StatusCode") == sts.Code
    orderby cu.Field<string>("FullName"), ord.Field<long>("ID")
    select new { CustomerID = cu.Field<long>("ID"),
    CustomerName = cu.Field<string>("FullName"),
    OrderID = ord.Field<long>("ID"),
    OrderStatus = sts.Description,
    OrderDate = ord.Field<Date>("OrderDate"),
    OrderTotal = ord.Field<decimal>("Total") };
```

   This query combines two *DataTable* instances (*customerTable* and *orderTable*, each decorated with the *AsEnumerable* extension method) with a collection of local object instances (*statusTable*). It forms implicit inner joins between the tables via the *where* clause and performs a projection of fields from each source table.

4. Just after the "Filter and display the orders" comment, add the following lines:

```
var result2 = result.Where(ord => ord.CustomerID ==
    long.Parse(CustomerID.Text));
AllOrders.DataSource = result2.ToList();
```

These statements filter the original query by selecting those records that include a user-specified customer ID. This segment uses LINQ extension methods and a lambda expression, which works well with the LINQ to DataSet provider. The second line displays the results.

5. Just after the "Just display the original full results" comment, add the following statement:

```
AllOrders.DataSource = result.ToList();
```

This code displays the query results when no further customer ID filtering is needed.

6. Run the program. To see orders, select the Include One Customer By ID option, enter **1** in the Customer ID field, and then click View.

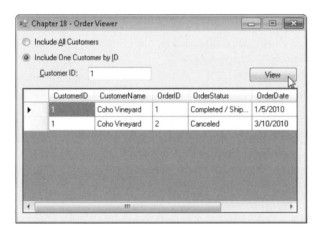

The grid displays content from each of the three source tables. For example, the *CustomerName* column shows a value from the ADO.NET *Customer* table, the *OrderDate* column comes from the *Order* table, and *OrderStatus* gets its information from the ad hoc in-memory *statusTable* collection.

Querying with LINQ to DataSet: Visual Basic

1. Open the "Chapter 18 VB" project from the installed samples folder. The project includes a *Windows.Forms* class named *OrderViewer*, which is a simple order-list viewer.

2. Open the source code view for the *OrderViewer* form. Locate the *GetConnectionString* function; this is a routine that uses a *SqlConnectionStringBuilder* to create a valid connection string to the sample database. It currently includes the following statements:

```
sqlPortion.DataSource = "(local)\SQLExpress"
sqlPortion.InitialCatalog = "StepSample"
sqlPortion.IntegratedSecurity = True
```

Adjust these statements as needed to provide access to your own test database.

3. Locate the *ActView_Click* event handler. This routine displays a list of orders for either all customers in the database or for a specific customer by ID number. Just after the "Retrieve all customer orders" comment, add the following statement:

```
Dim result = From cu In customerTable.AsEnumerable(),
    ord In orderTable.AsEnumerable(),
    sts In statusTable
    Where cu.Field(Of Long)("ID") = ord.Field(Of Long)("Customer") _
    And ord.Field(Of String)("StatusCode") = sts.Code
    Select CustomerID = cu.Field(Of Long)("ID"),
    CustomerName = cu.Field(Of String)("FullName"),
    OrderID = ord.Field(Of Long)("ID"),
    OrderStatus = sts.Description,
    OrderDate = ord.Field(Of Date)("OrderDate"),
    OrderTotal = ord.Field(Of Decimal)("Total")
    Order By CustomerName, OrderID
```

This query combines two *DataTable* instances (*customerTable* and *orderTable*, each decorated with the *AsEnumerable* extension method) with a collection of local object instances (*statusTable*). It forms implicit inner joins between the tables via the *Where* clause and performs a projection of fields from each source table.

4. Just after the "Filter and display the orders" comment, add the following lines:

```
Dim result2 = result.Where(Function(ord) ord.CustomerID =
    CLng(CustomerID.Text))
AllOrders.DataSource = result2.ToList()
```

These statements filter the original query by selecting those records that include a user-specified customer ID. This segment uses LINQ extension methods and a lambda expression, which works well with the LINQ to DataSet provider. The second line displays the results.

5. Just after the "Just display the original full results" comment, add the following statement:

```
AllOrders.DataSource = result.ToList()
```

This code displays the query results when no further customer ID filtering is needed.

6. Run the program. To see orders, select the Include All Customers option and then click View.

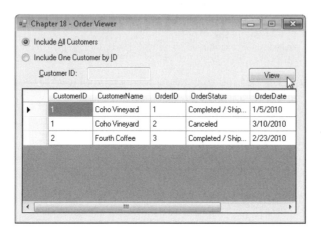

The grid displays content from each of the three source tables. For example, the *CustomerName* column shows a value from the ADO.NET *Customer* table, the *OrderDate* column comes from the *Order* table, and *OrderStatus* gets its information from the ad hoc in-memory *statusTable* collection.

Summary

This chapter introduced LINQ to DataSet, an ADO.NET-focused variation of LINQ to Objects. The implementation of the LINQ to Dataset provider shares a close relationship and syntax with the base LINQ to Objects implementation. By applying a few simple extension methods, *DataTable* objects can become part of independent or integrated data queries.

Beyond LINQ to Objects, LINQ to DataSet is probably the easiest of the LINQ providers to use in your application. Its only drawback is that it expects any queried data to be memory-resident, something not required by other LINQ providers that extract content from external databases.

Chapter 18 Quick Reference

To	Do This
Include a *DataTable* instance in a LINQ query	Call the *DataTable* object's *AsEnumerable* extension method.
	Pass the results of this call as a table source in the query.
Include a *DataTable* column in a LINQ query	Add the *DataTable* as a source within the query, adding a range variable.
	Call the range variable's *Field* extension method, indicating the generic data type and the name of the column.

Chapter 19
Using LINQ to Entities

After completing this chapter, you will be able to:

- Create LINQ queries that access content from an Entity Framework data model
- Call database-level functions from LINQ queries
- Understand how LINQ treats entities differently from other data sources

The Entity Framework (EF) is a model-based interface between your application and an external database. As discussed earlier in this book, the Framework presents logical, database-centric data content in a conceptual form expressed through object instances. This focus on objects makes the Entity Framework a great match for LINQ.

The LINQ to Entities provider brings the world of entities and LINQ queries together. This chapter introduces this EF-centric LINQ provider, a system that takes advantage of the Entity Framework's model-focused data and LINQ's capability to develop native language queries that target entities and their properties.

 Note The exercises in this chapter all use the same sample project, a tool that makes queries using LINQ to Entities. Although you can run the application after each exercise, the expected results for the full application might not appear until you complete all exercises in the chapter.

Understanding the LINQ to Entities Provider

The *ObjectSet(Of TEntity)* and *ObjectQuery(Of T)* classes—the two key collection-style base classes used in the Entity Framework—are ready to use in LINQ queries. Both collection types implement *IEnumerable(Of T)* and *IQueryable(Of T)*, the same interfaces that LINQ requires to enable query operations on a collection. Any entity collection exposed by an EF context or built from an *ObjectQuery* instance—such as a query processed with Entity SQL—can form the basis of a LINQ query.

EF entities referenced in a LINQ query expose properties that are available for projection, filtering, sorting, and other LINQ operations. LINQ to Entities queries are much cleaner than their LINQ to DataSet counterparts because each entity property already expresses its model-defined data type.

Like LINQ, the Entity Framework is a delayed-processing system. The actual retrieval of data (from the database) does not occur at the time you build a data query; instead, data is processed and returned to your application only when you attempt to reference specific entities and properties. When you write an EF query, the Framework prepares a T-SQL query (when SQL Server is used as the backend database) that it runs on the database server to obtain the desired records. That database action occurs only when you access the results of the query statement.

When you craft LINQ queries that involve EF objects, the application employs this same form of delayed processing. The clauses in a LINQ query—and ultimately the extension methods and lambda expressions that make up a LINQ expression tree—translate into SQL statements and clauses that are played out on the data server. For this reason, *all LINQ to Entities queries can involve only objects and data elements that can be represented within a remotely run SQL statement*. While other LINQ providers can be mixed—Chapter 18, "Using LINQ to DataSet," combined LINQ to Objects and LINQ to DataSet content—LINQ to Entities imposes restrictions on the type of data involved in the queries.

> **Note** One of the exercises in this chapter will demonstrate one way that LINQ to Entities can be used indirectly with other forms of LINQ.

Some LINQ features available with other LINQ providers are not supported by LINQ to Entities. Projections, comparisons, and joins that are based on a locally-defined function won't work in LINQ to Entities because the local function cannot be represented in a SQL query running elsewhere. Also, the *Last, SkipWhile*, and *TakeWhile* extension methods are not available; *Skip* and *Take* (in both their SQL-style and extension method forms) will work.

Writing Queries with LINQ to Entities

As with all LINQ providers, the general structure of LINQ to Entities queries varies only a little from the LINQ to Objects standard. In fact, looking at a LINQ to Entities query, it's hard to see that it isn't working with standard .NET objects. The telltale sign is the use of an active Entity Framework object context, either as a direct source for entities or as a way to run an *ObjectQuery* that will feed data into LINQ.

Here is a query that returns some properties from a *Customer* entity:

C#
```
using (SalesOrderEntities context = new SalesOrderEntities(connectionString))
{
    var results = from cu in context.Customers
        orderby cu.FullName
        select new { CustomerID = cu.ID, CustomerName = cu.FullName };
}
```
Visual Basic
```
Using context As New SalesOrderEntities(connectionString)
    Dim results = From cu In context.Customers
        Order By cu.FullName
        Select CustomerID = cu.ID, CustomerName = cu.FullName

End Using
```

Most of the standard LINQ clauses are included, in both their LINQ expression and their extension method/lambda expression forms, including *Where, Join, Group By,* and so on. As far as the LINQ syntax is concerned, LINQ to Entities is pretty full-featured. But there are limitations. Some, such as the inability to use the *SkipWhile* and *TakeWhile* extension methods, were listed previously. Others follow this general rule: *If it can't be converted easily into a storage-level function, it can't be used directly in LINQ to Entities.*

Querying with LINQ to Entities: C#

> **Note** This exercise parallels the exercise found in Chapter 18. It is nearly identical in functionality and purpose, but uses LINQ to Entities instead of LINQ to DataSet to process database content.

1. Open the "Chapter 19 CSharp" project from the installed samples folder. The project includes three *Windows.Forms* classes: *OrderViewer, StatesByYear,* and *Switchboard.* This example focuses on the *OrderViewer* form.

2. Open the source code view for the *General* class. Locate the *GetConnectionString* function; this is a routine that uses a *SqlConnectionStringBuilder* to create a valid connection string to the sample database. It currently includes the following statements:

```
sqlPortion.DataSource = @"(local)\SQLExpress";
sqlPortion.InitialCatalog = "StepSample";
sqlPortion.IntegratedSecurity = true;
```

Adjust these statements as needed to provide access to your own test database.

3. Open the source code view for the *OrderViewer* form. Locate the *ActView_Click* event handler. This routine displays a list of orders, either for all customers in the database or for a specific customer by ID number. Just after the "Retrieve all customer orders" comment, add the following statement:

```
var result = from cu in OrderContext.Customers
    from ord in OrderContext.OrderEntries
    where cu.ID == ord.Customer
    orderby cu.FullName, ord.ID
    select new { CustomerID = cu.ID,
    CustomerName = cu.FullName,
    OrderID = ord.ID,
    OrderDate = ord.OrderDate,
    OrderTotal = ord.Total,
    ord.StatusCode };
```

This query combines two entity collections, *Customers* and *OrderEntries*, both of which are members of the *SalesOrderEntities* class, a derived Entity Framework context. It forms implicit inner joins between the entity collections via the *where* clause and performs a sorted projection of fields from each source table.

4. Just after the "Add in the status code" comment, add the following query:

```
var result2 = from cu in result.ToArray()
    from sts in statusTable
    where cu.StatusCode == sts.Code
    select new { cu.CustomerID, cu.CustomerName, cu.OrderID,
    OrderStatus = sts.Description, cu.OrderDate, cu.OrderTotal };
```

This query extends the original query by linking in a local object collection. This is necessary because LINQ to Entities cannot transmit an entire local collection to the database for SQL processing. Instead, the original query must be converted into a regular .NET collection, as is done with the *result.ToArray()* clause. The original query is processed at that moment, and the results are placed in a standard anonymous array. The *result2* query is actually doing its work using LINQ to Objects.

5. Run the program. When the *Switchboard* form appears, click Order Viewer. When the *OrderViewer* form appears, select the Include All Customers option and then click View.

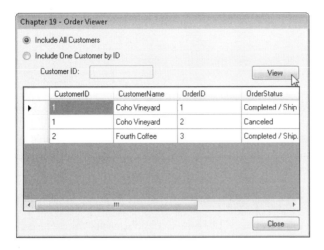

The grid displays content from the *Customer* and *OrderEntries* entities, plus a column from the local *statusTable* collection.

Querying with LINQ to Entities: Visual Basic

Note This exercise parallels the exercise found in Chapter 18. It is nearly identical in functionality and purpose, but uses LINQ to Entities instead of LINQ to DataSet to process database content.

1. Open the "Chapter 19 VB" project from the installed samples folder. The project includes three *Windows.Forms* classes: *OrderViewer, StatesByYear,* and *Switchboard.* This example focuses on the *OrderViewer* form.

2. Open the source code view for the *General* module. Locate the *GetConnectionString* function; this is a routine that uses a *SqlConnectionStringBuilder* to create a valid connection string to the sample database. It currently includes the following statements:

```
sqlPortion.DataSource = "(local)\SQLExpress"
sqlPortion.InitialCatalog = "StepSample"
sqlPortion.IntegratedSecurity = True
```

Adjust these statements as needed to provide access to your own test database.

3. Open the source code view for the *OrderViewer* form. Locate the *ActView_Click* event handler. This routine displays a list of orders, either for all customers in the database or for a specific customer by ID number. Just after the "Retrieve all customer orders" comment, add the following statement:

```
Dim result = From cu In OrderContext.Customers,
    ord In OrderContext.OrderEntries
    Where cu.ID = ord.Customer
    Select CustomerID = cu.ID,
    CustomerName = cu.FullName,
    OrderID = ord.ID,
    OrderDate = ord.OrderDate,
    OrderTotal = ord.Total,
    ord.StatusCode
    Order By CustomerName, OrderID
```

This query combines two entity collections, *Customers* and *OrderEntries*, both of which are members of the *SalesOrderEntities* class, a derived Entity Framework context. It forms implicit inner joins between the entity collections via the *Where* clause and performs a sorted projection of fields from each source table.

4. Just after the "Add in the status code" comment, add the following query:

```
Dim result2 = From cu In result.ToArray(), sts In statusTable
    Where cu.StatusCode = sts.Code
    Select cu.CustomerID, cu.CustomerName, cu.OrderID,
    OrderStatus = sts.Description, cu.OrderDate, cu.OrderTotal
```

This query extends the original query by linking in a local object collection. This is necessary because LINQ to Entities cannot transmit an entire local collection to the database for SQL processing. Instead, the original query must be converted into a regular .NET collection, as is done with the *result.ToArray()* clause. The original query is processed at that moment and the results are placed in a standard anonymous array. The *result2* query is actually doing its work using LINQ to Objects.

5. Run the program. When the *Switchboard* form appears, click Order Viewer. When the *OrderViewer* form appears, select the Include One Customer By ID option, enter **1** in the Customer ID field and then click View.

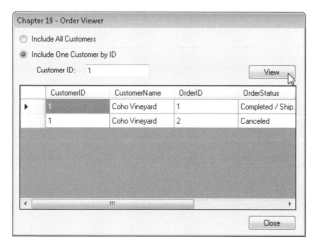

The grid displays content from the *Customer* and *OrderEntries* entities, plus a column from the local *statusTable* collection.

Working with Entity and Database Functions

Calling your own custom function within the *Where* clause isn't supported.

```csharp
C#
private decimal? AdjustTotal(decimal? origValue)
{
    // ----- Add tax to the amount.
    if (origValue.HasValue == false) return new decimal?();
    return Math.Round((decimal)origValue * LocalTaxRate, 2);
}


// ----- Later, try this code, although it will fail.
var result = from ord in context.OrderEntries
    where AdjustTotal(ord.Total) > 500M
    select new { ord.ID, ord.OrderCustomer.FullName, ord.Total };
```

```vbnet
Visual Basic
Private Function AdjustTotal(ByVal origValue As Decimal?) As Decimal?
    ' ----- Add tax to the amount.
    If (origValue.HasValue = False) Then Return New Decimal?
    Return Math.Round(CDec(origValue) * LocalTaxRate, 2)
End Function


' ----- Later, try this code, although it will fail.
Dim result = From ord In context.OrderEntries
    Where AdjustTotal(ord.Total) > 500@
    Select ord.ID, ord.OrderCustomer.FullName, ord.Total
```

But converting this code to use the calculation inline does work.

```csharp
C#
// ----- This will work.
var result = from ord in context.OrderEntries
    where Math.Round(ord.Total * LocalTaxRate, 2) > 500M
    select new { ord.ID, ord.OrderCustomer.FullName, ord.Total };
```

```vb
Visual Basic
' ----- This will work.
Dim result = From ord In context.OrderEntries
    Where Math.Round(ord.Total * LocalTaxRate, 2) > 500@
    Select ord.ID, ord.OrderCustomer.FullName, ord.Total
```

This works because although LINQ to Entities cannot easily migrate your custom and possibly complex *AdjustTotal* function to a SQL equivalent, it does know how to convert the *Math. Round* reference into something that the database engine will recognize (the T-SQL *ROUND* function).

Only certain .NET methods have database-level equivalents, and it's not always immediately clear which local methods will be passed to the database without your interaction. *Math.Round* converts to SQL Server's *ROUND*, but *Math.Sqrt* generates an error, even though Transact-SQL includes a *SQRT* function.

If you would like to have a little more confidence when writing your LINQ to Entities queries, you can forgo the automated conversion and decide up front which Entity Framework or database-level functions you want to include in your query.

LINQ to Entities includes a set of canonical functions which are all hosted in the *System.Data. Objects.EntityFunctions* class. These functions somewhat parallel the Entity SQL canonical functions discussed in the "Using Literals, Operators, and Expressions" section on page 249 of Chapter 15, although only a subset is available with LINQ.

- **Date and time functions**   All the *Add...* functions (such as *AddMinutes*) are included, as are *Diff...* functions that return an integral time span. *CreateTime, CreateDateTime,* and *CreateDateTimeOffset* build new date and time values from their components. *TruncateTime* maps to the Entity SQL *Truncate* function, which returns a date with the time portion removed.

- **String functions**   *Left* and *Right* return string subsets. *Reverse* returns the content of a string in reverse order. *AsUnicode* and *AsNonUnicode* perform Unicode-related conversions on existing strings. These two functions are specific to LINQ to Entities and do not have Entity SQL equivalents.

- **Math and statistical functions**   The *Truncate* canonical function performs numeric rounding. Three statistical functions—*StandardDeviation, Var,* and *VarP* are also included.

To use the canonical functions, be sure to have a *using* (C#) or *Imports* (Visual Basic) reference to *System.Data.Objects* and then prefix the function calls in your query with the *EntityFunctions* class name.

```csharp
C#
var result = from cu in context.Customers
    where EntityFunctions.Left(cu.FullName, 1) == "A"
    select cu;
```

```vbnet
Visual Basic
Dim result = From cu In context.Customers
    Where EntityFunctions.Left(cu.FullName, 1) = "A"
    Select cu
```

Beyond the canonical functions, LINQ to Entities also exposes database-level functions. The SQL Server functions appear in the *System.Data.Objects.SqlClient.SqlFunctions* class and parallel their T-SQL counterparts. The following list touches lightly on the functions available.

- **Server identity functions**   *HostName, CurrentUser,* and *UserName* equate to the T-SQL *HOST_NAME, CURRENT_USER,* and *USER_NAME* functions, respectively.

- **Math functions**   Most, but not all the native SQL Server math functions are included: *Acos, Asin, Atan, Atan2, Cos, Cot, Degrees, Exp, Log, Log10, Pi, Radians, Rand, Sign, Square, SquareRoot* (a renaming of *SQRT*), and *Tan.* Missing from this list are *ABS, CEILING, FLOOR, POWER,* and *ROUND,* although each of these can be accomplished either by using their *System.Math* or *EntityFunctions* equivalents.

- **String functions**   Various string and string-conversion functions from SQL Server can be called from LINQ: *Ascii, Char, CharIndex, Difference* (a Soundex-related function), *IsDate, IsNumeric, NChar, PatIndex, QuoteName, Replicate, SoundCode* (more Soundex), *Space, StringConvert* (known as *STR* in T-SQL), *Stuff,* and *Unicode.*

- **Date and time functions**   This set includes some of the query-level and system-level date-related functions: *CurrentTimestamp* (known as *CURRENT_TIMESTAMP* in the database), *DateAdd, DateDiff, DateName, DatePart, GetDate,* and *GetUtcDate.*

- **Other functions**   The *Checksum* and *DataLength* functions map to their *CHECKSUM* and *DATALENGTH* function counterparts in SQL Server.

The database functions work just like the canonical functions. First include an *Imports* (Visual Basic) or *using* (C#) reference to *System.Data.Objects.SqlClient* and then attach the *SqlFunctions* class name to the start of each database function used in your query.

C#
```
var result = from ord in context.OrderEntries
    select new { ord.ID, ord.OrderCustomer.FullName,
    LateDate = SqlFunctions.DateAdd("day", 90, ord.OrderDate) };
```

Visual Basic
```
Dim result = From ord In context.OrderEntries
    Select ord.ID, ord.OrderCustomer.FullName,
    LateDate = SqlFunctions.DateAdd("day", 90, ord.OrderDate)
```

Working with Custom Database Functions

In addition to calling database-supplied functions from your LINQ queries, you can also call user-defined functions added to SQL Server with the *CREATE FUNCTION* command. Like standard stored procedures, custom functions let you add business logic within the database with standard Transact-SQL syntax, or with Visual Basic or C# via SQL Server's support for the Common Language Runtime (CLR).

Making direct calls to database-level functions through a LINQ to Entities query involves four distinct steps:

1. Create the target function in SQL Server using the *CREATE FUNCTION* DDL command. Make note of the exact spelling and capitalization of the function name and its parameters because you will need to replicate them within your application. The exercise shown later in this section references *AdmittedInYear*, a custom function from the book's sample database. Here is its T-SQL definition:

```
CREATE FUNCTION AdmittedInYear(@whichDate AS DATETIME)
RETURNS int AS
BEGIN
  ----- Return the number of states admitted to the union
  --     during the year of the specified date.
  DECLARE @result int;

  SELECT @result = COUNT(*) FROM StateRegion
    WHERE DATEPART(year, Admitted) = DATEPART(year, @whichDate);
  RETURN @result;
END
```

This function returns a count of the number of states admitted to the United States during the year specified by the supplied date.

2. Add a reference to the function within your Entity Framework storage model layer design for the target database. The storage model uses the Store Schema Definition Language (SSDL) and will appear in an .ssdl file in your project or within the storage portion of the .edmx file generated by the Entity Data Model Wizard. When using the Wizard, add the function by selecting it from the Stored Procedures tree branch on the Choose Your Database Objects panel.

The *AdmittedInYear* function, when imported using the Entity Data Model Wizard, generates the following SSDL content:

```
<Function Name="AdmittedInYear" ReturnType="int" Aggregate="false"
        BuiltIn="false" NiladicFunction="false" IsComposable="true"
        ParameterTypeSemantics="AllowImplicitConversion" Schema="dbo">
    <Parameter Name="whichDate" Type="datetime" Mode="In" />
</Function>
```

3. Add a *static* (C#) or *shared* (Visual Basic) function to your application that parallels the database-level function in its name, arguments, and return type. While the actual database function is remote and inaccessible to LINQ during compilation, this local definition provides LINQ with a valid function to call and enables full IntelliSense during LINQ query development.

You don't need to include any of the function's logic in this stub, but you must decorate the definition with the *System.Data.Objects.DataClasses.EdmFunctionAttribute* attribute. The *EdmFunctionAttribute* class accepts two arguments: (1) the function's namespace, which matches the namespace of the storage level; and (2) the name of the function, with the original spelling and capitalization intact. See the following exercise for examples on how to build this stub in both Visual Basic and C#.

4. Call the function in your LINQ query. The syntax is the same as calls to the canonical and database functions shown earlier in this chapter on page 323.

Although LINQ to Entities is limited in its capability to call custom functions defined within your application, this limitation can be remedied in part by adding relevant logic directly to the database within a custom function and using the preceding steps to enable LINQ to call the custom functionality.

Calling Custom Database Functions: C#

> **Note** This exercise continues the previous exercise in this chapter.

1. Open the source code view for the *StatesByYear* form. This form will access the *AdmittedInYear* database function. Your sample database should already have this function defined.

> **Note** The *SalesOrder.edmx* project file includes the SSDL definition of the function within the storage model layer. The code for both appears in the discussion immediately before this example.

2. Within the *StatesByYear* class, add the following static method:

```
[EdmFunction("SalesOrderModel.Store", "AdmittedInYear")]
public static int? AdmittedInYear(DateTime? whichDate)
{
    // ----- This is a stub for the true AdmittedInYear function
    //       in the database.
    throw new NotSupportedException("Direct calls are not supported.");
}
```

This routine defines the function stub that both LINQ and Visual Studio's IntelliSense will use to recognize the database function. This function cannot be called directly, as evidenced by the thrown exception within the function body. Instead, the *EdmFunction* attribute notifies LINQ that it should locate the *AdmittedInYear* function exposed in the *SalesOrderModel.Store* namespace of the model and call that function instead. The date parameter and the return value for the stub are both nullable types because the query can pass *NULL* values to the actual database function.

3. Locate the *StatesByYear_Load* event handler; this is a routine that loads the data onto the form. Add the following code as the body of the routine:

```
var result = from st in context.StateRegions
    orderby st.Admitted
    select new { StateName = st.FullName,
    AdmitYear = SqlFunctions.DatePart("year", st.Admitted),
    TotalAdmittedInYear = AdmittedInYear(st.Admitted) };

StateAdmittance.DataSource = result.ToList();
```

This query includes a call to both a native database function (*SqlFunctions.DatePart*) and the custom function (*AdmittedInYear*) that matches the function stub added in the previous step. When LINQ to Entities processes this query, it builds a SQL statement that includes a T-SQL call to the database-level *AdmittedInYear* custom function.

4. Run the program. When the *Switchboard* form appears, click States By Year. When the *StatesByYear* form appears, the query results will display in the form's main grid.

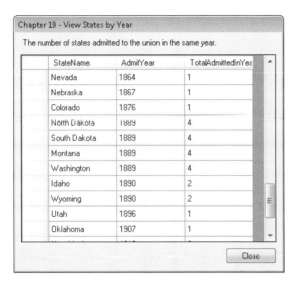

The *TotalAdmittedInYear* column displays an integer value generated by the logic in the custom database function.

Calling Custom Database Functions: Visual Basic

> **Note** This exercise continues the previous exercise in this chapter.

1. Open the source code view for the *StatesByYear* form. This form will access the *AdmittedInYear* database function. Your sample database should already have this function defined.

> **Note** The *SalesOrder.edmx* project file includes the SSDL definition of the function within the storage model layer. The code for both appears in the discussion immediately before this example.

2. Within the *StatesByYear* class, add the following shared method:

```
<EdmFunction("SalesOrderModel.Store", "AdmittedInYear")>
Public Shared Function AdmittedInYear(
        ByVal whichDate As Date?) As Integer?
    ' ----- This is a stub for the true AdmittedInYear function.
    '        in the database.
    Throw New NotSupportedException("Direct calls are not supported.")
End Function
```

This routine defines the function stub that both LINQ and Visual Studio's IntelliSense will use to recognize the database function. This function cannot be called directly, as evidenced by the thrown exception within the function body. Instead, the *EdmFunction* attribute notifies LINQ that it should locate the *AdmittedInYear* function exposed in the *SalesOrderModel.Store* namespace of the model and call that function instead. The date parameter and the return value for the stub are both nullable types because the query can pass NULL values to the actual database function.

3. Locate the *StatesByYear_Load* event handler; this is a routine that loads the data onto the form. Add the following code as the body of the routine:

```
Dim result = From st In context.StateRegions
    Select StateName = st.FullName,
    AdmitYear = SqlFunctions.DatePart("year", st.Admitted),
    TotalAdmittedInYear = AdmittedInYear(st.Admitted)
    Order By AdmitYear

StateAdmittance.DataSource = result.ToList
```

This query includes a call to both a native database function (*SqlFunctions.DatePart*) and the custom function (*AdmittedInYear*) that matches the function stub added in the previous step. When LINQ to Entities processes this query, it builds a SQL statement that includes a T-SQL call to the database-level *AdmittedInYear* custom function.

4. Run the program. When the *Switchboard* form appears, click States By Year. When the *StatesByYear* form appears, the query results will display in the form's main grid.

Chapter 19 - View States by Year

The number of states admitted to the union in the same year.

StateName	AdmitYear	TotalAdmittedInYea
Nevada	1864	1
Nebraska	1867	1
Colorado	1876	1
North Dakota	1889	4
South Dakota	1889	4
Montana	1889	4
Washington	1889	4
Idaho	1890	2
Wyoming	1890	2
Utah	1896	1
Oklahoma	1907	1

Close

The *TotalAdmittedInYear* column displays an integer value generated by the logic in the custom database function.

Summary

This chapter introduced LINQ to Entities, a LINQ provider that allows you to run queries against entity types within a generated Entity Framework conceptual model. Because entities and their properties are strongly typed, it's simple to include them in LINQ queries without additional data type conversion code. Also, the syntax used in the query is nearly identical to the basic LINQ to Objects form.

If there is a downside to LINQ to Entities, it is its inability to include client-side content within the query. Because its queries are processed within the database using that platform's native SQL language, locally defined logic and data content can't always make the transition to the processing layer. Fortunately, LINQ to Entities exposes both predefined and custom database functions that let you move any needed logic to the database level.

Chapter 19 Quick Reference

To	Do This
Include an Entity Framework entity in a LINQ query	Generate the entity container from the conceptual model, storage model, and mapping layer.
	Create an *ObjectContext* instance for the generated model.
	Use the context's exposed entity collections within the *From* clauses of a LINQ query.
Include a custom SQL Server function within a LINQ to Entities query	Add the function to the storage layer of the Entity Framework model.
	Generate the entity container for the model that contains the function.
	Create a *static* (C#) or *shared* (Visual Basic) function stub that has the same name, arguments, and return value (or a reasonable .NET equivalent) as the original function.
	Call the function within a LINQ query.

Chapter 20
Using LINQ to SQL

After completing this chapter, you will be able to:

- Build LINQ queries that use the LINQ to SQL provider

- Understand how LINQ to SQL prepares queries for processing

- Determine when to use LINQ to SQL over LINQ to Entities

LINQ is an extensible system, enabling a consistent querying experience against different data platforms. Sometimes these different systems overlap, providing access to the same target platform through different providers. SQL Server is one such database platform. LINQ to DataSet and LINQ to Entities both allow you to build LINQ queries that interact with data sourced from SQL Server, either directly (LINQ to Entities) or indirectly (LINQ to DataSet). LINQ to SQL, also included as a native LINQ provider within the .NET Framework, provides a third option for processing SQL Server data.

This chapter focuses on the LINQ to SQL provider and the benefits it supplies to your data-focused application. In many ways, LINQ to SQL feels like LINQ to Entities, especially when using its class-generation feature. However, LINQ to SQL was built specifically to interact with SQL Server database tables, and its queries reflect that closer relationship.

Note In October 2008, soon after the announcement of its plans for Visual Studio 10 and the related .NET Framework 4.0 release, Microsoft provided guidance on the future of its LINQ to SQL provider. This "Update on LINQ to SQL and LINQ to Entities Roadmap" blog entry posted by the ADO.NET team (*http://blogs.msdn.com/b/adonet/archive/2008/10/29/update-on-linq-to-sql-and-linq-to-entities-roadmap.aspx*) indicated that the Entity Framework would be the "recommended data access solution for LINQ to relational scenarios." The posting also included a commitment to evolve the LINQ to SQL product based on customer feedback.

Note The exercises in this chapter all use the same sample project, a tool that makes queries using LINQ to SQL. Although you will be able to run the application after each exercise, the expected results for the full application might not appear until you complete all exercises in the chapter.

Understanding the LINQ to SQL Provider

LINQ to SQL is a LINQ provider that targets SQL Server databases. Its simple configuration needs and its focus on the logical organization of the underlying tables make it a useful tool for applications that need easy access to a specific SQL Server database.

Comparing LINQ to SQL with LINQ to Entities

The LINQ to SQL provider first appeared with the initial release of LINQ, part of Visual Studio 2008 and the .NET Framework 3.5. It preceded the release of LINQ to Entities, which was delivered as part of the .NET Framework 3.5 SP1. The two platforms share many similarities, including the following:

- Modeling of data entities using an XML-based schema language
- A Visual Studio–hosted visual designer that simplifies XML model creation
- Generation of a language-specific class layer from the model
- Support for database updates using custom stored procedures
- Delayed query processing through LINQ-constructed SQL statements

Despite these similarities, the two systems diverge significantly in many respects. These differences often help determine which of the two solutions is best for a given application. The two systems differ in four key areas:

- **Platform support** The Entity Framework and its LINQ to Entities extension include support for a wide range of database platforms. In contrast, LINQ to SQL communicates only with SQL Server 2000 and later, including SQL Server Compact 3.5.

> **Note** The visual designer used to set up LINQ to SQL models does not work with SQL Server Compact 3.5.

- **Model focus** LINQ to Entities queries focus on the Entity Framework conceptual model, which is an abstraction of the underlying logical database model. This model can differ significantly from the organization presented within the database. In LINQ to SQL, the model closely reflects the database tables that support it.

- **Overhead** LINQ to SQL is extremely lightweight compared with its Entity Framework counterpart. EF's three model layers allow for tremendous flexibility, but such design comes at a performance and memory overhead cost.

- **Extensibility** While the query features available in both LINQ to Entities and LINQ to SQL are comparable, the Entity Framework's design offers many opportunities for third-party enhancement that aren't currently possible with LINQ to SQL.

Using LINQ to SQL, especially when building models with its visual designer, is straightforward and often much quicker than setting up a LINQ to Entities environment. Microsoft's official encouragement to use the Entity Framework option may help guide your decision, but for applications that have simple needs and access to SQL Server data, LINQ to SQL may be the best query platform.

Understanding the Components of LINQ to SQL

The focus of an Entity Framework model is the XML-based definition of the three different layers: conceptual, storage, and mapping. While LINQ to SQL can use an XML definition as the basis for a specific data implementation, the focus of each table definition is the *entity class*, a standard .NET class decorated with attributes from the *System.Data.Linq.Mapping* namespace.

```csharp
C#
[Table(Name="UnitOfMeasure")]
public class UnitOfMeasure
{
    // ----- As defined in the database:
    //          ID          bigint
    //          ShortName   varchar(15)
    //          FullName    varchar(50)

    [Column(IsPrimaryKey = true)] public long ID;
    [Column] public string ShortName;
    [Column] public string FullName;
}
```

```vbnet
Visual Basic
<Table(Name:="UnitOfMeasure")>
Public Class UnitOfMeasure

    ' ----- As defined in the database:
    '          ID          bigint
    '          ShortName   varchar(15)
    '          FullName    varchar(50)

    <Column(IsPrimaryKey:=True)> Public ID As Long
    <Column> Public ShortName As String
    <Column> Public FullName As String
End Class
```

Attributes, such as the *TableAttribute* and *ColumnAttribute* shown in this code block, inform LINQ to SQL how to map class members to tables and columns in the database. Additional attributes identify storage-level data types, intertable relationships, stored procedure definitions, and other key items that let the application communicate cleanly with the external data source.

The *System.Data.Linq.DataContext* class binds these class definitions with actual data and acts much like the *ObjectContext* class in the Entity Framework. Derived versions of *DataContext* include instances of the decorated classes, forming a class-style representation of the actual database.

```csharp
C#
public class SalesOrderLink : DataContext
{
    // ----- Constructor establishes database connection.
    public SalesOrder(string connectionString):
        base(connectionString) {}

    // ----- Table definitions to link with database.
    public Table<Customer> Customers;
    public Table<OrderEntry> Orders;
    public Table<UnitOfMeasure> UnitsOfMeasure;
}
```

```vbnet
Visual Basic
Public Class SalesOrderLink
    Inherits DataContext

    ' ----- Constructor establishes database connection.
    Public Sub New(ByVal connectionString As String)
        MyBase.New(connectionString)
    End Sub

    ' ----- Table definitions to link with database.
    Public Customers As Table(Of Customer)
    Public Orders As Table(Of OrderEntry)
    Public UnitsOfMeasure As Table(Of UnitOfMeasure)
End Class
```

After you have a defined context, using it with LINQ is a simple matter of creating an instance of the context and adding its exposed members to a query.

C#

```csharp
using (SalesOrderLink context = new SalesOrderLink(connectionString))
{
    var results = from cu in context.Customers
        orderby cu.FullName
        select new { CustomerID = cu.ID, CustomerName = cu.FullName };
}
```

Visual Basic

```vbnet
Using context As New SalesOrderLink(connectionString)
    Dim results = From cu In context.Customers
        Order By cu.FullName
        Select CustomerID = cu.ID, CustomerName = cu.FullName

End Using
```

Except for the replacement of an *ObjectContext* by a *DataContext*, this query is identical to the first LINQ to Entities query included in Chapter 19, "Using LINQ to Entities."

Like its Entity Framework complement, LINQ to SQL uses the clauses in the query (in either the standard LINQ form shown here or one built with extension methods) to craft SQL statements that retrieve, project, filter, and sort the data returned by the query. Because of this, you are limited in the types of non-LINQ-To-SQL data that you can include in the query. Only data content and functionality that can be represented easily in a SQL statement are candidates for inclusion in a LINQ to SQL query.

Despite this limitation, LINQ to SQL does a pretty good job at converting ordinary .NET elements into SQL equivalents. Comparisons with *null* (C#) and *Nothing* (Visual Basic) translate into the expected *IS NULL* and *IS NOT NULL* forms. Using the Visual Basic *Like* pattern-matching operator results in a similar *LIKE* comparison in the generated SQL. Including the *AddDays* method on a date value within a LINQ to SQL query properly converts the expression into one that uses the related *DATEADD* function in T-SQL. For a complete list of all .NET features that LINQ to SQL can use in database queries, see the "Data Types and Functions (LINQ to SQL)" entry in the Visual Studio online help.

Using the Object Relational Designer

Although you can handcraft your own entity classes, a better option for large databases (and even small ones) is to use the *Object Relational (O/R) Designer*, a drag-and-drop visual designer that generates LINQ to SQL classes based on a graphical database model. To use the O/R Designer, add a new "LINQ to SQL Classes" item to your Visual Basic or C# project.

The Designer adds a .dbml file to your project, which hosts the data model in XML form. It also adds two support files: (1) a *.dbml layout* file that stores some designer-specific information; and (2) a *.designer.vb* or *.designer.cs* file that holds the generated entity classes in either Visual Basic or C#. The Designer produces the designer file content as you make content-related changes to the visual design.

You build your data model by dragging classes (entities) and associations (relationships) to the left pane of the designer surface. These entity and relationship instances are either generic forms from the Visual Studio Toolbox or existing database elements from the Server Explorer (or Database Explorer in Visual Studio Express Editions) tool window, as shown in Figure 20-1. You can also include database-level stored procedures and custom functions in the model by dragging them to the Designer's right-side pane.

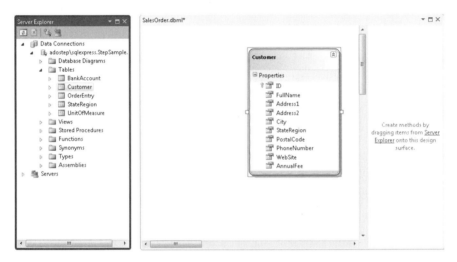

FIGURE 20-1 The Designer after dragging and dropping an existing database table.

Any changes you make to the model result in an immediate adjustment to the generated language-specific source code. You should not customize these generated class files because any future changes to the model will overwrite your changes.

Note You can generate both the XML model and the class layer from a source database without using the visual designer. The Windows SDK installed with Visual Studio includes a program named *SqlMetal.exe*. This tool generates output similar to that of the visual designer, but it does so through a command-line interface. See the "SqlMetal.exe (Code Generation Tool)" entry in the Visual Studio online help for information on using this application.

Building a LINQ to SQL Model

1. Open the "Chapter 20 CSharp" (C#) or "Chapter 20 VB" (Visual Basic) project from the installed samples folder. The project includes three *Windows.Forms* classes: *OrderViewer, StatesByYear,* and *Switchboard.*

2. Add a new LINQ to SQL data model to the application through the Project | Add New Item menu command. When the *Add New Item* form appears, select LINQ to SQL Classes from the list of templates and enter **SalesOrder.dbml** in the Name field. Click the Add button.

3. Visual Studio displays a blank Object Relational Designer. Open the Server Explorer (or Database Explorer) tool window (use the View | Server Explorer or View | Database Explorer menu if the window is not already present in Visual Studio) to display the contents of the book's sample database. If the sample database is not already present in the Data Connections tree, use the Connect To Database toolbar button within the Server Explorer to locate the database.

4. Expand the sample database tree in the Server Explorer and drag the following items to the left half of the O/R Designer surface: **Customer**, **OrderEntry**, and **StateRegion**.

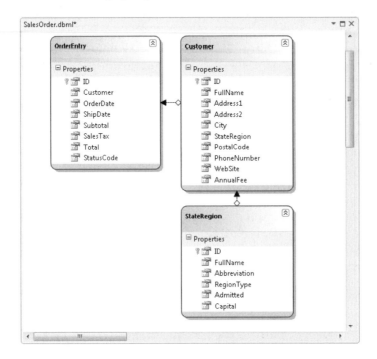

As you drag each item, the Designer automatically creates associations between the entities based on foreign key references defined in the database schema. Click each entity and association, and then view the Properties panel to review the different settings associated with each element.

5. Drag the *AdmittedInYear* custom function from the Server Explorer tree to the right half of the designer surface. This adds a reference to a database-level function, allowing it to be used in your LINQ to SQL queries.

6. Save changes to the file and close it. The Designer has already generated the class layer for the database objects dragged to the design surface. You can view the generated content by opening *SalesOrder.designer.cs* (C#) or *SalesOrder.designer.vb* (Visual Basic, although you may need to click the Show All Files button in the Solution Explorer to see the file).

Using Custom Database Functions in Queries

Although custom functions defined within a .NET application cannot participate directly in a LINQ to SQL query, these same queries can easily access functions written at the database level. When dragged to the design surface (as was done in the example shown previously), these T-SQL functions become part of the context that also hosts the entity classes.

LINQ to Entities includes a similar feature, but it requires you to create local .NET stubs in your own code. With LINQ to SQL, the functions are ready to use in your queries; simply reference the function name as a member of the instantiated context, passing the appropriate parameters as defined within the database.

```
C#
// ----- Assumes an AgedInvoices database function that
//       accepts a customer ID and a number of days,
//       returning a financial amount.
var result = from cu in context.Customers
    orderby cu.FullName
    select new { cu.ID, cu.FullName, context.AgedInvoices(cu.ID, 90) };
```

```
Visual Basic
' ----- Assumes an AgedInvoices database function that
'       accepts a customer ID and a number of days,
'       returning a financial amount.
Dim result = From cu In context.Customers
    Select cu.ID, cu.FullName, context.AgedInvoices(cu.ID, 90)
    Order By cu.FullName
```

You can also call these functions directly, as long as a valid context exists.

```
C#
decimal pending = context.AgedInvoices(whichCustomer, 90);
```

```
Visual Basic
Dim pending As Decimal = context.AgedInvoices(whichCustomer, 90)
```

Querying with LINQ to SQL: C#

> **Note** This exercise parallels exercises found in Chapter 19. The project is nearly identical in functionality and purpose, but it uses LINQ to SQL instead of LINQ to Entities to process database content.
>
> This exercise continues the previous exercise in this chapter.

1. Open the source code view for the *General* class. Locate the *GetConnectionString* function; this is a routine that uses a *SqlConnectionStringBuilder* to create a valid connection string to the sample database. It currently includes the following statements:

```
sqlPortion.DataSource = @"(local)\SQLExpress";
sqlPortion.InitialCatalog = "StepSample";
sqlPortion.IntegratedSecurity = true;
```

   Adjust these statements as needed to provide access to your own test database.

2. Open the source code view for the *StatesByYear* form. This form will access the *AdmittedInYear* database function, which was dragged into the model in the prior example.

3. Locate the *StatesByYear_Load* event handler; this is a routine that loads the data onto the form. Add the following code as the body of the routine:

```
using (SalesOrderDataContext context = new
        SalesOrderDataContext(GetConnectionString()))
{
    var result = from st in context.StateRegions
        where st.Admitted != null
        orderby st.Admitted.Value.Year
        select new { StateName = st.FullName,
        AdmitYear = st.Admitted.Value.Year,
        TotalAdmittedInYear = context.AdmittedInYear(st.Admitted) };

    StateAdmittance.DataSource = result.ToList();
}
```

   In addition to calling the custom function *AdmittedInYear*, this query also uses *!= null* as a condition, which will translate into the appropriate T-SQL comparison clause.

4. Run the program. When the *Switchboard* form appears, click States By Year. When the *StatesByYear* form appears, the results of the query will display in the form's main grid.

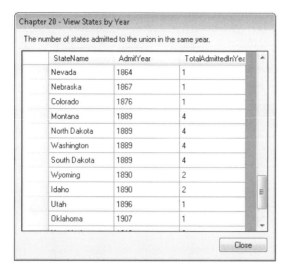

Querying with LINQ to SQL: Visual Basic

Note This exercise parallels exercises found in Chapter 19. It is nearly identical in functionality and purpose, but it uses LINQ to SQL instead of LINQ to Entities to process database content.

This exercise continues the previous exercise in this chapter.

1. Open the source code view for the *General* class. Locate the *GetConnectionString* function; this is a routine that uses a *SqlConnectionStringBuilder* to create a valid connection string to the sample database. It currently includes the following statements:

```
sqlPortion.DataSource = "(local)\SQLExpress"
sqlPortion.InitialCatalog = "StepSample"
sqlPortion.IntegratedSecurity = True
```

Adjust these statements as needed to provide access to your own test database.

2. Open the source code view for the *StatesByYear* form. This form will access the *AdmittedInYear* database function, which was dragged into the model in the prior example.

3. Locate the *StatesByYear_Load* event handler; this is a routine that loads the data onto the form. Add the following code as the body of the routine:

```
Using context As New SalesOrderDataContext(GetConnectionString())
    Dim result = From st In context.StateRegions
        Where st.Admitted IsNot Nothing
        Select StateName = st.FullName,
        AdmitYear = st.Admitted.Value.Year,
        TotalAdmittedInYear = context.AdmittedInYear(st.Admitted)
        Order By AdmitYear

    StateAdmittance.DataSource = result.ToList
End Using
```

In addition to calling the custom function *AdmittedInYear*, this query also uses *IsNot Nothing* as a condition, which will translate into the appropriate T-SQL comparison clause.

4. Run the program. When the *Switchboard* form appears, click States By Year. When the *StatesByYear* form appears, the results of the query will display in the form's main grid.

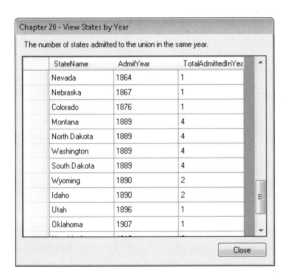

Summary

This chapter introduced the LINQ to SQL query provider. Although it shares many features with LINQ to Entities, its quick setup and close ties to SQL Server make it a useful choice for applications that target that platform.

LINQ to SQL sports its own visual designer: the Object Relational Designer, or O/R Designer. For developers looking for a more direct approach or who need the automation support available through command-line utilities, the provider also includes *SqlMetal.exe* as an alternative to the visual experience.

Chapter 20 Quick Reference

To	Do This
Include an entity class in a LINQ query	Add the entity class to your project by writing its code, using the Object Relational Designer, or employing the *SqlMetal.exe* command-line tool.
	Create a *DataContext* instance for the generated entity class.
	Use the context's exposed entity collections within the *From* clauses of a LINQ query.
Include a custom SQL Server function within a LINQ to SQL query	Drag the function to the right half of the Object Relational Designer surface or use equivalent code-based alternatives.
	Create a *DataContext* instance that contains the function.
	Call the function within a LINQ query.

Part V

Presenting Data to the World

Chapter 21: Binding Data with ADO.NET

Chapter 22: Providing RESTful Services with WCF Data Services

Chapter 21
Binding Data with ADO.NET

After completing this chapter, you will be able to:

- Bind data to controls in Windows Forms, WPF, and ASP.NET applications

- Understand the classes and technologies that make binding possible

- Create working database programs with simple drag-and-drop techniques

Data binding involves connecting display and data-entry controls with a data source in a way that somewhat automates the data management process. Rather than writing code that manually transfers data between, say, a *DataTable* instance and individual *TextBox* controls, you configure the controls to understand how they should obtain data from the *DataTable*. This simulated simplicity—the true complexity is hidden away inside of .NET controls and classes—brings Rapid Application Development (RAD) features from pre-.NET versions of Visual Basic into the .NET world.

This chapter provides brief demonstrations of using data binding in three types of .NET applications: Windows Forms, Windows Presentation Foundation (WPF), and ASP.NET. In each case, you'll create a sample application with simple drag-and-drop techniques, with no additional code added to enable data migration. A discussion of the technologies involved follows each example.

Binding Data in Windows Forms

The Windows Forms system supports two types of binding scenarios based on the features of individual controls: *simple* and *complex*. In simple data binding, a control hosts a single value from a single data record, such as a *TextBox* that supports displaying or editing a customer name. In this arrangement, a form typically hosts multiple controls, each of which is bound to a specific data row field.

In complex data binding, a single control expresses a list of records, perhaps all records in a table. The control can include features that indicate how to display the complexities of a data row in a single control entry. The *ListBox* control is a typical candidate for complex data binding.

Creating Complex-Bound Applications

You've already seen complex data binding demonstrated throughout this book. Starting with Chapter 4, many of the sample applications employed the *DataGridView* control to display data results. Assigning a compatible array or collection to that control's *DataSource* property renders the data within the control's visible grid.

The most interesting use of the control appeared in Chapter 11, "Making External Data Available Locally," where a data adapter-enabled *DataTable* instance was linked to the *DataGridView*. *DataSource* property. The sample code built a data adapter link to the *UnitOfMeasure* table, crafting each of the *INSERT, UPDATE,* and *DELETE* statements before making the assignment to the grid control.

```
C#
UnitAdapter.Fill(UnitTable);
UnitGrid.DataSource = UnitTable;

Visual Basic
UnitAdapter.Fill(UnitTable)
UnitGrid.DataSource = UnitTable
```

By having an active data adapter as part of the control's input source, changes made to data values within the grid propagate back to the external data source, essentially creating a miniature grid-based table editor. That sample could be shortened even more to use a *SqlCommandBuilder,* freeing you from even having to craft the three SQL data manipulation statements. But even with this change, you still need a bit of custom code to make the grid work.

For an even simpler grid-based solution, you can build an application that supports editing of database table values without writing a single line of code. Creating such a program involves little more than dragging tables from a wizard-configured data source to the surface of a form.

Creating a Complex Data-Bound Form

1. Create a new Windows Forms application using either Visual Basic or C#. The new project displays a single blank form.

2. Add a data source for the table to be edited. The "Connecting to External Data" section in Chapter 1, "Introducing ADO.NET 4," includes step-by-step instructions for creating such a data source. Follow those instructions. When you reach the Choose Your

Database Objects panel in step 14 of the instructions, select the CourseCatalog table from the list. Type **CourseDataSet** in the DataSet Name field. Click Finish to add the *DataSet* to the project.

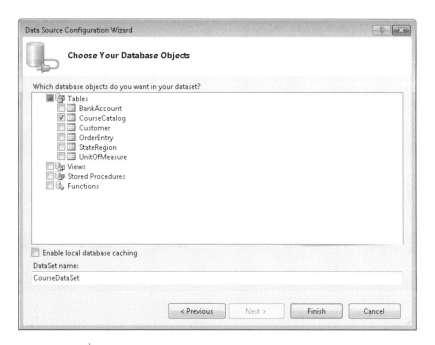

3. The Data Sources panel in Visual Studio now contains a *CourseDataSet* tree with the *CourseCatalog* table as a branch within it. Expand the *CourseCatalog* branch to see the individual fields associated with the table: four text fields and two Boolean fields.

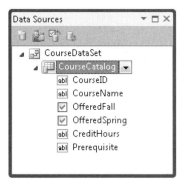

4. The *CourseCatalog* branch is actually a drop-down list; click its name to enable the list. Expand the list and ensure that *DataGridView* is selected.

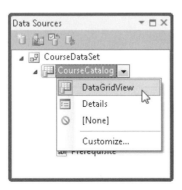

5. Drag the *CourseCatalog* name from the Data Sources panel and drop it on the blank form's surface. This action adds a *DataGridView* control to the form with columns for each of the table's fields. It also adds a toolbar-style control and several non-visual controls to the bottom of the design window. Resize the form and grid control as needed.

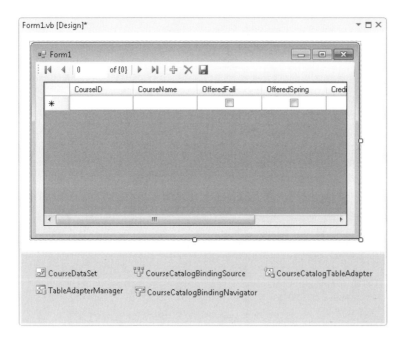

6. Run the program. When the form appears, the grid will display any records already found in the *CourseCatalog* table. Note that the data is fully editable; you can add, update, and delete records in the table through the form.

Creating Simple-Bound Applications

The *DataGridView* control and the accompanying VCR-style control in the complex-bound solution provide an editing experience reminiscent of Microsoft Access' default table editing environment. If a grid interface doesn't meet your data display and editing needs, Visual Studio can generate a data-bound form that hosts each data value in a distinct control. This method gives the form a more traditional data-editing look while still keeping the promise of no-custom-code simplicity.

Creating a Simple Data-Bound Form

1. Create a new Windows Forms application using either Visual Basic or C#. The new project displays a single blank form.

2. As in the prior example, use the Data Source Configuration Wizard to create a *CourseDataSet* data set that contains the *CourseCatalog* table.

3. In the Data Sources panel, click the drop-down for the *CourseCatalog* table branch and select *Details* from the list of choices.

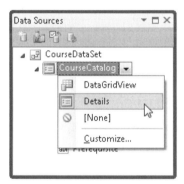

> **Note** The field names for each table as displayed in the Data Sources panel are also drop-down lists. These lists allow you to indicate what type of simple data-bound control will be used to display the data on the target form.

4. Drag the *CourseCatalog* name from the Data Sources panel and drop it on the blank form's surface. This action adds separate *TextBox* and *CheckBox* controls to the form for each column in the *CourseCatalog* table. It also adds a toolbar-style control, and several nonvisual controls to the bottom of the design window. Resize the form and data controls as needed.

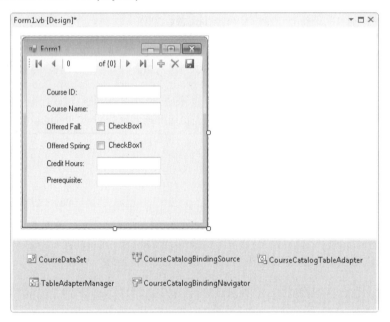

5. Run the program. When the form appears, it displays one record from the *CourseCatalog* table. The data is fully editable, and you can add, update, and delete records in the table through the form.

Understanding Windows Forms Data Binding

Although these simple applications work without the need for custom code, the form and its display controls, the data set, and the nonvisual controls added to the form each include sufficient code to enable source-to-user data management.

When you drag a table to the form's surface in either the complex-style or simple-style bindings, Visual Studio builds a hierarchy of classes that work together to transport data between the database and the user. The following list identifies the members of this chain, moving from the source-side to the form-side of the interaction.

- **TableAdapter**   As discussed in Chapter 11, a data adapter enables bidirectional movement of a table's content. Because the bound controls display data and accept updates from the user, the adapter keeps the database and the form in sync.

- **TableAdapterManager**   This object, added to the form by Visual Studio, assists the *TableAdapter* in hierarchical-data environments. The *CourseCatalog* examples shown above do not include hierarchical data.

- **DataSet**   This is the wizard-built *DataSet* instance added to the Data Sources panel. It's actually a strongly typed data set, which is not discussed in this book other than to point out how the Entity Framework (EF) expands on the basic strongly typed data set functionality.

- **BindingSource**   Although Windows Forms controls can bind directly to ADO.NET *DataTable* instances, such a relationship provides only minimal functionality. The *BindingSource* class enriches this relationship by adding change notifications, error management, and consistent movement functionality between the records of a source data table.

- **BindingContext**   The binding context doesn't appear as one of the controls added by Visual Studio, but it is present. It appears as a member of the form itself and exists in parallel in each of the controls that participate in the data binding operation. A single form (or some other equivalent data surface, such as a *Panel* control) can support multiple binding contexts, one for each source of incoming and outgoing data displayed on the form. Each context is defined by its *source* (typically a reference to the *DataSet* instance or other top-level data source) and the *path* within the source (for *DataSet* instances, this typically refers to the table name). The *BindingContext* instances manage the comings and goings of all data, keeping all controls that share a common context in sync with each other. It ensures that controls managing the same source table don't point to different rows.

- **Form** and controls   The form surface and the individual data control form one endpoint of the data-binding relationship. Each control exposes a *DataBindings* collection that maps bound data to specific properties of the control. For instance, in the preceding simple-bound example, the incoming *CourseCatalog.CourseName* field is mapped to the *CourseNameTextBox* control's *Text* property. But data can be bound to other properties as well. For example, you can map a control's *BackColor* property to a database field that tracks color values.

In addition to the grid or detail controls added to the form, dragging a data source table to a form adds a *BindingNavigator* control, a "VCR" control that lets the user move between the different rows of the table, adding and deleting rows as needed. One of the buttons on this toolbar, the Save button (with a floppy disk image), includes some code-behind in its *Click* event handler.

```
C#
this.Validate();
this.courseCatalogBindingSource.EndEdit();
this.tableAdapterManager.UpdateAll(this.courseDataSet);
```

Visual Basic
```
Me.Validate()
Me.CourseCatalogBindingSource.EndEdit()
Me.TableAdapterManager.UpdateAll(Me.CourseDataSet)
```

This code finishes up all pending edits and saves all changes to the database, bringing everything back in sync.

As convenient as these data binding examples are, it is rare that an application can meet usability needs without providing additional custom code. In addition to using these simple techniques, you can augment the generated controls and code with your own source code or use the generated source as a basis for designing your own data-bound environments.

Binding Data in WPF

Windows Presentation Foundation (WPF) applications use an XML-based schema language called XAML to define the user interface and behavioral aspects of an application. Visual Studio includes support for building WPF/XAML applications, presenting a design experience that is similar to standard Windows Forms development.

 Note An introduction to the Windows Presentation Foundation and its XML-based way of describing application elements is beyond the scope of this book.

Creating Data-Bound WPF Applications

WPF applications in Visual Studio support the same type of drag-and-drop data-bound application building features present in Windows Forms projects, albeit with some variations. The following examples guide you through the construction of a data-bound WPF project.

Creating a Data-Bound WPF Project

1. Create a new WPF Application project using either Visual Basic or C#. The new project displays a single blank window with associated XAML content below the visual representation.

2. As in the prior examples, use the Data Source Configuration Wizard to create a *CourseDataSet* data set that contains the *CourseCatalog* table.

3. In the Data Sources panel, click the drop-down for the *CourseCatalog* table branch and select Details from the list of choices.

4. Drag the *CourseCatalog* name from the Data Sources panel and drop it on the blank WPF window surface. This action adds a grid to the form that hosts separate *Label, TextBox,* and *CheckBox* controls for each column in the *CourseCatalog* table.

5. Run the program. When the form appears, it displays the first record from the *CourseCatalog* table.

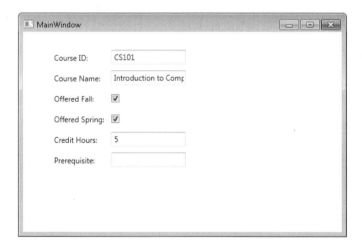

Building the WPF project is simple using drag-and-drop techniques, but as the example project demonstrates, it's possible to view only the initial record in the incoming table. The following language-specific projects add navigation features.

Adding Navigation to a Data-Bound WPF Window: C#

> **Note** This exercise continues the initial WPF exercise in this section.

1. Add four *Button* controls from the Toolbox panel to the WPF window surface. Name the buttons **ActFirst**, **ActPrevious**, **ActNext**, and **ActLast**; set their *Content* property values to **First**, **Previous**, **Next**, and **Last**, respectively.

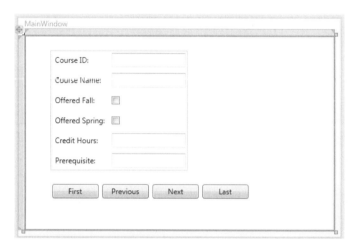

2. Double-click the *ActFirst* button control. When the event handler appears, add the following code:

```
// ----- Move to the first record in the table.
System.Windows.Data.CollectionViewSource catalogSource =
    (System.Windows.Data.CollectionViewSource)
    this.FindResource("courseCatalogViewSource");
catalogSource.View.MoveCurrentToFirst();
```

3. Back on the window design surface, double-click the *ActPrevious* button control. When the event handler appears, add the following code:

```
// ----- Move to the previous record in the table.
System.Windows.Data.CollectionViewSource catalogSource =
    (System.Windows.Data.CollectionViewSource)
    this.FindResource("courseCatalogViewSource");
if (catalogSource.View.CurrentPosition > 0)
    catalogSource.View.MoveCurrentToPrevious();
```

4. Back on the window design surface, double-click the *ActNext* button control. When the event handler appears, add the following code:

```
// ----- Move to the next record in the table.
System.Windows.Data.CollectionViewSource catalogSource =
    (System.Windows.Data.CollectionViewSource)
    this.FindResource("courseCatalogViewSource");
catalogSource.View.MoveCurrentToNext();
if (catalogSource.View.IsCurrentAfterLast)
    catalogSource.View.MoveCurrentToPrevious();
```

5. Back on the window design surface, double-click the *ActLast* button control. When the event handler appears, add the following code:

```
// ----- Move to the last record in the table.
System.Windows.Data.CollectionViewSource catalogSource =
    (System.Windows.Data.CollectionViewSource)
    this.FindResource("courseCatalogViewSource");
catalogSource.View.MoveCurrentToLast();
```

6. Run the program. When the form appears, it displays the first record from the *CourseCatalog* table. Use the new navigation buttons to move through the records in the bound table.

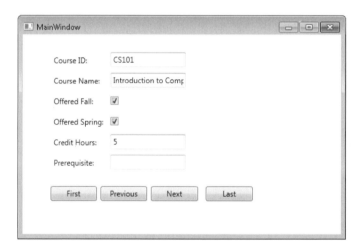

Adding Navigation to a Data-Bound WPF Window: Visual Basic

 Note This exercise continues the initial WPF exercise in this section.

1. Add four *Button* controls from the Toolbox panel to the WPF window surface. Name the buttons **ActFirst**, **ActPrevious**, **ActNext**, and **ActLast**; set their *Content* property values to **First**, **Previous**, **Next**, and **Last**, respectively.

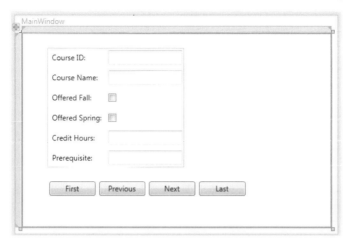

2. Double-click the *ActFirst* button control. When the event handler appears, add the following code:

```
' ----- Move to the first record in the table.
Dim catalogSource As System.Windows.Data.CollectionViewSource =
    CType(Me.FindResource("CourseCatalogViewSource"),
    System.Windows.Data.CollectionViewSource)
catalogSource.View.MoveCurrentToFirst()
```

3. Back on the window design surface, double-click the *ActPrevious* button control. When the event handler appears, add the following code:

```
' ----- Move to the previous record in the table.
Dim catalogSource As System.Windows.Data.CollectionViewSource =
    CType(Me.FindResource("CourseCatalogViewSource"),
    System.Windows.Data.CollectionViewSource)
If (catalogSource.View.CurrentPosition > 0) Then _
    catalogSource.View.MoveCurrentToPrevious()
```

4. Back on the window design surface, double-click the *ActNext* button control. When the event handler appears, add the following code:

```
' ----- Move to the next record in the table.
Dim catalogSource As System.Windows.Data.CollectionViewSource =
    CType(Me.FindResource("CourseCatalogViewSource"),
    System.Windows.Data.CollectionViewSource)
Dim totalItems = Aggregate vw In catalogSource.View
    Into Count(True)

If (catalogSource.View.CurrentPosition < (totalItems - 1)) Then _
    catalogSource.View.MoveCurrentToNext()
```

5. Back on the window design surface, double-click the *ActLast* button control. When the event handler appears, add the following code:

```
' ----- Move to the last record in the table.
Dim catalogSource As System.Windows.Data.CollectionViewSource =
    CType(Me.FindResource("CourseCatalogViewSource"),
    System.Windows.Data.CollectionViewSource)
catalogSource.View.MoveCurrentToLast()
```

6. Run the program. When the form appears, it displays the first record from the *CourseCatalog* table. Use the new navigation buttons to move through the records in the bound table.

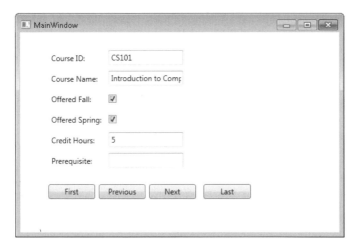

Understanding WPF Data Binding

The *DataSet, TableAdapter,* and *TableAdapterManager* instances used in the Windows Forms bound data example earlier in this chapter also appear in the WPF example. That's because those portions are generated by the Data Source Configuration Wizard; they are not dependent on the type of project in which they appear. In WPF, as in Windows Forms, they manage retrieving the data from the external data source and propagating any changes from the application back to the data source.

The binding elements that connect the *DataSet* content to the on-window fields vary significantly between WPF and Windows Forms. Much of a WPF application is declared using XAML, and data bindings are no different. To enable data binding, Visual Studio adds information on the data source to the *Grid* control that hosts the individual data controls.

```
<!-- Attributes not relevant to the discussion have been removed. -->
<Grid DataContext="{StaticResource CourseCatalogViewSource}" Name="Grid1" >
```

The *DataContext* attribute defines the data source for all subordinate elements, which in this case will be the individual data-bound controls found inside of the *Grid1* grid. *CourseCatalogViewSource* is defined a little earlier in the XAML.

```
<Window.Resources>
  <my:CourseDataSet x:Key="CourseDataSet" />
  <CollectionViewSource x:Key="CourseCatalogViewSource"
    Source="{Binding Path=CourseCatalog,
    Source={StaticResource CourseDataSet}}" />
</Window.Resources>
```

CourseCatalogViewSource is an instance of *CollectionViewSource* (actually, it's known as the *CollectionView* class by the time the XAML bubbles up into actual code), which is a wrapper around data sources that makes navigation of those sources convenient for WPF applications. In this case, that data source is the *CourseDataSet* data set, as identified in this same XML block.

The important part of the *CourseCatalogViewSource* definition is the *Binding* component.

```
{Binding Path=CourseCatalog, Source={StaticResource CourseDataSet}}
```

This content identifies the source of the data that will bind to the controls. As with the form-hosted *BindingContext* in Windows Forms applications, the *Binding* entry defines both a *source* (the *DataSet* instance) and a *path* within the source (the *DataTable* name).

Within the XAML definitions for an individual data-bound control, the *Binding* entry appears again to identify the path to the individual column hosted by that control. This code block defines the *TextBox* control that hosts the *CourseCatalog.CourseName* field.

```
<!-- Attributes not relevant to the discussion have been removed. -->
<TextBox Name="CourseNameTextBox" Text="{Binding Path=CourseName,
    Mode=TwoWay, ValidatesOnExceptions=true, NotifyOnValidationError=true}" />
```

This entry specifies the path (the *CourseName* column) relative to the *DataContext* established by the enclosing *Grid* control (*Grid1*). The binding ties to the *Text* attribute, which will display the bound content in the editable portion of the control. Part of XAML's power is that bound data can flow into almost any attribute exposed by a control. In fact, the entire XAML binding system extends to non-controls as well, allowing nearly any aspect of a WPF application definition to be configured by bound data from a variety of sources, both internal and external to the application.

Although the drag-and-drop operation that built the WPF window included enabled text boxes and clickable *CheckBox* controls, the application will not return any data changes to the database. Also, you cannot add or delete records through the default bound application. To enable these features, you must update the bound *DataSet* directly, adjusting the content exposed through each *DataTable* instance's *Rows* collection as needed. Calls to *DataSet.AcceptChanges* and the table adapter's *Update* method will send any changes back to the source and trigger a refresh of the displayed results.

Binding Data in ASP.NET

ASP.NET is Visual Studio's standard web application development solution. Although the development experience is similar to that of Windows Forms and other Visual Studio project types, running ASP.NET applications exist to generate valid HTML and related Web-centric scripting content for consumption by a web browser. All application components, including any data-bound controls, flow to the user's screen as ordinary web content.

> **Note** ASP.NET is not included in either the C# or the Visual Basic flavors of the Visual Studio 2010 Express Edition product. Express Edition users must instead obtain Visual Web Developer 2010 from Microsoft's Visual Studio Express web site *http://www.microsoft.com/express/Web/*.

Creating Data-Bound ASP.NET Applications

ASP.NET applications in Visual Studio support some drag-and-drop data-bound functionality, although the default data presentation options are not as varied as those found in either Windows Forms or WPF projects. The following projects guide you through the process of adding a read-only data-bound grid to a new ASP.NET project.

Creating a Data-Bound ASP.NET Page

1. Create a new ASP.NET web application project using either Visual Basic or C#. The new project displays an ASP.NET page in source view. Click the Design display mode button along the bottom of the *Default.aspx* page panel.

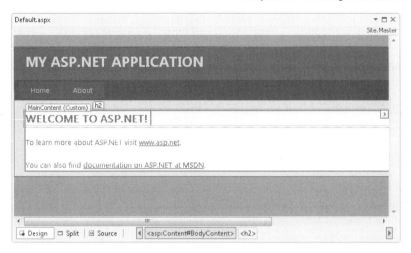

2. Clear out some of the default content to make room for the bound data content. Just above the "Welcome to ASP.NET" message in the page, click the MainContent (Custom) tab. This selects the content within the tab's panel. Press Delete to remove the content.

3. Access the Server Explorer panel (or the Database Explorer panel depending on your edition of Visual Studio). Expand the branch for the book's sample database. (You might need to add it as a new connection if it does not appear in the panel.) Within that branch, expand the Tables item. The *CourseCatalog* table should appear in the panel.

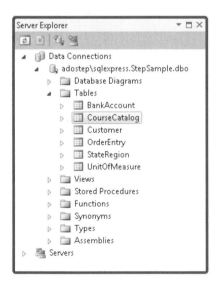

4. Drag *CourseCatalog* from the Server Explorer panel (or the Database Explorer panel) to the blank area within the *MainContent (Custom)* tab in the web page.

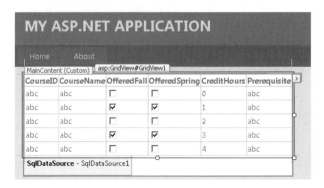

This action adds an ASP.NET *GridView* control to the page, already configured with the table's columns. It also adds a *SqlDataSource* control just below the grid.

5. Run the application. Visual Studio starts up a web browser session and displays the data-bound grid in the web page that appears in the browser.

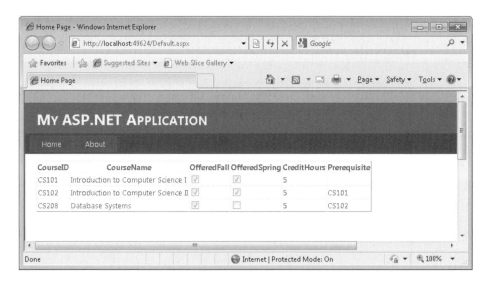

Understanding ASP.NET Data Binding

As with Windows Forms, a data-bound ASP.NET application uses controls that encapsulate database access and data-binding behaviors. But whereas the Windows Forms example earlier in this chapter added nearly a half-dozen data-enabled intermediate controls to work its binding magic, not to mention the final display controls, the ASP.NET sample gets by with only two controls: the data source and the grid control.

Within the markup for an ASP.NET application, controls appear as special HTML tags prefixed with "asp." Behind the scenes, the implementation for these special tags is a standard .NET class, a system that has a closer relationship with a WPF user interface than to a Windows Forms UI. The following code defines the data source that Visual Studio created when you dragged the *CourseCatalog* table to the page surface:

```
<asp:SqlDataSource ID="SqlDataSource1" runat="server"
    ConnectionString="<%$ ConnectionStrings:StepSampleConnectionString1 %>"
    DeleteCommand="DELETE FROM [CourseCatalog] WHERE [CourseID] = @CourseID"
    InsertCommand="INSERT INTO [CourseCatalog] ([CourseID], [CourseName],
        [OfferedFall], [OfferedSpring], [CreditHours], [Prerequisite]) VALUES
        (@CourseID, @CourseName, @OfferedFall, @OfferedSpring,
        @CreditHours, @Prerequisite)"
    ProviderName="<%$ ConnectionStrings:
        StepSampleConnectionString1.ProviderName %>"
    SelectCommand="SELECT [CourseID], [CourseName], [OfferedFall],
        [OfferedSpring], [CreditHours], [Prerequisite] FROM [CourseCatalog]"
    UpdateCommand="UPDATE [CourseCatalog] SET [CourseName] = @CourseName,
        [OfferedFall] = @OfferedFall, [OfferedSpring] = @OfferedSpring,
        [CreditHours] = @CreditHours, [Prerequisite] = @Prerequisite
        WHERE [CourseID] = @CourseID">
    <DeleteParameters>
        <asp:Parameter Name="CourseID" Type="String" />
    </DeleteParameters>
    <InsertParameters>
        <asp:Parameter Name="CourseID" Type="String" />
        <asp:Parameter Name="CourseName" Type="String" />
        <asp:Parameter Name="OfferedFall" Type="Boolean" />
        <asp:Parameter Name="OfferedSpring" Type="Boolean" />
        <asp:Parameter Name="CreditHours" Type="Int16" />
        <asp:Parameter Name="Prerequisite" Type="String" />
    </InsertParameters>
    <UpdateParameters>
        <asp:Parameter Name="CourseName" Type="String" />
        <asp:Parameter Name="OfferedFall" Type="Boolean" />
        <asp:Parameter Name="OfferedSpring" Type="Boolean" />
        <asp:Parameter Name="CreditHours" Type="Int16" />
        <asp:Parameter Name="Prerequisite" Type="String" />
        <asp:Parameter Name="CourseID" Type="String" />
    </UpdateParameters>
</asp:SqlDataSource>
```

This definition includes sufficient content to define both the *DataSet* instance and the *DataAdapter* that loads data into it. The *asp:SqlDataSource* control (as implemented through the *System.Web.UI.WebControls.SqlDataSource* class) includes the logic needed to create a *DataSet* instance and fill it with incoming data from a *DataAdapter*. The connection string, referenced in the control's *ConnectionString* attribute, appears in the project's *Web.config* XML file.

```
<!-- This is just the connection string portion of the Web.config file. -->
<connectionStrings>
    <add name="StepSampleConnectionString1"
        connectionString="Data Source=(local)\SQLExpress;
        Initial Catalog=StepSample;Integrated Security=True"
        providerName="System.Data.SqlClient" />
</connectionStrings>
```

The content can vary depending on your database configuration.

The actual data binding occurs through the data-enabled features of the *GridView* control.

```
<asp:GridView ID="GridView1" runat="server" AutoGenerateColumns="False"
    DataKeyNames="CourseID" DataSourceID="SqlDataSource1"
    EmptyDataText="There are no data records to display.">
    <Columns>
        <asp:BoundField DataField="CourseID" HeaderText="CourseID"
            ReadOnly="True" SortExpression="CourseID" />
        <asp:BoundField DataField="CourseName" HeaderText="CourseName"
            SortExpression="CourseName" />
        <asp:CheckBoxField DataField="OfferedFall" HeaderText="OfferedFall"
            SortExpression="OfferedFall" />
        <asp:CheckBoxField DataField="OfferedSpring" HeaderText="OfferedSpring"
            SortExpression="OfferedSpring" />
        <asp:BoundField DataField="CreditHours" HeaderText="CreditHours"
            SortExpression="CreditHours" />
        <asp:BoundField DataField="Prerequisite" HeaderText="Prerequisite"
            SortExpression="Prerequisite" />
    </Columns>
</asp:GridView>
```

The control's *DataSourceID* references the *SqlDataSource* instance that will supply the bound data. Within the control's *Columns* tag, a collection of *asp:BoundField* instances and their *DataField* attributes identify the path needed to locate the display data within the source. The control also includes an *EmptyDataText* attribute that adjusts the grid's content in the running application if the source lacks data records. It's a surprisingly small amount of code for the functionality it brings to the web page, and it works without adding a single line of custom C# or Visual Basic code.

Summary

This chapter introduced some of the data binding options available in different flavors of Visual Studio projects: Windows Forms, Windows Presentation Foundation, and ASP.NET. With little more than wizard-based database configuration followed by some mouse clicks, Visual Studio can generate a working application that displays—or in some cases enables editing of—data from an external source.

The samples included in this chapter provide only the most basic examples of what is possible with data-bound controls. If you forgo the simple drag-and-drop methods and use the examples as a starting point for data binding concepts, you can craft complex, interactive applications that depend on the intelligent data-linking features included in most Visual Studio user interface controls.

Chapter 21 Quick Reference

To	Do This
Create a simple data-bound Windows Forms application	Create a new Windows Forms project.
	Add a data source to the project that exposes the relevant data table(s).
	Drag a table from the data source to the surface of a form.
Create a simple data-bound Windows Presentation Foundation application	Create a new WPF application.
	Add a data source to the project that exposes the relevant data table(s).
	Drag a table from the data source to the surface of a window.
Create a simple data-bound ASP.NET application	Create a new ASP.NET application.
	Ensure that the target database is available in the Server Explorer (or Database Explorer).
	Drag a table from the Server Explorer (or Database Explorer) to the surface of a page.

Chapter 22
Providing RESTful Services with WCF Data Services

After completing this chapter, you will be able to:

- Create model-based data services
- Understand REST and its interaction with a data service
- Make database queries using specially constructed URIs

The Internet is a disconnected world. Except for brief moments of connectivity, web pages spend most of their time separated from the servers that provide their data. This reality makes it difficult, if not impossible, to implement a traditional client-server or n-tier database application. Instead, some Web-based applications use a new service-oriented model of requesting and updating data at the server.

This chapter introduces some ADO.NET-related technologies that take advantage of this service-focused methodology. *WCF Data Services* provides a standardized way of exposing Entity Framework (EF) data and other ADO.NET data content to Web-based clients. *REST*, short for *representational state transfer*, provides a method of querying and updating data service content using URIs and other standardized Web-based interfaces.

Getting to Know the Service Layers

Exposing entity data through a service-oriented RESTful interface involves multiple layers of data libraries. Some of them have already been covered in this book, including the Entity Framework modeling layer that provides the core access to the data. WCF Data Services and the REST interface provide two additional layers that make the service-based movement of data to a web client a reality.

Introducing WCF Data Services

Windows Communication Foundation (WCF) Data Services began its life as ADO.NET Data Services in Microsoft's version 3.5 update to the .NET Framework and in the accompanying Visual Studio 2008 SP1 release. The library is Microsoft's implementation of the *Open Data Protocol*, a Web-based standard for querying and updating data from a wide array of data sources. The Open Data Protocol is sponsored by Microsoft.

Note Learn more about the Open Data Protocol and its objectives at the specification's official web site: *www.odata.org*.

WCF Data Services are ASP.NET services as expressed through a .svc service file in an ASP.NET project. Clients make query and data-update requests by accessing the service using standard HTTP operations.

Note In addition to ASP.NET, WCF Data Services can be expressed directly through Microsoft's Internet Information Services (IIS), through a standalone WCF service, or through any other network service that supports the *IDataServiceHost* interface. This chapter discusses only the ASP.NET service interface.

The goal of a WCF Data Service is to present a collection of data, such as an EF model, in a form that can be queried by something as basic as a specially formed web page address. The system has a strong preference for EF conceptual models, making exposure of model data as easy as creating a derived class instance.

WCF Data Services uses a set of source providers to express different types of source data. The Entity Framework provider handles EF conceptual models. Services can also expose data from standard .NET objects that implement the *IQueryable* interface via the Reflection provider. (If a model supports the *IUpdatable* interface, clients will be able to update source data as well through that same provider.) Custom Data Service Providers let you create late-bound data services that indicate the available data collections as they are accessed.

Note This chapter examines only the Entity Framework provider.

By default, data exposed by the service is in the form of an Atom Publishing Protocol (AtomPub) XML document. JavaScript Object Notation (JSON) is also supported. Queries of individual scalar properties return data either in a simple XML wrapper (the default) or as plain-text data.

All classes involved in setting up WCF Data Services appear in the *System.Data.Services* namespace.

Introducing REST

Representational state transfer is a software architecture for managing distributed text and media content in a client-server environment. It documents a standardized interface for requesting distributed hypermedia content in a stateless manner.

The type of content being retrieved is not REST's concern. Instead, the architecture focuses on the rules and tools used to locate and transfer the content. If you've ever browsed the Internet, you are already well versed in REST because the World Wide Web is, with its distributed content and its standardized set of request verbs, the largest implementation of a REST-based (or "RESTful") system.

WCF Data Services—and the Open Data Protocol on which it is based—is a RESTful system. The services you create in ASP.NET can expose a variety of source data, but the interfaces and commands used to access that data are standardized. For the convenience of discussion in this chapter, RESTful refers to the HTTP transport and the constructed URIs or HTTP requests that access data from an exposed service.

The URIs for REST requests use a syntax that reflects the structure of the data and the query capabilities inherent in an EF model. Data components, such as entity and property names, are added to the URI after the service address. For example, a request to return all entities in the "Customers" entity set might use the following URI:

```
http://example.com/ExampleService.svc/Customers
```

In a more complex example, the following URI returns the ID numbers and totals (in descending order) for all of a specific customer's orders:

```
http://example.com/ExampleService.svc/Customers(3492L)/
    OrderEntries?$orderby=OrderTotal desc&$select=ID,OrderTotal
```

Setting Up a Data Service

WCF Data Services implementations typically appear as web services and are built as part of an ASP.NET application. You can create a new service based on an Entity Framework model in just a few steps:

1. Create a new ASP.NET web application using either C# or Visual Basic.

2. Add an ADO.NET Entity Data Model to your project and generate the conceptual model from a database. The "Using the Entity Data Model Wizard" section of Chapter 14, "Visualizing Data Models," walks you through this process.

3. Add a new WCF Data Service item to your project. This action adds a new class file to your project that derives from *System.Data.Services.DataService(Of T)*. The new file includes some boilerplate code that you can modify to meet the needs of your service. At the very least, you must modify this template to identify the name of your EF entity container (for the "Of T" part of the generic definition).

4. Configure the new data service to indicate which portions of the entity model are available for use by clients. These changes occur in the *InitializeService* method of the new service class. The method already appears in the generated class code; you just need to customize it.

The following exercise exposes an Entity Framework data model as a WCF Data Service.

Creating a Data Service from an EF Model: C#

> **Note** If you are using Microsoft Visual C# 2010 Express as your development tool, you must download and install Microsoft Visual Web Developer 2010 Express to complete the exercises in this chapter. Visit *www.microsoft.com/express* to download Express products.

1. Create a new ASP.NET web application project.

2. Add a new ADO.NET Entity Data Model to the project. (See the "Importing Database Tables as Entities" exercise on page 227 in Chapter 14 for step by step instructions.) Name the model file **SalesOrder.edmx**. When the Entity Data Model Wizard prompts you to store the connection string in the *Web.config* file, select that option.

3. On the wizard's Choose Your Database Objects panel, add the *Customer*, *OrderEntry*, and *StateRegion* tables to the model. Set the Model Namespace field to **SalesOrderModel**. Click Finish to complete the wizard.

4. In the properties for the *SalesOrder.edmx* model, make sure that the *EntityContainerName* property is set to **SalesOrderEntities**. Save and close the model file.

5. Add a new WCF Data Service item to the project, naming it **SalesOrder.svc**. The new file appears in your project with the following class code already included (comments removed for clarity):

```
public class SalesOrder : DataService<  >
{
    public static void InitializeService(DataServiceConfiguration config)
    {
        config.DataServiceBehavior.MaxProtocolVersion =
            DataServiceProtocolVersion.V2;
    }
}
```

6. In the initial class definition clause, replace the *DataService< >* base class definition (and any content contained within the angle brackets) with **DataService<SalesOrder Entities>**. This change tells the service which Entity Framework model to use as the data source.

7. Add the following statement to the *SalesOrder* class in the *InitializeService* method:

```
config.SetEntitySetAccessRule("*", EntitySetRights.AllRead);
```

This line tells the service to allow full read access to all the model's entities.

8. Run the application. Visual Studio starts the service using its built-in web server. Next, it opens a web browser and points it to the address of the new service. The service returns information about the service's available features in the default AtomPub format.

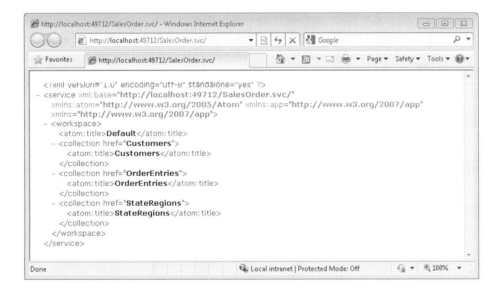

Note Depending on the configuration of your web browser, the XML content might or might not appear in the browser window.

Creating a Data Service from an EF Model: Visual Basic

Note If you are using Microsoft Visual Basic 2010 Express as your development tool, you must download and install Microsoft Visual Web Developer 2010 Express to complete the exercises in this chapter. Visit *www.microsoft.com/express* to download Express products.

1. Create a new ASP.NET web application project.

2. Add a new ADO.NET Entity Data Model to the project. (See the "Importing Database Tables as Entities" exercise on page 227 in Chapter 14 for step-by-step instructions.) Name the model file **SalesOrder.edmx**. When the Entity Data Model Wizard prompts you to store the connection string in the *Web.config* file, select that option.

3. On the wizard's Choose Your Database Objects panel, add the *Customer, OrderEntry,* and *StateRegion* tables to the model. Set the Model Namespace field to **SalesOrderModel**. Click Finish to complete the wizard.

4. In the properties for the *SalesOrder.edmx* model, make sure that the *EntityContainerName* property is set to **SalesOrderEntities**. Save and close the model file.

5. Add a new WCF Data Service item to the project, naming it **SalesOrder.svc**. The new file appears in your project with the following class code already included (comments removed for clarity):

```
Public Class SalesOrder
    Inherits DataService(Of [[class name]])

    Public Shared Sub InitializeService(ByVal config
            As DataServiceConfiguration)
        config.DataServiceBehavior.MaxProtocolVersion =
            DataServiceProtocolVersion.V2
    End Sub
End Class
```

6. In the *Inherits* clause of the *SalesOrder* class definition, replace *[[class name]]* with **SalesOrderEntities**. This change tells the service which Entity Framework model to use as the data source.

7. Add the following statement to the *SalesOrder* class in the *InitializeService* method:

```
config.SetEntitySetAccessRule("*", EntitySetRights.AllRead)
```

This line tells the service to allow full read access to all of the model's entities.

8. Run the application. Visual Studio starts the service using its built-in web server. Next, it opens a web browser and points it to the address of the new service. The service returns information about the service's available features in the default AtomPub format.

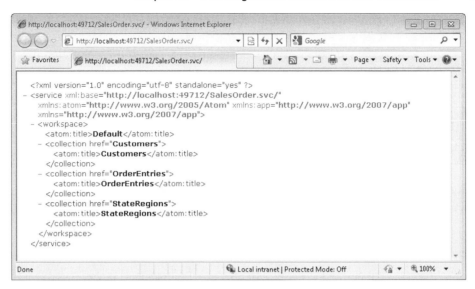

Note Depending on the configuration of your web browser, the XML content might or might not appear in the browser window.

Defining Service Rights

By default, the WCF Data Service exposes none of the entity sets included in a model for client queries. To access any data, you must configure the data rights available to RESTful callers. This configuration occurs in the derived *DataService(Of T)* class' *InitializeService* method. The service host calls this routine once at startup to determine the features activated for the service.

When you add a new WCF Data Service to your project, the *InitializeService* method already includes one configuration setting, which is updated using the passed-in *config* parameter, an instance of *DataServiceConfiguration*.

C#
```
config.DataServiceBehavior.MaxProtocolVersion =
    DataServiceProtocolVersion.V2;
```

Visual Basic
```
config.DataServiceBehavior.MaxProtocolVersion =
    DataServiceProtocolVersion.V2
```

This setting indicates which features are available to clients based on the release version of those features. For example, the ability to project properties in a query (with the *Select* extension method) is not available before Version 2. (Version 2 is the current release level as of this writing.)

For entity permissions, the key configuration setting is the *DataServiceConfig.SetEntitySet AccessRule* method, as used in the previous example. You pass this method the name of an entity set and a set of rights from the *EntitySetRights* enumeration.

C#
```
config.SetEntitySetAccessRule("Customers", EntitySetRights.AllRead);
```

Visual Basic
```
config.SetEntitySetAccessRule("Customers", EntitySetRights.AllRead)
```

Call this method for each entity set you plan to make available or use an asterisk ("*") as the entity name to simultaneously set rights for all entities at once. Table 22-1 lists the rights available for each entity set. Combine multiple rights together with a bitwise-Or operator to use a combination of rights.

TABLE 22-1 Rights Available for Data Service Entities

EntitySetRights Member	Description
None	Removes all access rights for the indicated entity set. This is the default for all model entities.
ReadSingle	Clients can query a specific entity instance by its primary key.
ReadMultiple	Clients can retrieve a set of all entities in an entity set. This right does not permit selection of an individual entity by primary key, although a filter may retrieve similar results.
WriteAppend	Clients can add new entity records to an entity set.
WriteReplace	Clients can update entities. When updating an individual entity, only those new property values supplied by the client are updated. Other property values are cleared or set to their default values. The client replaces the original record completely.
WriteDelete	Clients can delete existing entity records.
WriteMerge	Clients can update entities. When updating an individual entity, only those new property values supplied by the client get updated. Other property values are left unchanged. The client modifies the existing record in-place.
AllWrite	Combination of all the write-specific rights.
AllRead	Combination of all the read-specific rights.
All	Combination of all the read-specific and write-specific rights.

If your entity model exposes database-side or model-defined procedures, you can set their rights using the *DataServiceConfig.SetServiceOperationAccessRule* method.

Accessing a Data Service using REST

REST uses standard HTTP verbs to retrieve data and make updates to entities. Data queries that return content in either AtomPub (the default) or JSON format use the *GET* verb. Data updates use the *PUT, POST, MERGE,* and *DELETE* verbs, depending on the update operation.

> **Note** This section documents some typical examples of querying and updating entities through REST. For detailed information and examples, visit the Open Data Protocol web site at *www. odata.org.*

Querying Entities with REST

REST queries use the HTTP *GET* verb to identify the content to retrieve. The easiest way to use *GET* is to build a URI that includes all the query components and enter it in the address bar of a web browser. In the exercise shown earlier in this chapter, the running service displayed its available entity sets by making an address-based *GET* request through the browser.

```
http://example.com/SalesOrder.svc/
```

> **Note** In lieu of an exercise that demonstrates REST queries, run the service created earlier in this chapter and use its web browser session to test the URIs documented throughout this section.

REST queries start with this URI base and add additional entity information and operators to adjust the query. The simplest query involves appending the name of an entity set to the URI base.

```
http://example.com/SalesOrder.svc/Customers
```

Assuming that the Customers entity set is enabled for multiple-read access, this request returns all available entities in AtomPub format.

```xml
<?xml version="1.0" encoding="utf-8" standalone="yes" ?>
<feed xml:base="http://localhost:49712/SalesOrder.svc/"
    xmlns:d="http://schemas.microsoft.com/ado/2007/08/dataservices"
    xmlns:m="http://schemas.microsoft.com/ado/2007/08/dataservices/metadata"
    xmlns="http://www.w3.org/2005/Atom">
  <title type="text">Customers</title>
  <id>http://localhost:49712/SalesOrder.svc/Customers</id>
  <updated>2010-08-11T01:16:42Z</updated>
  <link rel="self" title="Customers" href="Customers" />
  <entry>
    <id>http://localhost:49712/SalesOrder.svc/Customers(1L)</id>
    <title type="text" />
    <updated>2010-08-11T01:16:42Z</updated>
    <author>
      <name />
    </author>
    <link rel="edit" title="Customer" href="Customers(1L)" />
    <link rel="http://schemas.microsoft.com/ado/2007/08/
      dataservices/related/State" type="application/atom+xml;type=entry"
      title="State" href="Customers(1L)/State" />
    <link rel="http://schemas.microsoft.com/ado/2007/08/
      dataservices/related/OrderEntries" type="application/atom+xml;
      type=feed" title="OrderEntries" href="Customers(1L)/OrderEntries" />
    <category term="SalesOrderModel.Customer"
      scheme="http://schemas.microsoft.com/ado/2007/08/dataservices/scheme" />
    <content type="application/xml">
      <m:properties>
        <d:ID m:type="Edm.Int64">1</d:ID>
        <d:FullName>Coho Vineyard</d:FullName>
        <d:Address1>123 Main Street</d:Address1>
        <d:Address2 m:null="true" />
        <d:City>Albany</d:City>
        <d:StateRegion m:type="Edm.Int64">32</d:StateRegion>
        <d:PostalCode>85000</d:PostalCode>
        <d:PhoneNumber m:null="true" />
        <d:WebSite>http://www.cohovineyard.com</d:WebSite>
        <d:AnnualFee m:type="Edm.Decimal">200.0000</d:AnnualFee>
      </m:properties>
    </content>
  </entry>
  <entry>
    <!-- Another entry here -->
  </entry>
  <!-- And so on... -->
</feed>
```

Note Internet Explorer 8, the latest version of Microsoft's web browser (as of this writing), applies a user-friendly interface to AtomPub feed content that hides the underlying XML. You can still access the XML by viewing the page source. Another option is to disable the interface conversion on all feeds. To do this, select Tools | Options from the menu in Internet Explorer. On the Options dialog box, select the Content tab and click the Settings button in the Feeds And Web Slices section. When the Feed And Web Slice Settings dialog box appears, clear the Turn On Feed Reading View field.

This content includes an *<entry>* tag for each returned entity, with distinct XML tags for each of the entity's properties. This is the typical format any time your query is based on an entity set. Queries to retrieve a single entity append the primary key in parentheses at the end of the URI.

```
http://example.com/SalesOrder.svc/Customers(3L)
```

This result, as with most results that return a single entity instance, uses the *<entry>* tag as the top-level XML tag, instead of *<feed>*. Otherwise, the content is generally the same as the multi-entity results.

> **Note** The schema used by REST defines formats for literals, such as the primary key value. For example, text-based primary keys must be surrounded by single quotes. If your primary key is a long (64-bit) integer, you must add an uppercase "L" to the end of the number. Otherwise, the WCF Data Service will not succeed in locating the record.

To return content in JSON format instead of AtomPub, append the *$format=json* system query option to the URI.

```
http://example.com/SalesOrder.svc/Customers(3L)?$format=json
```

If you build your own *GET* packet, you can also set the *accept* request header to the *application/json* MIME type.

By default, a query for a single entity returns all properties for that entity. To limit the result to a single scalar property, append the property name to the query.

```
http://example.com/SalesOrder.svc/Customers(1L)/FullName
```

This query returns simplified XML content that contains the requested data:

```
<?xml version="1.0" encoding="utf-8" standalone="yes" ?>
<FullName xmlns="http://schemas.microsoft.com/ado/2007/
    08/dataservices">Coho Vineyard</FullName>
```

The *$value* query option removes the XML wrapper and returns only the data:

```
http://example.com/SalesOrder.svc/Customers(1L)/FullName/$value
```

This query returns just the retrieved content:

```
Coho Vineyard
```

Navigation properties work just like scalar properties within the URI, although they return results formatted more like a multi-entity feed.

```
http://example.com/SalesOrder.svc/Customers(1L)/OrderEntries
```

Several query options modify the returned returns. These options translate into Entity Framework extension methods that filter, project, or sort the results. The *$orderby* option sorts multi-entity results by the indicated properties or expressions.

```
http://example.com/SalesOrder.svc/Customers?$orderby=FullName desc
```

The *$filter* and *$select* options limit and project the results using the instructions provided after the equal signs.

```
http://example.com/SalesOrder.svc/Customers/
    ?$filter=City eq 'Albany'&$select=ID,FullName
```

Most traditional operators don't work in REST; instead, you use a set of abbreviated operators, such as:

- **Math operators**: *add, sub, mul, div, and mod*
- **Logical operators**: *and, or, not*
- **Comparison operators**: *eq, ne, lt, gt, le, ge*

For example, the following query returns orders that have a post–8.75 percent taxed amount of 500 or more.

```
http://example.com/SalesOrder.svc/OrderEntries?$filter=
    (Subtotal mul 1.0875) ge 500
```

Other query options include the *$top* and *$skip* operators that work like their extension method counterparts. The *$count* option returns the number of records in the entity or query.

```
http://example.com/SalesOrder.svc/Customers/$count
```

The query returns just the numeric count as a string, without any XML wrapper.

> **Note** The *$count* operator is disabled by default. To enable it, set the *config. DataServiceBehavior.AcceptCountRequests* property to *True* in the *InitializeService* method.

The *$expand* option returns a related set of entities for a result. For instance, the following query returns the specified *Customer* entity, plus that customer record's associated *OrderEntries* entities as a *<feed>* tag subordinate to the customer's *<entry>* tag block.

```
http://example.com/SalesOrder.svc/Customers(1L)?$expand=OrderEntries
```

Malformed query strings result in an HTTP error code 400: "Bad Request." In all cases, the query options, operators, entity names, and all other elements of the query are case-sensitive.

For more query examples and to discover other query options and formats, see the "Addressing Resources (WCF Data Services)" and "Query Functions (WCF Data Services)" pages in the Visual Studio online help. The *www.odata.org* web site also contains numerous query examples, plus full documentation on the format of all query components.

Updating Entities with REST

REST also includes features that let you modify the entities exposed by a WCF Data Service—assuming that write permissions have been enabled for the entities. Creating a REST request that updates content is a little more involved than writing a simple *GET*-based query. Beyond the basic URI, you must also add details on what to update in the HTTP request's payload section.

> **Note** This section provides general information on building REST updates. Specifics on how to package and transmit the request will vary depending on the client libraries used to communicate with the service. Specific implementation details on transmitting HTTP requests are beyond the scope of this book.

To add a new entity, you send a *POST* request that includes all new property values in AtomPub or JSON format. The following AtomPub-formatted request adds a new *Customer* entity to the database via the data service.

```
POST /SalesOrder.svc/Customers HTTP/1.1
Host: example.com
DataServiceVersion: 1.0
MaxDataServiceVersion: 2.0
accept: application/atom+xml
content-type: application/atom+xml
Content-Length: 937

<?xml version="1.0" encoding="utf-8"?>
<Entry xmlns:d="http://schemas.microsoft.com/ado/2007/08/dataservices"
    xmlns:m="http://schemas.microsoft.com/ado/2007/08/dataservices/metadata"
    xmlns="http://www.w3.org/2005/Atom">
  <title type="text"></title>
  <updated>2010-08-31T23:45:12Z</updated>
  <author>
    <name />
  </author>
  <category term="SalesOrderModel.Customer"
    scheme="http://schemas.microsoft.com/ado/2007/08/dataservices/scheme" />
  <content type="application/xml">
    <m:properties>
      <d:FullName>Southridge Video</d:FullName>
      <d:Address1>789 Washington Parkway</d:Address1>
      <d:City>Phoenix</d:City>
      <d:StateRegion m:type="Edm.Int64">3</d:StateRegion>
      <d:PostalCode>90909</d:PostalCode>
      <d:WebSite>http://www.southridgevideo.com</d:WebSite>
      <d:AnnualFee m:type="Edm.Decimal">350.0000</d:AnnualFee>
    </m:properties>
  </content>
</Entry>
```

When the new record is successfully inserted, the service returns an image of the new record in AtomPub or JSON format (as indicated by the *accept* request header) and an HTTP status code of 201.

Updates to existing entities follow the same pattern, but use the *PUT* verb instead of *POST*. This action replaces the existing record with the new content. To perform a merge operation—modifying just those properties specified in the request payload—use the *MERGE* verb instead of *PUT*.

```
MERGE /SalesOrder.svc/Customers(4L) HTTP/1.1
```

Updates to a single property use a shortened form of the *PUT* request. The following code updates the *AnnualFee* property for a *Customer* entity:

```
PUT /SalesOrder.svc/Customers(4L)/AnnualFee HTTP/1.1
Host: example.com
DataServiceVersion: 1.0
MaxDataServiceVersion: 2.0
accept: application/xml
content-type: application/xml
Content-Length: 259

<?xml version="1.0" encoding="utf-8" standalone="yes"?>
<d:AnnualFee xmlns:d="http://schemas.microsoft.com/ado/2007/08/dataservices"
    xmlns:m="http://schemas.microsoft.com/ado/2007/08/dataservices/metadata"
    m:type="Edm.Decimal">400.0000</d:AnnualFee>
```

An even shorter form uses the *$value* query option to indicate that the payload is stripped down to just the bare data content.

```
PUT /SalesOrder.svc/Customers(4L)/AnnualFee/$value HTTP/1.1
Host: example.com
DataServiceVersion: 1.0
MaxDataServiceVersion: 2.0
accept: application/xml
content-type: application/xml
Content-Length: 3

400
```

To remove an entity, issue an HTTP *DELETE* request, including the query path to the entity in the request.

```
DELETE /SalesOrder.svc/Customers(4L) HTTP/1.1
```

An HTTP return code of 200 indicates success.

Summary

This chapter provided a brief introduction to WCF Data Services and REST, which are service-oriented programming tools that make it simple to expose Entity Framework model content to fully disconnected, remote consumers. WCF Data Services is an implementation of the Open Data Protocol (OData) standard that provides a consistent request mechanism for different types of server-hosted content.

REST combines the power of traditional database queries with the simplicity of web addresses. By forming simple text-based HTTP requests, you can query or update data from a WCF Data Service without the need to know or understand the underlying structure of the data.

Chapter 22 Quick Reference

To	Do This
Expose an EF model as a service	Create an ASP.NET web application project.
	Add the entity model to the project.
	Add a WCF Data Service item to the project.
	Change the generic class definition of the new service to include the entity container name.
	Modify the service's *InitializeService* method to set access rights.
	Make the .svc file available on a web server.
Provide read access to an entity	Add the EF model and WCF Data Service to an ASP.NET project.
	Locate the data service's *InitializeService* method.
	In that method, call *config.SetEntitySetAccessRule*, passing it the name of the entity set and the enumerated value *EntitySetRights.AllRead*.
Issue a REST query for a single entity instance	Create an HTTP *GET* request.
	In the URI, after the path to the .svc hosted file, add /xxx(ID), where "xxx" is the entity set name, and "ID" is the primary key of the instance.

Index

G

About the Author

Tim Patrick is an author and software architect with over 25 years of experience in software development and technical writing. He has written seven books and several articles on programming and other topics. In 2007, Microsoft awarded him with its *Most Valuable Professional* (MVP) award in recognition of the benefits his writings bring to Visual Basic and .NET programmers. Tim earned his undergraduate degree in Computer Science from Seattle Pacific University.

What do you think of this book?

We want to hear from you!

To participate in a brief online survey, please visit:

microsoft.com/learning/booksurvey

Tell us how well this book meets your needs—what works effectively, and what we can do better. Your feedback will help us continually improve our books and learning resources for you.

Thank you in advance for your input!

Stay in touch!

To subscribe to the *Microsoft Press® Book Connection Newsletter*—for news on upcoming books, events, and special offers—please visit:

microsoft.com/learning/books/newsletter